MW00623230

GOLD MATTERS

Real Solutions to Surreal Risks

Egon von Greyerz & Matthew Piepenburg

Gold Matters © Copyright 2021 Egon von Greyerz & Matthew Piepenburg

All rights reserved. No part of this publication may be reproduced, distributed or transmitted in any form or by any means, including photocopying, recording, or other electronic or mechanical methods, without the prior written permission of the publisher, except in the case of brief quotations embodied in critical reviews and certain other noncommercial uses permitted by copyright law.

Although the authors and publisher have made every effort to ensure that the information in this book was correct at press time, the authors and publisher do not assume and hereby disclaim any liability to any party for any loss, damage, or disruption caused by errors or omissions, whether such errors or omissions result from negligence, accident, or any other cause.

Adherence to all applicable laws and regulations, including international, federal, state and local governing professional licensing, business practices, advertising, and all other aspects of doing business in the US, Canada or any other jurisdiction is the sole responsibility of the reader and consumer.

Neither the authors nor the publisher assumes any responsibility or liability whatsoever on behalf of the consumer or reader of this material. Any perceived slight of any individual or organization is purely unintentional.

The resources in this book are provided for informational purposes only and should not be used to replace the specialized training and professional judgment of a financial professional.

Neither the authors nor the publisher can be held responsible for the use of the information provided within this book. Please always consult a trained professional before making any decision regarding your own individualized financial planning.

For more information, email: contact@goldswitzerland.com.

ISBN: 978-0-578-28839-0

To that which has a value beyond measure: Our family, friends, and the wonder, visible and invisible, forever surrounding us.

Table of Contents

Foreword – By Grant Williams & Ronald-Peter Stoeferle

Grant Williams (*RealVision TV* Co-Founder and publisher of *Things That Make You Go Hmmm*)

When looking up the definition of 'matter,' one finds two very distinct assessments. The first pertains to the realm of physical property:

Matter: physical substance in general, as distinct from mind and spirit; (in physics) that which occupies space and possesses rest mass, especially as distinct from energy.

The second, deals with more ephemeral issues:

Matter: a subject or situation under consideration.

In this important and entirely timely book, Egon von Greyerz and Matthew Piepenburg take the former and place it under the latter, dissecting the history of the precious metal which has been used as money for thousands of years but which, in an age of infinite fiat currencies, remains understood by too few and disregarded by far too many.

As the era of quantitative easing and extensive monetary accommodation on the part of central banks reaches the end of its useful life, rising inflationary pressure is demanding a different set of solutions to the very different set of problems it poses.

Sadly, the world's central banks have created a set of conditions whereby the entire global financial system has become reliant upon the maintaining of historically low interest rates via the over-creation (and hence debasement) of fiat currencies. This has become necessary as a means to refinance the inordinate amount of debt the world has taken on in order to forestall a series of rolling crises - each more dangerous than the last.

In *Gold Matters*, Egon and Matthew help the reader easily understand gold's history as money, its critical place in the present-day financial system and its potential role as the post-Bretton Woods era comes to a close.

From its earliest days as the fulcrum of innumerate local currency systems to its role as the anchor of the modern-day global monetary system when the Gold Standard allowed Western society to be built from the ground up, Egon & Matthew will take you on a journey through time, explaining how and why gold became the most important monetary metal of all, showing you the risks that have multiplied in the financial system as gold has been marginalized over the last half-century and outlining the threats faced by the pension system, the banking system, the currency system and a series of bankrupt Western governments

From the monstrous leverage provided by the gold futures market as a means to suppress the natural price of the metal to the methods used by policymakers to suppress and underreport inflation calculations, Egon and Matthew lay bare the manifold ways in which the public's understanding of both the monetary system and money itself are deliberately manipulated in order to mask the damage done to many developed nations' finances by decades of financial mismanagement and promise-and-spend politics.

Amidst all this, gold stands stoic and immutable as the purest representation of financial independence in a world filled with reliance and fragility. Gold has preserved and protected wealth and purchasing power for centuries - characteristics that, while under-appreciated in an age of FOMO and manic speculation in risk assets, are about to be proven once again as essential to the protection and preservation of capital.

Gold Matters.

Ronni Stoeferle (Incrementum, AG, Managing Partner and author of the *In Gold We Trust* report)

Back in September of 2008, I was a newbie in the gold world. My second *In Gold We Trust* report had just been published, I was a junior analyst at Erste Bank, and had a limited understanding of the monetary system, Austrian Economics, and the stock market. It was during this month that I attended the Denver Gold Show in Zürich and met Egon von Greyerz for the first time. The two of us clicked, and it quickly became clear that we had many shared passions. We ended up diving into a long conversation about gold, entrepreneurship, values, family and more. I was impressed that such a star of the gold scene was humble enough to take time to talk at such length to a young analyst.

A few months before, gold had broken through the USD 1,000 mark for the first time. Egon and I shared a fascination with the precious metal, and our enthusiasm was strengthened by that recent price milestone. Over the subsequent 14 years, Egon and I have developed a close personal friendship, and he has become something of a mentor to me. I remember fondly many conversations with Egon in periods of market turbulence, over a period where we have seen the gold price double in USD terms.

In 2013, when I took the leap into self-employment and co-founded the Liechtenstein-based Incrementum AG, Egon was always ready to provide advice and support. In the concluding chapter of this book, Egon quotes Confucius, who states that gold possesses the outstanding qualities of "loyalty and good faith." Over the years of our friendship, I've come to appreciate that the Confucian sentiment about gold very much applies to Egon himself!

With *Gold Matters*, Egon von Greyerz and Matthew Piepenburg present a comprehensive work on gold that looks set to become a standard text on the subject. The authors display a deep understanding of both economic history and present market conditions: Indispensable prerequisites for making sound investment decisions. The result of their efforts is a tour de force that is both enlightening and entertaining.

Today we live in a world of economic turmoil where Covid-19 looks to turn endemic. It should be remembered, however, that Covid-19 was only an accelerant rather than the root cause of our present troubles. After all, even before the outbreak of the pandemic, the unprecedented rise in global debt had already started to cause economic difficulties for governments, companies and households alike. For this reason, we should not regard central banks' reckless monetary policies as being recent and temporary. Rather, we should see them as an expression of a fundamental "Monetary Climate Change," a phrase that we chose as the theme of our 2021 *In Gold We Trust* report. This monetary climate change is threatening the wealth of large sections of the population, and the rise of inflation in recent months to multi-decade highs could just be a taste of the economic turmoil to come.

For this reason, the publication of *Gold Matters* is timely. In an era of rapid structural change, increasing geopolitical uncertainty and a pandemic with all its imponderables, gold radiates stability, continuity and reliability. Governments, companies and currencies come and go; but gold, as Egon and Matthew impressively demonstrate, is not only here to stay, but is experiencing a revival. The authors make a compelling case that gold remains an essential component of any portfolio. As it has done throughout history, gold stands to protect investors against some of the worst economic and political calamities that could be on our horizon.

Gold Matters – no doubt about that, and so does friendship.

Introduction

Are You Prepared?

Never before in the history of global markets have the international currency and financial systems which impact each of our lives been at greater risk of unprecedented mis-direction and distortion leading to increased controls and eventual implosion.

As dramatic or over-stated as this may sound, the following pages are not designed to sensationalize, but to candidly share objective facts and, better yet, offer realistic solutions to the economic realities which confront us all. As Swiss-based principals to *the* world's largest private wealth management service for High-Net-Worth investors dedicated exclusively to precious metal ownership outside of an increasingly fractured banking system, we speak from decades of personal and professional experience at the highest levels of public and private investing. Between us, we share over 70-years of combined experience in the financial industry, having worked within international banks, directed a highly successful FTSE 100 enterprise and managed billions of dollars for wealthy clients around the world as directors to private family offices as well as alternative investment vehicles.

From our offices in Zurich, Switzerland, we are now exclusively dedicated to serving individual and institutional clients in over 80 countries by offering the most historically-confirmed means of protecting amassed wealth against undeniable and increasing currency debasement and systemic market risk. Toward this end, we emphasize wealth preservation solutions through the private ownership of allocated, segregated and fully-insured *physical* gold and silver stored in jurisdictions free of counterparty or capital control risk and held in the safest and largest private vault in the world.

In short, we take the ownership, transportation, insurance, storage and ultimate liquidity of precious metals seriously.

Why?

The answer is simple: Regardless of how one's wealth is acquired, if it is measured only in paper currencies (be they U.S., Canadian, or Australian dollars, Japanese yen or western euros etc.), the inherent purchasing power of that hard-earned wealth is deteriorating by the month, minute and second. Stated more simply, paper wealth is effectively devolving into no wealth at all.

Again, this may seem difficult to fully conceptualize or believe. We understand such reticence, and for years shared a similar skepticism while acquiring and managing our own and others' wealth via traditional investment approaches and equally traditional understandings of risk management and wealth preservation. But as wealth increases, so does individual responsibility. It soon became increasingly clear to each of us that measuring security and income in fiat currencies was a common yet dangerous misconception.

As global policy makers and central bankers fall deeper and deeper into unsustainable as well as unignorable levels of national, corporate and household debt, they have turned more and more toward the desperate expansion of fiat currencies created literally out of thin air to "manage" that debt. This mouse-clicked money creation, or "liquidity assistance," has been done at levels never witnessed before in the pages of economic history, from the days of Ancient Rome to the S&P's infamous collapse in 2008. Such extreme currency creation bought time, even good times, but in the end, and like a bucket of water added to a glass of wine, this reckless, as well as global, monetary policy has caused (and continues to cause) the slow dilution of the purchasing power of the currency in one's hand, bank account or security portfolio.

This is not fable but fact, one which became increasingly impossible for us to ignore. In the pages and chapters below, we detail this open secret with careful attention to math and history rather than hyperbole or fear-selling. As a store of value, global fiat currencies will simply not protect you in the coming years from the gradual and then extreme risks to your acquired wealth as measured by national currencies. Fortunately, physical gold offers an elegant, market-ignored yet historically-confirmed anti-dote to the disease of dying paper (i.e., "fiat") currencies taking place right now.

Most importantly, and given the natural reluctance to face such risks, we have chosen to *show* rather than *tell* you this. Measured against a single milligram of gold, for example, the purchasing power of the world's major currencies have lost greater than 80% of their value in just the last twenty years alone, as the graph below, repeated throughout this book, confirms:

Purchasing power of main currencies valued in gold (log), 01/1971-09/2020

Source: Reuters Eikon, Nick Laird, goldchartsrus.com, Incrementum AG

Our promise to those who approach these pages is simple: If you read the objective data, examples, history, math and blunt advice provided herein to the very last page, you will no longer doubt that a key component of preserving your future wealth must involve some meaningful ownership of physical gold as an insurance policy against currencies already burning to the ground. Once you have closed this book, you will have acquired the peace of mind that only informed (albeit often uncomfortable) knowledge provides. Regardless of your individual wealth level, you will acquire the confidence to weather the coming financial and currency storms with insights, tools and assets which the vast majority of uninformed yet otherwise diligent investors simply won't possess.

Never has the need for such blunt information been greater, yet never has the window to protect yourself via still-affordable access to physical gold been more opportune. But that window, like all windows, will eventually close, and the time for considering the themes and solutions presented herein is indeed now. Hence our expedited effort to gather and present these pages.

Toward this end, we begin by asking one simple question: Are you prepared for what's ahead?

Confucian Insights—Superior Men, Superior Planning

Whenever and however risk asset bubbles in stocks and bonds burst, the world suddenly discovers the scarcity of what Confucius described as "superior men." Such a term has nothing to do with gender, ancient dueling skills, stunning good-looks, amassed wealth, expensive educations or otherwise lofty public credentials. Instead, "superior men" were (and always will be) characterized more by certain philosophical measures and temperaments, most notably their ability to realistically recognize and accept life's altering currents, both headwind and tailwind, and therefore prepare for the same calmly and rationally. Specifically, Confucius said this of "superior men:"

"The superior man, when resting in safety, does not forget that danger may come. When in a state of security, he does not forget the possibility of ruin. When all is orderly, he does not forget that disorder may come. Thus, his person is not endangered, and his States and all their clans are preserved."

Superior men can exist within many different contexts not otherwise linked to currencies or investments. There will be, and have always been, many, for example, without much money or interest in portfolio risk management or wealth preservation who were and are prepared at a psychological level for whatever slings and arrows the world may throw at them. These people are often the happiest of all, regardless of their wealth.

A Wealth Preservation Focus

Throughout this book, however, we will be speaking primarily to the theme of preserving wealth in a backdrop of historically unprecedented currency risk and increasingly distorted financial markets. Again, our aim is not to dazzle or frighten, but to inform and *prepare* investors by using realistic data and blunt-speak from two authors who have spent their entire careers managing and preserving their own as well as others' financial wealth around the world. The hundreds of investors we have met from our offices in Zurich are risk aware and therefore focused on wealth preservation, heeding the now infamous observation that "return *of* capital is more important than return *on* capital." Prepared investors buy physical gold not to get rich quick on a speculation spread, but because they are aware of the excessive risks in markets, governments, currencies and banks (central and commercial), all of which are openly discussed in the chapters below. These informed market-watchers endeavor to protect and insure their already acquired wealth against inevitable yet largely media and market-ignored headwinds. Like ourselves, such investors consider physical precious metals, stored outside of fragile, distorted and increasingly centralized banking systems and command-control economies, as a critical component of their wealth preservation.

Despite such risks now hiding in plain sight, many otherwise sophisticated investors are blind to what lies ahead. Investment gold represents less than 0.5% of world financial assets. There is, as all market veterans understand, immense power behind such scarcity. But knowledge too is a scarce commodity, which explains why only a very small minority of informed and hence highly successful investors insure their wealth in physical gold. This has always troubled (yet not surprised) us given the equally ignored fact that physical gold is the only asset that has ever survived as real money in the last 5000 years. History has repeatedly shown, without exception, that every nation, empire or regime which found itself in a debt trap from which it could never escape, has consistently resorted to debasing its currency to inflate away its debts. Every market cycle, every economy, every time. And within this sad pattern, gold has always emerged as the primary asset which protected "superior men" when the once sane world around them became suddenly, well: Insane. Again, this was true of every currency and systemic collapse, every time.

In the pages and chapters below, we use objective data rather than dramatic statements to evidence how the grossly distorted global markets, debt levels and currency regimes heading into the 2020's were and are no exception to this historical pattern. In fact, and despite valiant efforts by global policy makers to ignore or downplay such irreversible risks, financial conditions in the 21st century represent the *worst* debt levels, currency dilutions and broken financial models ever witnessed in the long history of capital markets, from the first Persian trade huts to the modern derivatives desks in the global COMEX markets.

That is, a global economy facing over $300 trillion in debt against just $88 trillion in global income (i.e., "Gross Domestic Product" or "GDP") suddenly found itself with its back against an insurmountable debt wall. The "solution" offered by policy makers from DC to Tokyo was as predictable as it was disastrous: Inflate away (and "pay" for) their debt by creating more increasingly debased, fiat currencies. And as we show throughout the following pages, gold shines brightest in such desperate backdrops.

There are, of course, other real assets like certain real estate holdings that have held their values very well over time. As the 2020's brace for major inflation in food prices, for example, agricultural land is likely to do well in coming years. By the end of 2020, we were already seeing high inflation in agricultural and other soft commodities.

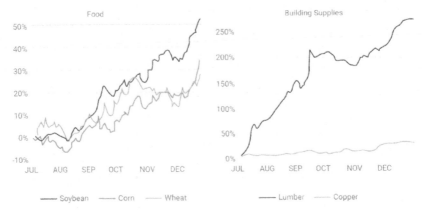

Past performace dies not guarantee future results. Source: Bloomberg, U.S. Global Investors

Bonds Yields Do Not Represent Current Risk Levels

But commercial and residential property is a different matter. The incessant and deliberate repression of interest rates and bond yields by global central banks to dramatically increase credit access since 1971 has driven commercial and residential property prices ever higher. In addition, central banks have given select corporate borrowers the best leg up by charging virtually nothing for borrowed money.

In the Switzerland of 2021, for example, one could get a 15-year mortgage at a fixed rate of 1%. This was effectively handing out money for free. As for corporations, including those rising to all-time highs in the backdrop of zero profits and earnings, cheap debt was there for the taking as debt-driven markets reached unprecedented levels despite a global recession and viral pandemic. But rather than use that free money for operational and capital expenditures at the business level, CEO's (whose salaries are based upon share prices) have simply used their borrowed dollars to buy more of their own stocks, thus sending stock prices (and Wall Street bonuses—*See* Chapter 4) way past anything even remotely resembling honest valuation for honest effort.

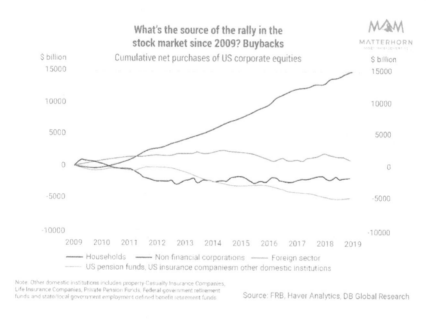

What's the source of the rally in the stock market since 2009? Buybacks

Cumulative net purchases of US corporate equities

Note: Other domestic institutions includes property Casualty Insurance Companies, Life Insurance Companies, Private Pension Funds, Federal government retirement funds and state/local government employment defined benefit retirement funds

Source: FRB, Haver Analytics, DB Global Research

But low interest rates in no way represent the generosity or fiscal strength of governments or central banks. Instead, they are merely the sad, artificial and desperate cause, consequence and symptom of profligate spending by governments and corporate entities who ignored this simple lesson of financial history, namely: Extreme debt slowly and then abruptly destroys every economy and currency.

With incessant deficit spending, governments must finance new debt at virtually no cost (thanks to artificial and unsustainable interest rate suppression) in order to service old debt and hence avoid default and/or insolvency. Bond prices (and hence interest rates) were so artificially overbought and over-valued due to central bank support (i.e., bond purchasing with "printed" currencies), that bond yields (which move inversely to price) are going *negative*, something *never seen before* in the history of money. By 2021, the world witnessed over $19 trillion of *negative yielding* government bonds with no Western borrower paying above 2% for any maturity.

Interest rates, of course track bond yields, and the absolute absurdity of such an artificially repressed yield and interest rate setting is reflected in the example of Greek versus U.S. rates for 30-Year bonds. In 2021, Greece launched a massively over-subscribed (i.e., central bank supported/purchased) 30-Year bond issue at a yield of 1.95%. By comparison, yields on the 30-Year U.S. Treasury bond for the same period were 2.36%. What's staggering to us (yet ignored by most), is that both of these sovereign borrowers are virtually bankrupt; equally absurd is the fact that a financially insolvent Greece, whose comical credit score has been known to the world for years, was able (due to European Central Bank "accommodation") to borrow at a lower rate than the U.S. But this is what happens when central banks, rather than natural market forces, artificially set the price for bonds by purchasing the same with printed (and hence increasingly debased) currencies. In short, the government bond market, itself fully "supported" by central banks rather than natural demand, had grown into the biggest and most artificial asset bubble ever witnessed by two-legged creatures on the planet earth. But sadly, that didn't stop this bogus securities bubble and sovereign debt party from expanding further.

U.S. Government Debt: $40+ Trillion by 2025?

Just consider the United States. When President Trump was elected in November of 2016, U.S. debt was $20 trillion. That same year, we forecast that it would reach $28 trillion by January of 2021 and $40 trillion by 2025. Thus far, we've been proven correct, despite the fact that the majority of market observers found this forecast unthinkable. Sadly, however, those same critics (mostly armed with marketing degrees rather than market experience) hadn't studied much math or history in school, which told us precisely what would happen.

Based on further deteriorating economic conditions and rapidly rising debt levels leading into the 2020's, we are now convinced that the $40 trillion debt levels we forecasted in 2016 for the U.S. in 2025 were in fact too low; we are anticipating public debt levels to go even higher.

Seem hard to believe? Well, let's just get back to basic history and the patterns of desperate policy makers. When president Reagan took office in 1981, U.S. debt was under $1 trillion. But, fast-forward 40 years later and that same debt level had already skyrocketed to $30 trillion by 2021, a multiple of 30X, proving yet again that debt levels have gone from the exuberant to the insane in a relatively short window of time. Also, keep in mind that our $40+ trillion projection doesn't even include potential defaults in credit or derivative markets (Chapter 10) which could increase that $40+ trillion forecast exponentially. Total combined corporate, public and household debt in the U.S. was already at $84 trillion by 2021, a sum that can never be repaid nor its interest expense ever serviced without open manipulation of the interest rates and expanding the U.S. money supply by increasingly desperate and experimental central bankers.

Unfortunately, such unpayable debt levels and such unsustainable rate suppression and monetary expansion policies eventually fail, as the amount of printed (and inflationary) dollars needed to buy the bonds to repress interest rates and bond yields eventually becomes too extreme, too discredited and too debased. At such historical yet inevitable tipping points, credit markets tank, rates and yields spike and stock markets crash, along with the national and global economies and currencies chained to their speculative ankles. The only alternative to such an immediate market implosion would be full-on centralized control of our banks, economies, currencies and markets by governmental agencies. In short, the complete death of free-market capitalism, which is precisely what was happening to markets crawling into the 2020's (*See* Chapter 3).

When bond bubbles burst (despite every desperate, central-bank effort to postpone the same), the domino effect is incalculable. In addition to debt defaults in the $10s of trillions, derivative defaults, which are very likely, could add trillions and trillions more to the default pyre. In the interim, we are confident that the Fed and other central banks are already cranking up the printing presses or expanding the memory of their computers to cope with all the additional zeros they will need to creatively add to their already bloated central bank balance sheets. In other words, trillions more fiat currencies will be created by one mouse click after the next at a central bank near you. Such grotesque, yet inevitable increases in the broad money supply are the very definition of inflation and currency debasement, for which gold, as underscored in Part II of this work, is the ultimate counter-measure.

Hyperinflation is a Currency Event

Despite such defining inflation characteristics and forces, there will always be a number of respected market observers who believe that we will not see high inflation or hyperinflation, as discussed in Chapter 17. In their often cogent yet flawed analysis, they conveniently avoid the effect that such abused levels of money printing and fiscal (i.e., deficit) spending have on currencies, regardless of whether the global stage be officially labeled as inflationary or deflationary. As we have regularly pointed out, every single event of hyperinflation in history has arisen as a result of the currency collapsing. In other words, it is not an increase in the demand for goods and services (nor even central bank manipulation of dishonest inflationary reporting) that causes rising or even hyperinflation. Instead, it is the total mismanagement of the economy and the consequent debasement of the currency that creates fatal levels of inflation.

Just consider the table and data below. All the major currencies have lost 80-86% in real purchasing power (when measured against a milligram of gold) since 2000, and 96-99% since 1971 when Nixon closed the gold window. And if we look at a hyperinflationary economy like Argentina, its Pesos has lost 99.99% since 2000.

THE CURRENCY RACE TO THE BOTTOM

GOLD PER OZ	1971	2000	2021	DROP IN CURRENCY 2000-2021	DROP IN CURRENCY 1971-2021
USA	USD 35	USD 288	USD 1740	84%	98%
UK	GBP 15	GBP 177	GBP 1260	86%	99%
GERMANY/EUR	EUR 65	EUR 286	EUR 1470	80%	96%
CANADA	CAD 35	CAD 417	CAD 2184	81%	99%
ARGENTINA		ARS 288	ARS 159k	99.99%	GoldSwitzerland

Few Are Prepared for Disorder

Whether it is ordinary investors or the so-called experts, almost everyone naturally believes that ruin won't happen to them. Therefore, they are not in a Confucian state of preparedness for the coming (and, in fact, *current*) economic and currency collapse discussed throughout these pages.

Toward this end, let us share a recent anecdote about hyperinflation closer to home in Europe. Last year, for example, in the small town of Ticino, (Italian part of Switzerland), co-author Egon von Greyerz was dining with his wife and friends in a secluded restaurant. The owner approached Egon and said he recognized him from his many articles and interviews. The owner then explained that he had fled from Yugoslavia in the 1990s and that his family had lost a significant part of its wealth during the 1992-94 hyperinflation period which helped bring Yugoslavia's government out of debt while placing its economy, and hence citizens, on their knees. The annual level of inflation in Yugoslavia in January 1994 had reached 116 billion percent! In case this seems hard to imagine, below is a 500 billion Yugoslav Dinar note.

Fortunately, the restaurant owner had some of his savings in gold rather than just national currencies. This simple decision had allowed him to start afresh in Switzerland. He told Egon and his dinner companions to never keep any money in the bank but to only hold physical gold. Needless to say, Egon could only nod and smile, as he has been saying this for years to his numerous clients around the globe.

This former witness to Yugoslavian inflation was a Confucian hero in that he was prepared for the "possibility of ruin." He was not a market expert, hedge fund manager, global banker or Harvard graduate. He simply understood and foresaw, in real time, the inevitable failure of policy makers pretending that a massive debt problem can be solved with even more debt. As for Egon's erudite and wealthy friends who were at the restaurant that same night, they still don't hold any gold. Like 99.5% of other "sophisticated" investors, they prefer the comfortable illusion that policy makers are wise and that trees grow to heaven together with stocks, crypto's and property. In short: The "Yugoslav problem" could never happen to *them*...

And based on the stock market in the prior 40 years, who could blame such thinking, as this was an understandable delusion. Indeed, most investors in such central-bank-supported markets could not avoid making money and never feared a crisis. But beneath such an understandable and common complacency, lies a dangerous reality. As of this writing, almost no investors are in a Confucian state of preparedness. As such, they will inevitably be taken by a painful surprise whenever and however the next financial crash accelerates.

Initially, of course, most investors will expect central banks to save them yet again, as they had done in 1998, 2003, 2009, 2018 and 2020. But when the next V-shaped recovery doesn't happen and the markets just continue downward, most investors will ride that once proud Titanic market all the way to the cold and humble ocean floor.

We however, are not blind to such policy-making ignorance (hubris) and hence such inevitable as well as real reversals, despite how difficult they can be to imagine, accept and then time with any precision, especially given the still powerful ability of central banks and financial sell-siders to promulgate a propaganda-like narrative that modern bankers know how to run deficits without tears or print trillions in currencies without inflation destroying the currencies they hold. We, however, would not be surprised if markets in the coming years fell by as much as 80% to 90% like in the U.S. of 1929-32 or the Japan of 1989. Again, the only alternative to such a *natural* scenario would be far worse: The total command and *un-natural* control of our markets, economies and lives by increasingly centralized governments and central banks. As we are all seeing in real time today, such increasingly autocratic and command-control practices are rising all around us.

Heading into the close of 2021, the Buffett indicator (or ratio) of market cap to GDP (198%) was already giving us another major warning. As the graph below shows, stocks were at an all-time high valuation in relation to GDP.

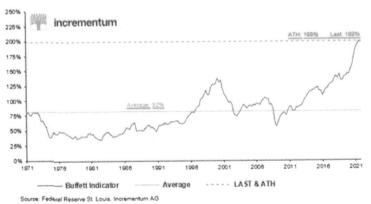

Buffett Indicator (Wilshire 5000/US GDP), in %, Q1/1971-Q4/2021

If we look at the Shiller Cape index, it too was at an historical high (excluding the Dot Com bubble) at 2X the historical average.

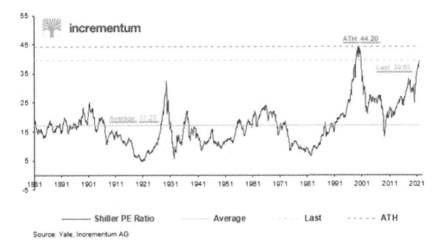

Shiller PE Ratio, 1880-2022

Source: Yale, Incrementum AG

So, yes, overbought positions can extend beyond any rational measure of valuation, but the subsequent crash which follows *every* market bubble, *every* time, will ultimately be long and vicious.

Sell Stocks and Buy Gold—A Seminal Decision

Finally, there were other indicators that reminded us of Confucius' warning that "danger, disorder and ruin may come." The Dow, for example, peaked against gold in 1999. That ratio came down from 44 to 6 (or 87%) by 2011. We have since seen a 10-year correction whereby the DOW has fallen by 58% when compared against the valuation of gold.

By the time this book reaches you, we could even see a further melt-up in the Dow, or the entire exchange could fall dramatically tomorrow. No one can time a market's tipping point toward disaster. No one. Regardless, the time for Confucian preparedness is now.

We know that stocks are massively overbought by every traditional measure, including the discounted value of future dividend streams. To catch the last few points of the rise in these rigged markets was and is an extremely seductive yet dangerous exercise that ultimately leads to ruin. Market tops, rather than confirmed bottoms, are the time to take profits in stocks and protect assets from extreme pain. Sadly, almost no one sells at tops or buys at bottoms, despite the commonsense clarity and historical confirmations of such wisdom. Heading into the 2020's, more and more investors were buying at tops, as they have always done for centuries. In sum: They were grossly over-paying and setting themselves up for long-term pain at the expense of short-term gain.

As of 2021, however, gold was as cheap in relation to the U.S. money supply as it was in 1970 at $35 per ounce or in 2000 when gold was at $290 an ounce. This was a clear invitation to get out of stocks and hold physical gold; a seminal decision, one that heeds 2,500 years of wisdom shared by none other than Confucius, who walked the earth long before the first hedge fund manager or Yugoslav restaurant owner stared down the barrel of a modern currency debasement in motion. In short, one doesn't need to be a market professional, economist, commodity trader or Swiss wealth manager to simply ask one critical question: Am I prepared?

Are you?

Part I

The Problems Facing Distorted Financial Markets

Chapter 1

Everything Is on Fire

"Everything is on fire" – Heraclitus (535-475 BC)

What Heraclitus meant by the foregoing observation is that the world is in a constant, "burning" state of flux. Unfortunately, the danger of that flux and current "fire" is going to become a massive as well as self-evident problem in the coming years. In short: The world will experience an economic fire of a magnitude never seen before in history. Again, this may seem extremely hard to accept or believe. We understand this, and for years were equally reticent to face hard facts otherwise hidden from public view and discourse. However, as we slowly looked at the evidence and events taking place in the global economy, the data became harder to ignore.

In the many articles and interviews since our concerns were confirmed by math and history rather than doom and gloom, we have repeatedly pointed out how predictable events (and people) truly are. This requires no sophistry or sensationalism and is particularly true of actors in the world economy. Empires come and go, economies boom and bust and new currencies equally come and go without fail. Again, all this happens with historically-confirmed regularity, as we show in the chapters below.

A Global Fire Is Coming

But at certain times in history, the fire becomes cataclysmic. Sadly, and without exaggeration, this is where the world is today.

Explosive fires have already started all around us. Stock markets are on fire and so are property and crypto markets, as well as bond and debt markets. The problem is that these fires are initially *explosive*, and even enjoyable/profitable, but they always end up as *implosive*.

At least as of this writing, we are in the explosive phase with markets all going parabolically exponential—or rather exponentially parabolic...

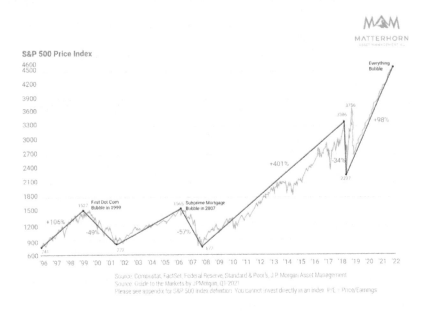

S&P 500 Price Index

Source: Compustat, FactSet, Federal Reserve, Standard & Poor's, J.P. Morgan Asset Management
Source: Guide to the Markets by JPMorgan, Q1 2021
Please see appendix for S&P 500 Index definition. You cannot invest directly in an index. P/E = Price/Earnings

We are now approaching the end of a secular bull market in the world economy which on a global level has reached extremes never seen before in history, fueled by uber-profligate money printing and credit (i.e., debt) expansion by central and commercial banks.

We have warned clients for years about asset price inflation running wild, and not just with regard to stocks. Property markets are literarily exploding, especially at the high end, from Malibu to St. Moritz. We see this all over the world as opposed to just in the US. In the UK, for example, HSBC stated that March 2021 (just one year after the COVID-induced market crash of March 2020) saw the highest number of mortgages ever issued. At the same time in Sweden, properties sold at 40% above asking price in a frenzied bidding war as second-hand leisure boats enjoyed such high demand that they cost virtually the same as a new boat. And even if you wanted a new boat, there were literally none available until 2022. Apparently, people were equally desperate for companionship after the lockdowns; prices for puppies in the UK were up to 100% higher than the previous year. Fortunately, Matt bought his Labrador in 2018...

Yes, nearly everything from housing to Labradors was literally on fire as consumers were desperate to just spend, spend, and spend after countless months of lockdowns and restrictions.

An Economic Bubble of Air

But such explosive, and even enjoyable, fires always end with economies, currencies and risk assets burning down or imploding. Sadly, this is precisely what we foresee in the coming years, a forecast that may make us unpopular at dinner parties today, but calm nevertheless in preparing for tomorrow. A massive economic forest fire is not just inevitable, but also an absolute necessity in clearing (burning) out the toxic excesses and distortions which fueled such conflagrations.

That is, burning economic bubbles consist primarily of highly flammable and toxic air—lots and lots of it. When economic systems or countries, for example, run out of money, all they have to replace it with is more artificially created money and false promises—i.e., more toxic air to keep the fire going.

Since new fiat money, like air, is free, governments can produce unlimited amounts of it. And without exception, gullible citizens want to believe that such newly (mouse-click) created money is actually real money and not just empty air. The beauty for the fork-tongued policy makers behind such toxic, fiat money schemes is that they can just produce and borrow trillions of these fiat currencies at ZERO cost. Furthermore, by manipulating interest rates, they can borrow even more of the fake, debased money at virtually ZERO cost.

The Ultimate of All Ponzi Schemes

So, first the government manufactures the money at no cost and then they pay NOTHING for the privilege of borrowing that money. This, ironically, boils down to an otherwise "respectable" policy which is nothing more than the ultimate of all Ponzi schemes. No wonder, therefore, that bank(er)s, hedge funds and wealthy investors were raking it in—and buying more homes, boats and even puppies...

Of course, the same toxic money obviously creates massive bubbles in stocks and other assets. Just look, for example, at how the Dow had risen exponentially and parabolically in an historically unprecedented straight line into 2021.

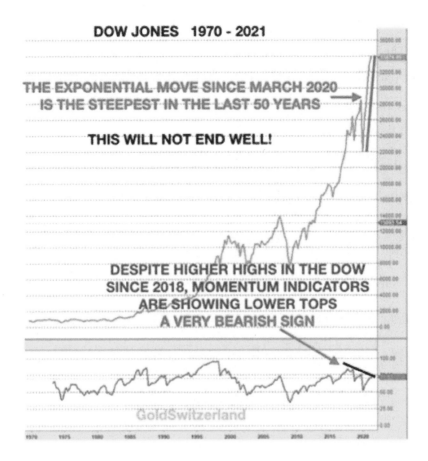

DOW JONES 1970 - 2021

THE EXPONENTIAL MOVE SINCE MARCH 2020
IS THE STEEPEST IN THE LAST 50 YEARS

THIS WILL NOT END WELL!

DESPITE HIGHER HIGHS IN THE DOW
SINCE 2018, MOMENTUM INDICATORS
ARE SHOWING LOWER TOPS
A VERY BEARISH SIGN

GoldSwitzerland

The U.S. Is Bankrupt

But as markets reached new and nosebleed highs, the toxic wind (air) beneath their wings was ignored by the vast majority of investors and policy makers with almost unthinkable levels of hubris and self-delusion, a topic we address more carefully in Chapters 6 and 18. In short, what was ignored during these "burning good times" was the otherwise objectively obvious fact that the US and other leading economies were and are totally bankrupt. With less than a handful of exceptions, the U.S. federal debt had been rising every year since 1930 to increasingly unsustainable levels, as we discuss and evidence with candid realism throughout these pages.

So, here we have the biggest economy in the world which can only hold on to this position by printing itself to a false prosperity at an ever-faster pace. To allow such candor and realism to sink in, just consider the simple math and facts below to understand what a government can create out of thin air.

After the Gold window was closed in 1971, US federal and total debt as well as money supply has gone exponentially parabolic and the dollar, the world's reserve currency has lost 98%. Other key figures to consider since 1971:

US federal debt is up by 74X;

Total U.S. debt is up by "only" 49X;

M2 Money Supply is up by greater than 29X;

U.S. Debt to GDP: In 1971, 37%, by 2021, that embarrassing ratio had risen to 135%.

But like all exponential curves of a big sample, this one will end in tears. Bubbles are called bubbles because they consist of air. And when bubbles become too big, they ALWAYS and without fail "pop," a pattern which becomes clear rather than theoretical in the chapters to follow. Sadly, such an implosion is precisely what the US economy as well as the rest of the world can expect next.

Fundamentally, and as discussed throughout Part I, US and global stocks are massively overvalued. Of course, we also know that such overvaluations can last longer than we can rationally expect, especially when approaching the end of a very long super-cycle. Central banks will not give up too easily nor ever admit their failures to otherwise outlaw market crashes. Nevertheless, markets are fundamentally, historically and technically giving very clear signals that THE END IS NIGH.

Whether that ending means days, weeks, months or years ahead is frankly irrelevant. We know from the data shared throughout these pages that we are at the end of the most remarkable period in history in regards to global currencies, markets and economies. At the same time, we also know that socially, morally and politically we are reaching a low point in history, the measurements of which we address in Chapters 3-7.

The World Needs a Big Fire

So, back to the fire. We actually need a proper and very big forest fire that gets rid of all the foregoing excesses, be they financial or social. Only then will the world again create new green shoots, free from debt and false values, both political and financial. Realistically, however, before such a fire-clearing cleanse can occur, the implosion of most debt and asset values will create a very difficult period of transition for the world. It could last one decade or several. How long it will actually last, only future historians can tell us.

Already, and in the years to come, there will be more and major suffering around the world which will not just be financial but also social. We will see increasing levels of centralized control over our lives, more distracting proxy wars (i.e., Ukraine), civil strife, famine, disease and migration. But there will be virtually no money for social security or aid of any kind. Citizens will be forced into greater dependence on governments who had previously ignored them. Nor will there be viable pensions and efficient markets. Again, we recognize that this sounds (and is) dire, but realistically we know that cycles are part of life. And some cycles are more extreme and painful than others. What has made this one potentially worse than any the world has ever experienced is that governments and central banks have so grossly interfered with the natural cycles of ebb and flow, supply and demand, good times and cleansing bad times. By extending the "good times" well beyond their rational expiration dates, policy makers have only made the "tough times" ahead far more extreme.

In trying to stay popular, beloved and hence credible, electable and praised, policy makers have promised more than can be delivered by sound economic principles. They have effectively tried to telegraph an openly dishonest and frankly shameless message that recessions and bad times can be outlawed by artificial money creation and central bank magic. Investors, like children, of course want to believe in such fairy tales, and thus, until now, have operated under the delusion that central banks and governments have their backs. What John F. Kennedy said in his infamous inaugural address of 1961 has sadly been entirely up-turned. That is, the famous declaration: "Ask not what your country can do for you, but what you can do for your country," has been inverted within a more selfish era and generation that declares instead: "Ask not what you can do for your country, but what your central banks can magically do for you."

Evidence of such delusional promises from on high are now ubiquitous, from every policy pulpit of nearly every developed nation. Gordon Brown, the UK Chancellor of the Exchequer (Finance Minister) famously stated in 1999, for example, that he had abolished "Boom and

Bust." A few months later, stocks and the economy crashed. Just months before the Great Financial Crisis of 2008, Fed Chairman Bernanke saw no signs of concern.

This fatal combination/trend of comforting words and toxic monetary policies has grossly interfered in natural market and even sociological cycles, especially within the US, whose rise and fall has undeniable implications for the rest of the world. By foolishly trying to abolish cycles, governments have exacerbated the problem to a degree that will create unnecessary suffering for the world, most of which will be falsely (and conveniently) attributed to COVID (death rate of 0.5%) rather than policy makers (death rate of global currencies >99%).

Ultimately, it is our stance that the most important remedy in periods of such crisis is family and friends. These are the key lessons of difficult times (from the 1941 bombing of London to the Live Aid concerts for Africa in 1985), namely: That people learn to support each other rather than just chase material values or point fingers at other groups.

In addition to family and close friends, there are so many wonderful things in life that are virtually free, including nature, music and books. We will soon find that these pursuits and settings are much more fulfilling than our iPads, Netflix or talking-head pundits de jour.

Gold and Wealth Preservation

Aside from such invisible and truly meaningful values, the task (as well as priority) of securing the tangible value of your finances in such current and looming periods of crisis will equally involve the ownership of *physical* gold and silver, which is the core theme of this carefully prepared book. Everyone can afford some gold or silver. As of this writing, an ounce of silver is $30; and one gramme of gold is $60. Saving in precious metals will not only be very useful, but essential at whatever level you can afford. For larger investors, physical gold and silver will be one of the few ways to avoid the total destruction of their acquired wealth. Again, and as we have advised so many times, gold is currently as cheap today as it was in 1970 at $35 or in 2000 at $290 when measured in relation to US money supply.

Gold and silver pricing, for reasons outlined in Part II below, have not at all (or yet) reflected the massive creation and hence debasement of money in the last 50 years. That catchup phase is likely to start very soon based on both fundamental and technical indicators. The upside potential for gold and silver is multiples of the current prices. Hyperinflation could take the price of metals to unfathomable heights.

But holding physical gold, as opposed to say Bitcoin (*See* Chapter 18), should not be seen or entered into simply as a speculative investment, but far more simply as the best protection against the coming destruction of paper assets and the imminent disorder in the financial system in general and fiat currency system in particular. As we'll see in the following chapter, great nations, economies and currencies can and do implode if they ignore the debt cancers flowing beneath the surface of their "boom years."

Chapter 2

History's Warnings: Old France

It's Ithaca, New York, the winter of 1912 and multiple jet streams, acquiring energy from low-pressure areas in the Gulf, have sent record-cold winds across Cayuga Lake and over the glacial erratics which formed several hundred thousand years prior. Gaining speed, these invisible gusts rose into the Hemlock Gorge and beyond the ice-caped Finger Lakes toward the heights above Fall Creek where a now forgotten academic began writing (and warning) of market weather patterns and broken currencies which persist to this day.

White's Ghost

His name was Andrew Dickson White, and perhaps this early 20th century historian and educator could already feel the currents of time pressing against his pen as those same winds pressed against the creaking walls of his campus home. The crackle from a massive fireplace sent a glow over endless bookshelves as the bibliophile's den filled with the scent of burning oakwood. Surrounded by texts dating back from the Latin of ancient Rome to the modern languages of Renaissance Italy, the Enlightenment of Voltaire and the theological range of Germany's Friedrich Schleiermacher to Friedrich Nietzsche, professor White had a lot on his mind in 1912. Perspective came easily to this aging scholar. Outside, the frigid gusts of February strained against windows overlooking a still young but ambitious Cornell University, which the same professor had founded decades prior in 1865.

Professor White was not only a student of history and its cyclical windspeeds, but an integral part of it, as each of us, ultimately, are. A great Civil War between his nation's Northern and Southern states had ended the very year his university came to fruition. Yet on Cornell University's Quadrangle, like other parks and campus greens across that still adolescent country, one cold still see grey-bearded men leaning on canes or smoking slow-burn pipes, the battle memories of Manassas, Gettysburg, Antietam or Cold Harbor still fresh in their memories. Alas, the winds of time and human behavior seemed to move with an instructive rhythm as Professor White considered the lessons of financial history while putting pen to paper amidst a winter storm.

At the same time, and across the world on the docks of Southampton, workers commissioned by the White Star Line were putting the finishing touches on the rivets, wall art and dining tables of the RMS Titanic, considered to be the safest and most luxurious passenger vessel of its day. Deemed unsinkable by the press and its creators, the great liner (much like the financial markets entering the 2020's) seemed immortal. But just two months later in April, the proud and unsinkable ship would carry both hubris and irreplaceable lives to the bottom of the Atlantic on its maiden voyage. Time, like the winter storm blowing against Professor White's windows, thus continued her perpetual motion, riddled with glories, reminders, tragedies and warnings.

Then as now, of course, the primal question facing Professor White remained as timeless as history itself, namely: Who would head her lessons? Who would be prepared for the currents and cycles of the past, present and future?

For Professor Andrew Dickson White of Cornell University, such questions never left his thoughts. From the ivory tower of an Ivy League campus on the edge of a town still flourishing in an industrial age that would eventually come crashing down, his thoughts were forever turning toward the patterns of yesterday and their prognosis for tomorrow. On this particularly cold day in 1912, Professor White's thoughts had turned to currencies, politicians, war debts, over-paid bankers, desperately broke sovereigns and profit-mad speculators, a theme for which we are all too familiar today--at least, if we, like White's example, are paying careful attention.

The manuscript pages strewn across Professor White's desk in early 1912 would soon be published that same year under the otherwise innocuous and academic title, *Fiat Money Inflation in France*. Today, more than a century later, if you were to make any pilgrimage to a modern bookstore, their shelves riddled with trending diet secrets, political face shots and the dross of identity politics and celebrity virtue-signaling masquerading as cultural insight, you would never, not ever, find a copy of White's compelling book of warnings among such titles and contemporary pablum. Like the author himself, his otherwise brilliant work and warnings have largely been absorbed, and for most, forgotten by time and lost in an era where insight is deemed "elitist" and patient, hard-won knowledge has been replaced by tweets authored by those who possess neither the patience nor knowledge of longer word counts and deeper considerations of facts rather than hype.

But like all things precious, from gold and silver to the affections of a spouse, child or friend, such assets are deemed as such precisely because they are, alas: Scarce, and *timeless*. In this brief chapter, as we blow the dust of the forgotten warnings of a forgotten book and equally forgotten author, let us therefore bring the precious lessons of White's ghost back to the current, and arguably, embarrassing moment in global economies. In doing so, we rediscover the intrinsic value of timeless lessons and timeless assets while endeavoring to provide a store of intelligent value to all who will take the necessary time to listen. In short, let us invite the ghost of Andrew White, as well as the pages of his 1912 warning, into the 21st century and the paragraphs gathered here. The reward, like anything rare and valuable, is worth the time spent.

In particular, White's 1912 examination of the fall of 18th century France is a fascinating as well as fitting place to begin, as it warns of a sincere (yet disastrous) attempt by the world's then strongest empire to tackle otherwise unsustainable military, private and public debts through the excessive printing of money and the extension of promised debt obligations otherwise too staggering in depth to ever repay.

Sound eerily familiar?

Equally worth noting is that the French National Assembly of 1789 of which Professor White had written, much like the Congress of 2008 Washington or the bureaucratic swamp of the European Union's Brussels headquarters of the same era, was comprised of the most educated minds and alleged "experts" of its time– including Charles Maurice de Talleyrand-Perigord, Jacques Necker, the Compte de Mirabeau, Jean Sylvain Bailly, Pierre Samuel DuPont de Nemours, and Dominique de La Rochefoucauld.

But as White's ghost reminds, even those 18th century titans of educational firepower and oratorical savvy were unable to thwart the natural laws of markets, including the simple lesson (harkened by philosopher-mathematicians from David Hume in 1752 to John Hussman in 2017) that extreme debt destroys all nations, with *zero* exceptions.

As White noted in 1912, these 18th century policy makers, "like every supporter of irredeemable (i.e., fiat) paper money then or since, seemed to think that the laws of Nature had changed since previous disastrous issues," including the currency diluting debacle of the John Law era of 1720. Today, this law of nature/markets is as plain to see in the 2020's as it was in 1789 Paris or 1912 Ithaca: Nations simply can't print and borrow their way out of debt in the short-term without unleashing a longer-term disaster to both their currency and economy.

Reading the pages of White's compelling yet now forgotten 1912 warnings of 1789 France from the current lens of the 2020's is in many respects a journey into the surreal. That is, one could easily change the names, venues or dates of old France and substitute them with the headline-makers of modern America, Europe or Asia, proving indeed: "*la plus ca change, la plus c'est le meme chose.*" That is: The more things change, the more they stay the same.

The past, like Professor White's ghost and pages, haunts us, warns us. Most importantly, such pages can also *prepare* us. As Mark Twain famously observed of history, it may not repeat itself, but it certainly rhymes. In short, there are cycles, from the psychological and financial to the rebellious and absurd, which move, like the weather patterns from Upstate New York to the sun rising and setting over the Swiss Matterhorn, *in predictable patterns.* In re-visiting the warnings of White's pages and ghost below, we can quickly track these cycles, all of which we have simplified below into nine distinct phases.

Let's begin.

Phase 1: A Deep Problem in Search of a Shallow Fix

The France of 1789, much like the U.S. of 2008, had found itself, as White observed, "in deep financial embarrassment." Namely, markets had crashed, deficits had grown beyond repayment and the population was slowly losing faith in its leaders. In this 1789 French backdrop, as in 2008 America, White wrote in 1912 of a "growing desperation among the national leadership to find a miracle solution." As White observed, "there was a general search for some short road to prosperity" (i.e., speedy calls for the printing of new money) to give the ailing nation a "little boost," what we and our financial leadership today would call "stimulus," or even more comically (and euphemistically) "accommodation."

The French Finance Minister at the time was a politician named Jacques Necker. Unlike our Monsieurs Bernanke of the 2008 Federal Reserve or the Mario Draghi of the European Central Bank, the Necker of 1789 recognized the short-term seduction yet long term (and fatal) danger of printing too many paper currencies to temporarily place a debt-soaked economy out of harm's way. Thus Necker, and other policy makers including Nicolas Bergasse (deputy from Lyons), Jacques Antoine de Cazales and Jean-Sifrein Maury, initially sought to fight off the seductive call of free printed money with classical oratory at the National Assembly. They proclaimed that the ultimate result of such money creation, "could only be disastrous," as printing fake currencies was nothing more than "a panacea...a way of securing resources without paying interest." These blunt-speakers of the 1790's reminded their gathered politicians of recent history, 70 years prior, in the era of John Law when it was learned how easy it was to print money, yet how difficult it was, as Necker warned, "to check its over-issue" and how "securely it creates a class of debauched speculators, the most injurious class that a nation can harbor."

Sound familiar?

By the 2020's, clearly the warnings of White's ghost or these French Assemblymen had been forgotten, as the vast majority of American policy makers and investors had indeed grown to become such an "injurious class" already "all-in" and looking to make their fortunes in a stock market bubble that had, in the prior decades, morphed into what was little more than a casino, filled with an entire new class of what Necker described as "debauched speculators."

In our modern markets, the price of Tesla, for example, proves this point without rancor but simple math. By 2020, we saw an entity with a nosebleed market cap of greater than $700B yet a free cash flow in the basement.

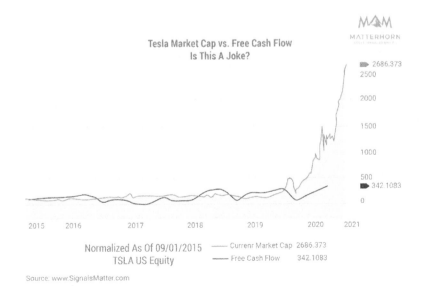

Tesla Market Cap vs. Free Cash Flow
Is This A Joke?

Normalized As Of 09/01/2015 —— Current Market Cap 2686.373
TSLA US Equity —— Free Cash Flow 342.1083

Source: www.SignalsMatter.com

Such disconnects between speculative price and intrinsic value warned of an undeniable trend of dangerous, and indeed, unprecedented speculation and hence grotesque over-valuation, making one class of speculators rich as the nation's economy slowly rotted from the bottom up. In short, market conditions in modern America looked a lot like the desperate world of 1789 France. And against these ultimately prophetic warnings in the late 1700's, hope peddlers and fantasy-chasing media leaders like Jean-Paul Marat, "friend of the people," and others in his speculative circles were more than able and willing to seduce the French investors with even more fantasy promises of "stimulating" the economy with just the right amount of French money printing and interest rate suppression.

Sound familiar?

Remember the Hank Paulson, Tim Geithner, and Ben Bernanke of 2008? Or the "Do-whatever-takes" Mario Draghi of 2012? Or how about China's bloated central bank or Japan's Haruhiko Kuroda ever since 2013? Just look at the massive amounts of mouse-click-created fiat money they collectively created between 2007 and 2021 to keep markets and "debauched speculators" happy.

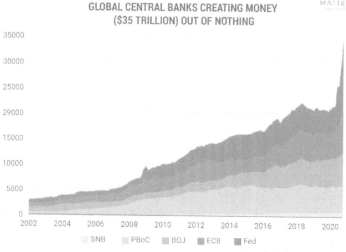

Turning back to White's ghost, he reminds us that in 1790, France made its first real toe-dip into printing money (the equivalent then of America's first try at "Quantitative Easing," or "QE1") with the issue of 400 million in new money (a relative hiccup compared to the 2008 equivalent in the US). The result? As expected, the free French money creation felt wonderful, as all new money initially does. The fake currencies were originally backed by French real estate confiscated from the nobles and the church and was promised (like our current sovereign IOU's/U.S. Treasury bonds) to "be free of default risk."

Needless to say, the French Treasury of 1790 was understandably relieved to see this new "money" pour into its coffers. Old debts were paid with new yet artificial "liquidity," easy and cheap credit was revived, trade was increased, markets surged and the French were quite euphoric—much like the post-09 "V-shaped" and money-printed recovery which markets in the U.S. enjoyed in the wake of its "QE" new normal.

Phase 2: From "Emergency Measure" to Addiction

But just like those accustomed to one too many martinis, the buzz of free money began to slowly lose its impact or "buzz," and thus within a short time, the French Assembly, along with that growing and "injurious class" of speculators and traders from Bordeaux to Marseilles, wanted another round of more fake and quick-fix money printing.

Sound familiar?

Despite original promises by Marat and Necker to temper the printing (as Bernanke had equally promised in 2009), the addiction to printed new money became too tempting, and thus another round of money was created (a veritable "QE2" of its day) in the form of another 800 million in what the French called "*assignants*," aka fake money.

The parallels then to the flirtation with printed money in post-08 America (as a proxy for Europe and Asia), for example, are striking. Yet then, as now, a small cadre of blunt-speakers tried to warn the so-called "experts" of the long-term destruction wrought by short term printing (think, today, of David Stockman, Steve Keen, Grant Williams or your current authors). Andre Mirabeau, for example, spoke of the printed money as "a nursery of tyranny, corruption, and delusion; a veritable delirium...a loan to an armed robber," with inevitable dangers of inflation or a bursting debt bubble.

Frankly, we could not describe the current era any better.

But soon, even Mirabeau (like Bernanke, Yellen and Powell) got hooked on the drug of quick fixes and easy French money printing, and later declared that "just one more round" of free money would be permissible...but nothing more.

Again: Sound familiar?

Just as Federal Reserve Chairman, Ben Bernanke, promised that the initial money printing of 2009 was only an "emergency measure" to be quickly phased out by 2010, the addictive need for "just one more shot-glass" of fake money trumped prior cautions and promises of restraint. As Professor White later observed in 1912: "the current toward paper money had become irresistible."

Americans have seen that same "irresistible" current from the Eccles building in Washington DC as the money printing euphemistically described as "Quantitative Easing" from its US Central Bank evolved from a one-time "emergency-measure" injection of TARP and QE1 into a permanent drug dispenser of new money and artificially suppressed, low-rate debt for years and years to follow—creating and extending an identical exuberance, market bubble and class of "debauched speculators" as seen in 18th century France right here at home. Meanwhile, and as expected, modern U.S. and global markets inevitably and predictably reached record highs.

Phase 3: The Good Times

As for the modern mania in the post-08 "new normal," even the most delirious bull of the 2020's could not deny the direct correlation of rising/inflating markets to the equally astounding rise in the artificial money supply (Fed Reserve Assets).

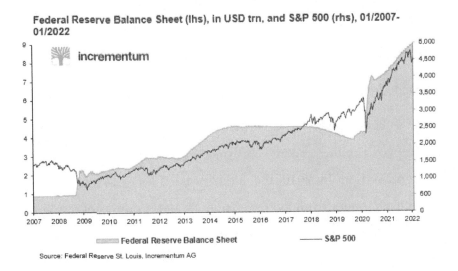

Federal Reserve Balance Sheet (lhs), in USD trn, and S&P 500 (rhs), 01/2007-01/2022

Source: Federal Reserve St. Louis, Incrementum AG

As indicated above, such short-term "good times" were and remain familiar components of the fatal pattern within which the global economy (and psychology) became thoroughly trapped (addicted) by the 2020's. As of this writing, global central banks have already created over $30 trillion in fake (fiat) currencies to provide artificial liquidity so essential to keeping otherwise over-levered and poorly managed global banks (Chapter 10) and risk assets (Chapter 9) artificially supported/elevated.

Phase 4: Keep the Fantasy Going with Fantasy "Data"

This same pattern, seen from 1790's France to the global 2020's, also contains the false comfort (i.e., lies and distortions) of policy experts whose bullish rhetoric kept the herd marching obliviously, even comfortably, toward financial debt cliffs. The France of the 1790's didn't have CNN, televised FOMC releases, the latest puff piece from the ECB or the Private Wealth Management teams of the primary dealer banks to keep investors artificially calm despite the growing risks. Instead, they had even more talented orators at the National Assembly and public newspapers to keep the delusion of easy money going.

One bullish dreamer, a certain Monsieur Gouy d'Arsy, even suggested the French simply liquidate their entire national debt by printing a large amount of money to be used, in his own words, to solve the nation's debt problems, "by one single operation, grand, simple, magnificent."

These were of course comforting and tempting words, which sound a lot like the fantasy which characterizes what so-called economists now describe as Modern Monetary Theory today. Such myopic seductions for easy answers to otherwise impossible debt burdens appeared throughout France and with understandably great appeal. Endless pamphlets and more seductive speeches spread throughout the nation, promising to stimulate the economy and offering dashing projections of how printed money and cheap debt leads to growth and prosperity while totally omitting any references to currency debasement and hence currency risk.

Sound familiar?

Remember Yellen's promise that we'd never see another recession in her lifetime? Remember Bernanke's promise that trillions in printed dollars would come "at no cost" to the currency system? But as history confirms, extreme money creation debases currencies and does, in fact, create considerable harm. Again, and when measured against a single milligram of gold, the world's major currencies have fallen by greater than 80% in just the last two decades.

Milligramm Gold per USD & EUR, 01/1999-09/2020

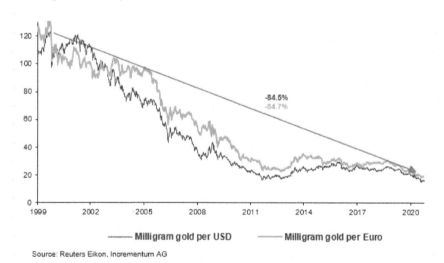

Source: Reuters Eikon, Incrementum AG

But as Andrew White noted in 1912, educated or famous people don't necessarily understand monetary policy, and calling upon "experts" just because they show seductive boldness and optimism "was like summoning a prize fighter to mend a watch."

Phase 5: Minority Voices of Reason Ringing the Warning Bells

Then, as now, there were lone voices of dissent, even exasperation. Necker, the finance minister who permitted the first rounds of printed money, ultimately resigned in frustration over excessive French money creation. Economists like Jean Maury attempted in vain to illustrate how the first issues of printed money always bring prosperity, but "those that follow bring only misery." A profoundly frustrated and farsighted Charles Lebrun then, much like the modern Ron and Rand Paul of the U.S. Congress today, openly attacked the entire scheme of addictive and artificial money creation in the noisy Assembly, prophetically declaring "that the proposal, instead of relieving the nation, would wreck it." Thereafter, additional lone wolfs like Francois de Boislandry and Paul du Pont de Nemours published pamphlets, predicting with haunting accuracy, "that doubling the quantity of money [and debt] simply increases prices, distorts values, alarms capital, diminishes legitimate enterprise and so decreases *real* rather than *speculative* demand that the only persons helped by it are the rich who have large debts to pay."

Again: Sound eerily familiar?

Stated in the 1790's, but such warnings are no less true in the 2020's as extreme money creation and the predictably extreme asset bubbles (and wealth inequality) which followed amounted to nothing more than a massive wealth transfer, making the rich even richer while the rest of the ignored population fell into a system that amounted to little more than financial feudalism (*See* Chapter 4). As this familiar graph reminds us, the only real beneficiaries of totally drunken and fake "market recoveries" lead by *speculative* rather than *real* demand have been the wealthy, not the rest of the nation. What was so true of France in the 1790's is equally and sadly the case in the America stumbling into the 2020's, where the top 10% of the nation's wealthiest enjoyed greater than 85% of the bloated shares in its central-bank-supported (i.e., inflated) S&P. Then, as now, wealth disparity became an open, as well as dangerous, embarrassment.

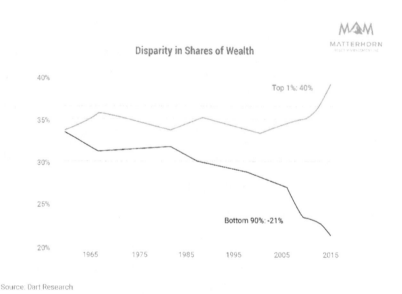

Source: Dart Research

Of course, then as now, such sober and blunt warnings and calls for restraint were not as popular as those promising continued prosperity, free money and, as one 18th century expert declared with a confidence foreshadowing such hope peddlers like Allan Greenspan, Janet Yellen, Ben Bernanke, Jerome Powell or Mario Draghi, "the end of further concern." France in the 1790's, like the US and other global economies crawling into the 2020's, was thus fully committed to a delusional yet popular policy of debt and printed money. Again, and for a while, the economy moved along and even prospered. As Professor White observed from his desk in 1912 Ithaca, "the great majority of Frenchmen became desperate optimists, declaring that printing and debt is prosperity...The nation was becoming inebriated with false hope."

Again: Sound familiar?

When we began writing these pages in 2020, total global debt had skyrocketed from $5T in 1971 to $258T.

Chart 1: Global debt topped $258 trillion in Q1 2020

MATTERHORN

$ trillion

% of GDP, weighted avg.

— % of GDP (rhs)   —— Global debt (in USD)

Source: IIF, BIS, IMF, National Sources

Now, just over a year later and as of this writing, total global debt has already passed $300 trillion, with global GDP (i.e., income) tallying in at well below 1/3 of that staggering figure.

Global Debt by Sector, in USD tn, Q1/1999-Q3/2021

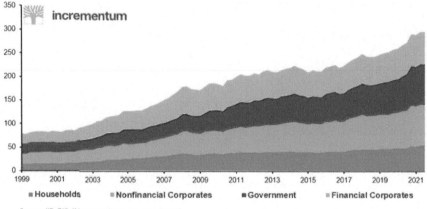

Source: IIF, BIS, IMF, World Bank, Incrementum AG

Such observations remind us of an S&P that never seemed to stumble, a DOW hitting all-time highs in the height of an otherwise global health pandemic and economic shutdown, and a bond-market so overbought by artificial demand form global central bank money printers that all of the major sovereign bonds of the world offered *negative* real yields, which technically meant those sovereign IOU's were in fact nothing more than *defaulting* bonds in the backdrop of a the greatest credit bubble ever seen.

10-year government yields, in %, 01/1995-09/2020

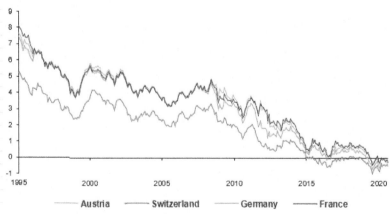

Source: Reuters Eikon, Incrementum AG

Such open yet largely ignored or misunderstood distortions in risk asset markets defied all laws of sound management or even intuitive common sense. Sadly, modern investors, like the delusional crowds of 18th century France, still felt protected by their equally delusional experts.

Again...Sound familiar?

Leading into the 2020's, global markets and investors mis-perceived the short-term safety-nets of central bank money creation as a long-term (and understandably seductive) miracle solution. But what Professor White was arguing in 1912, and what we are warning again *today*, is that these types of "solutions" can only appeal to those who have completely lost sight of market forces, courage, humility and alas: History.

Phase 6: Ignoring Reality—and Data

In fact, history tells us that the debt-and-print party which continued into the 2020's could not and would not last forever; this is simply because our "safety nets" were full of monetary policy weak-spots. Now as in 18th century France, "troublesome holes" began to appear. As White noted of that debt-soaked and market-topping France, "soon the markets were glutted and demand began to diminish."

In other words, bubbles were approaching their apex and the natural, as well as painful, forces of market-cleansing crashes were approaching. Almost no one in the old France, however, wanted to face these facts. Delusion still carried the day, until, well...reality creeped in.

Phase 7: The First Signs of Panic

And then, without warning, panic set in among the once "recovered" and grand empire that was France. In the years after the easy money started to lose its punch, the markets began to see a series of sudden and steep falls.

Sound Familiar?

Remember September of 2015? December of 2018? March of 2020?

Phase 8: Calm the Panic with More Fantasy

The French "solution" to these scary symptoms of pending collapse was no great surprise. More French money printing, more lower rates and thus more debt expansion followed. In short, the 18th century solution was to keep the monetary liquor (i.e., "liquidity") flowing, a policy reaction which boiled downed to this: Enjoy the inebriation and ignore (as well as postpone) the otherwise inevitable hangover.

Again: Sound familiar?

Think of Powell in the fall of 2019 and the Fed's multi-trillion repo market "stimulus" or the COVID crash of March 2020, followed predictably by more debt paid for by more money printing in a span of 8 months in 2020 than all the money printing that had preceded it from 2009 to 2014.

In short, the French, like the FED's sudden open policy of "Unlimited QE," went back to the printing press to create even more fake currency to pay for even more unpayable debts and more rising stock markets. By 1793, hundreds of millions in new *assignants* were created. That is, more fake money was desperately sought to solve rising debt obligations and rising social tensions. As Professor White noted of the French: "Out of this easy money came more speculating and gambling and luxury, and out of this, corruption and false economic data which grew as naturally as a fungus on a muck heap. It was first felt in business operations and markets, but soon began to be seen in the legislative body and in journalism."

Again: Sound familiar?

In 2020, even in the midst of a global pandemic, tanking economic indicators, record-breaking unemployment levels and stagnating growth from Seattle to Sydney, speculators, with the aid of central bank "accommodation" and an openly bullish financial media were pushing stocks like Amazon, Tesla and Bitcoin to levels which no sane, risk-savvy or value-educated buyer would have hitherto ever considered or imagined. Markets reached all-time highs as global economic conditions sank to undeniable as well as record-breaking lows.

And just like the French of the 1790's, the so-called market "journalism" of the 2020's became less and less about the reporting of facts and risks than a pulpit for market-making salesmanship bordering upon outright propaganda. Predatory buy and sell orders came from the tweets of CEOs like Elon Musk and Michael Saylor rather than from genuine experts in risk, history or common sense. In short, a new frenzy followed. At one point in 2021, Tesla made more money in a single day of Bitcoin front-running than it did from car sales in the prior fiscal quarter. Musk had essentially bought the Bitcoin and then made his own market for the same by publicly tweeting his buy order, which sent the digital currency to the moon on headlines rather than substance—a classic sign of the type of market insanity which *always* precedes a market bust.

As to the extraordinary dishonesty and collusion of the Wall Street spin sellers, media bobble-heads and Washington politicos, this is and was not part of some grand or evil conspiracy. Instead, it was merely par for the course human behavior in an industry that thrives on buy rather than sell orders and an historically confirmed weather pattern of human nature prone to delusion (*See* Chapter 6) by preferring seductive fantasy over uncomfortable reality.

In the France of the 1790's, like the US of the early 2020's, a corruptive luxury was enjoyed by bankers, share-price-compensated CEO's and allegedly expert market consultants whose entire survival depended on keeping investors "all-in, all the time." Nearly every analyst recommendation from the primary dealer banks in 2021 was a "buy." Then, as today, executive salaries and income were entirely incongruent with their actual "expertise" as retail investors were exploited by these market big boys in the same manner that plankton is used by open-water whales—to fatten the predator.

Again, this same pattern was seen as markets reached higher highs in the France of the 1790's. In short, White's ghost is worth consideration for the simple reason that history does indeed rhyme.

Heading into 2020's, investor cash levels (lower line) had already sunk to all-time lows as central-bank-supported markets (upper line) reached nosebleed levels of over-valuation. When it came to the market casino of risk assets, everyone was "all-in."

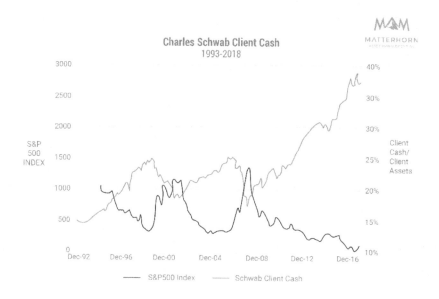

Charles Schwab Client Cash
1993-2018

Such behavior screamed of market distortion and risk ahead. In 2008, for example, had the natural laws of markets been allowed to do their natural cleansing ("constructive destruction") from the crime of too much free money printing, Fed intervention and artificial rate suppression (i.e., debt creation), the majority of those very same bankers and experts would have been deservedly *au chomage...* That is: out of a job—alas, constructively and naturally destroyed. Instead, they were bailed out with more printed dollars from American taxpayers--the ultimate definition and example of a national as well as financial moral hazard. By 2021, in the backdrop of the highest social unrest, unemployment dislocation and government intervention seen in decades, bonuses on Wall Street had reached new highs.

Phase 9: Blood in the Streets…

But as for the mania in France then, and the open mania leading into the 2020's today, the ending was, and is, always the same. The French money printing experiment all came crashing down in dramatic fashion. We have no guillotine in Brussels, Washington DC or Tokyo, but economic heads will roll in one metaphorical way or another soon enough; it's simply a question of how long powerful central banks and completely unaccountable and irresponsible policy makers can extend and pretend that their free money charade is a viable policy. In France, the disaster was so massive that heads literally did roll …Such economic, social and political unrest, unleashed by openly insane monetary and fiscal policies, set the stage for autocracy and created a red-carpet for the arrival of a freedom-destroying era under autocratic figures like Napoleon, whose extreme control over France rose from the rubble of the extreme money printing failures which preceded him.

We expect, and see even now, a slow trend toward increased autocracy (censorship, propaganda etc.) as our financial system slowly unravels.

History Lessons and Current Realities

The lesson of 18th century French money printing (or subsequent collapses in Germany, Poland, Brazil, Bolivia, Yugoslavia etc.) is that EVERY debt party comes to an abrupt and tragic end once artificially supported markets run out of monetary steam and hence suffocate under the growing weight of their own massive debt and massively debased currencies. Today, the major economies of the world are all drowning simultaneously under the greatest debt bubble in recorded history. That should be an immediate cause for concern, no? Policy makers cannot massively print money and increase debt levels without grossly distorting markets as well as free-floating currencies, no matter how long the intoxication or how delusional the delayed hangover. Eventually, the printed money *inflates* asset classes while *deflating* real economies and *debasing* national currencies. The credit and equity bubbles pop. Markets collapse. Currencies lose their inherent value. Societies, angered by economic distress, fracture, and governments respond by increasing their grip and control over individual liberties. The evidence of these trends today is ample enough and all around us, but the collective courage to look at it openly and honestly is temporarily lacking.

But again folks, here's our staggering (and unsustainable) global debt:

Global Debt by Sector, in USD tn, Q1/1999-Q3/2021

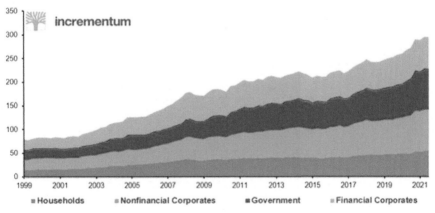

Source: IIF, BIS, IMF, World Bank, Incrementum AG

Again, here's our good-time "intoxication" evidenced by an S&P that just kept rising:

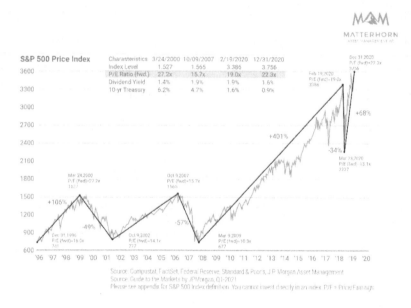

And here's global **GDP** flatlining and hence the ratio of debt to **GDP** skyrocketing around the world as the global market party raged into the 2020's:

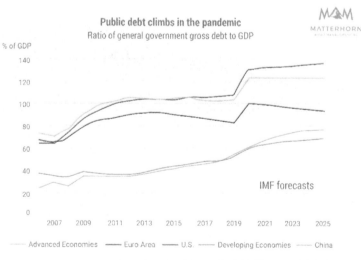

At some point, however, faith in this unprecedented print/debt experiment simply becomes too hard to maintain. The policy lies that once worked are no longer believed. When that faith dies, the markets and economy perish with it. It only takes one of an otherwise vast list of possible "exogenous" events to trigger a collective panic that sends the entire house of financial cards to the ground. Nothing has sustained our inflated markets heading into the 2020's but a misguided faith in artificially suppressed low rates which the central bankers dishonestly managed with one finger on a money printer and the others in a broken credit dyke backstopping the largest pool of toxic debt ever witnessed by mankind.

In the interim, it was (and remains) normal for the majority of investors to ignore such facts and questions. Delusion, as we further examine in Chapter 18, is a powerful *human* as well as *market* force. The cold facts and historical warnings are often too upsetting for those otherwise enjoying a speculative mania to confront. For individuals reading this book's many facts, lessons and warnings, "viewer discretion is therefore advised." Just consider the following hard realities, which serve as a kind of highlight reel of history "rhyming:"

• Since 2008, the US has increased its aggregate money supply (M2 and M3) by greater than 500%, printing 10X more money in just over a decade than was cumulatively created since the birth of that nation.

• In the same period, the US has more than tripled its public debt levels to over $30T; when we include un-funded liabilities to the balance sheet, the number is far greater than $200T. Bubbles are always and everywhere fed by debt/easy credit. The greater the credit preceding (feeding) the bubble, the greater the "pop" which always follows. Current global debt levels, at $300T, are the highest in history; just follow the algebra.

• In that same period of excessive printing and debt creation, actual GDP growth has been anemic at less than 2%. For every dollar of sovereign debt created, the US sees 3 pennies worth of growth.

• Actual, bread-winner US employment (U2 and U3) is at depression levels; despite reporting tricks as to the "civilian labor force" definition, which does not include the millions who have given up looking for work, the true percentage of the working age population that is in fact unemployed is closer to 25%. Today, more than 31 million Americans live off of unemployment benefits and well over 45 million are on food stamps.

• Despite Main Street's woes, Wall Street's speculators have singularly benefited from debt-sustained markets (equity, bond, real estate) which are in fact bubbles of unprecedented size poised for an eventual and cyclical collapse. The correlation of QE (money printing) stimulants and interest rate repressions to S&P peaks is 1:1. Meanwhile, five of the six "too big to fail" private banks have exploited zero-bound interest rate policies and are more levered today than during their pre-08 excess. They share over $270T (conservative) in derivative exposure; today, for each dollar of economic growth, there's 30 dollars of bank debt (a 30:1 ratio; in 1980 that ratio was 2:1).

• At over $1.5 *quadrillion*, the Current gross value of derivatives (i.e., levered paper) trading in global markets simply dwarfs global GDP. The current ratio of stock market capitalization to GDP is a bewildering 200+%. (In 1929 the pre-crash ratio was 84%.) These numbers simply defy reason and, as complexity theory suggests, are way beyond the measure of even the most sophisticated risk management systems.

In other words, having printed more money and incurred more debt than at any other time in world history, all we had to show for this staggering monetary experiment by 2021 was higher unemployment, weaker GDP growth, historically inflated stock/bond markets, extreme currency debasement and an historically unmatched and over-levered central and private banking system. Each of these facts points to a higher level of excess (and hence risk) than anything seen in 1790 France or even 1929 America, and yet the majority of investors, drunkenly stumbling into the 2020's, still believed themselves protected in a new normal of central bank miracles. They, of course, were and are not protected. Instead, they were and remain in an "historical cycle," a nightmarish bubble whose implosion has been postponed rather than outlawed. Such set-ups, of course, always end badly, as White's ghost reminded us in a book commenced (ironically) just one year before the founders of the U.S. Federal Reserve convened on Jekyll Island...

Bears or Just Blunt?

Do the foregoing facts, histories and warnings make us bears, prophets of panic or peddlers of doom and gloom? Are we hiding in caves, loading our guns and collecting gold, water and rice?

No. We are just blunt, and like Andrew White, we respect history and her lessons. Writing in 1912, Professor White was looking over his shoulder at the past with an almost breath-taking awe at the manner in which even the most esteemed policy makers and those who trusted them could single-handedly destroy themselves and their nation from within by grasping at desperate monetary straws-- deluding themselves with diluted currencies to pay for unsustainable and openly disgraceful debt levels.

It's to be assumed, moreover, that White's infamous bookshelves also contained equal chronicles of Ancient Rome, including the periods of the 2nd and 3rd century crisis begun after Commodus, son of Marcus Aurelius, took the throne in 180 AD. At that time, the silver content of the Denarius coin was almost 90%. But as costs gradually soared and revenues declined, the Roman Empire of the 200's, like the French of 1790's or the U.S. of the 2020's, was running out of funds. More and more money was required to bribe a disloyal army and keep infrastructure functioning. By 235 AD, the situation became openly serious as many Roman legions were spread too thin to fight endless and losing wars. The finances of Rome declined so rapidly and debts increased so substantially that taxes were continuously raised, but inevitably, the debts were just too large to solve with taxation alone. By 250 AD there was also a plague that killed major parts of the population.

Does any of this sound like history rhyming?

The similarity between ancient Rome and modern America is equally astonishing. The real (and then unthinkable) decline for Rome started in 235 when the Crisis of the 3rd century began. At that time the Denarius had a 50% silver content which, over the next 50 years, declined to 5%, representing a 90% fall. Emperor Gallienus presided over this final currency debasement in the 260s AD.

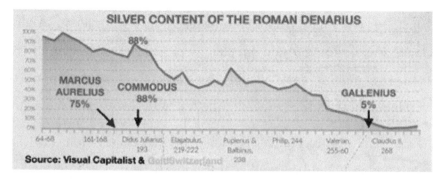

The situation in modern economies is even worse than the fall of Rome. In the 50 years between 1971 and today, the dollar has lost 98% of its real value, measured in gold. The fall is now accelerating as the critical and much-repeated graph below shows. The dollar has lost a staggering 83% in just the last 20 years since 2000.

In addition to the lessons of Roman history, White's private library contained the writings of American leaders who shared his respect for history as well as echoed his warnings for the future. Thomas Jefferson, the nation's third President, for example, had lived in and (personally witnessed) the era of the French National Assembly described above and understood all too well its timeless lessons. In his much-chronicled dispute with Alexander Hamilton over the subject of a private central bank ever finding its way into American policy and hence American economics, he famously wrote to John Taylor in 1816:

"*I sincerely believe* that banking establishments [like a private central bank] are more dangerous than standing armies, and that the principle of spending money to be paid by posterity under the name of funding is but swindling futurity on a large scale."

Just 16 years later, another outspoken U.S. President, Andrew Jackson, was far less prosaic but equally passionate, observing in 1832 that such a central bank would "represent the prostitution of our government for the advancement of the few at the expense of the many."

Less than a century after Jackson's spirited observation, Professor White's understanding, as well as warnings, were no less informed and no less ignored. What is equally telling, and, again, profoundly ironic, is that at the very time Professor White had penned his 1912 warnings of the disastrous example of 1793 France, the rhyming winds of history were already converging against its equally cyclical warnings.

Just 2 years prior to the day when White's book saw its first publication in 1912, the winds of bad banking, bad politics and myopic self-interest began gathering force yet again, this time blowing from a small island off the coast of Georgia straight toward Washington DC and the birth of what is now our so-called *Federal* Reserve, which finally came into a law one year after the publication of White's ignored lessons. The very central bank and polices of which Andrew White had warned (and which would later send the U.S. economic system through a series of disasters culminating in the excesses of the 2020's) was slowly coming to life, conceived by nothing less than a cabal of insider bankers who either ignored or never studied the painful lessons of economic history.

The Fed's Not-So Immaculate Conception

On November 23, 1910 seven powerful men with insider ties to government, banking and extreme wealth gathered in secret at a train station in Hoboken, New Jersey to enjoy a ride in Senator Nelson Aldrich's luxurious private railroad car. Their destination was an equally luxurious and private club on Jekyll Island, off the coast of Georgia. So concerned were they for their nefarious schemes, this cabal of insider bankers agreed to arrive at the station in darkness, using only their first names lest they be noticed by any curious reporters at a time when journalists actually questioned rather than acquiesced to powerful interests or a corporate-controlled media. Once their cigar and brandy-filled train car reached Jekyll Island, this "first-name club" of bankers and politico's spent nine days plotting the birth of the Federal Reserve Act and hence the clever over-throw of the U.S. Constitution's expressed aim of keeping the power of the U.S. currency within the hands of elected officials rather than a corrupt circle of private bankers masquerading as something "federal."

But the powerful personalities gathering at Jekyll Island were more than equipped with the right financial and political clout to pull off what amounted to nothing more than a financial coup d'état. Senator Aldrich, with direct ties to the Rockefeller family and J.P. Morgan, was joined by Abraham Andrew of the Treasury Department, Frank Venderlip and Charles Norton, each presidents of major New York banks, Henry Davison and Benjamin Strong, two senior executives of J.P. Morgan/Banker's Trust Co., and finally, Paul Warburg, a partner at

Kuhn, Loeb & Company with direct ties to the massive Rothschild banking empire.

The mechanizations and tricks schemed on this appropriately named island more resemble the plot of a crime-thriller than a moment of historical realism, and would require many pages to fully unpack, as author Edward Griffen, thankfully, has already done for us. We strongly urge anyone doubting the dubious work, as well as origins, of the Federal Reserve to read his critically important work, *The Creature of Jekyll Island*, as it demonstrates, rather than speculates, that the world's most powerful central bank was illegitimately conceived with an aim toward serving a minority of insiders rather than a nation of citizens, laws and capitalistic values. Three years after their Jekyll Island meeting, the Federal Reserve was signed into law by a cowering Woodrow Wilson. Alas, the creature now known as the Federal Reserve was born in 1913, a private bank conceived by private bankers who, from the stroke of one reluctant yet pressured Presidential pen, were given the immense power to control the cost and supply of the U.S. Dollar. And from that unholy alliance of insiders, a sordid and rigged history of financial engineering, wealth disparity and market distortions continue unabated to this day, the grotesque consequences of which we shall track throughout the chapters and pages to follow.

Stated simply, the road ahead is filled with change and discomfort for the broader economy and markets. For informed citizens and investors of the global economy, however, such a crisis also offers tremendous opportunities. For those armed with stubborn facts, common sense and patience, we wrote the following pages to prepare and protect any who are willing to soberly confront cold data, absorb their implications and thus prepare for their consequences. Once so informed, investors can thereby make the otherwise uncomfortable journey ahead far less volatile, surprising and painful. And as we discover in the following chapter, such hazardous roads, are nothing new, just more extreme today.

Chapter 3

History's Rhymes: Modern America

In Chapter 2, we looked in some detail at the tragic history of extreme debt colliding with extreme liquidity (i.e., money creation) in the backdrop of late, 18th century France. In this chapter, we turn to a nation and era far more familiar, namely: The post-Fed setting of the United States. As you will quickly discover, there are familiar patterns worth noting in the current environment which can help you identify, and hence prepare for, open signs of current and future market, economic and currency risk.

Within just 16 years of its formation, the U.S. Federal Reserve stood by as America entered the Great Depression, a soon-to-be global disaster unleashed by the very same central bank whose public promise in 1913 was to avoid it. Instead, the easy credit and wanton speculation made possible by the "hot money" of central bank "accommodation" during the 1920's–namely cheap and easy access to credit–had sent the debt-soaked U.S. economy and markets to their knees by the early 1930's.

The credit bubble which marked the roaring 1920's ended in an historical disaster on Black Monday of October 28, 1929–precisely as history, as well as the pens and ghosts of Jefferson, Jackson and White had forewarned. As we examine below, the boom to bust cycle marked by the Great Depression in the U.S. was no historical aberration, but rather part of a pre-existing template to be oft repeated in the many decades to follow. In particular, we uncover a pattern of short-sighted leaders using self-centered policies of debt and spend-to-bust euphoria to prolong artificial markets (and garner personal fortunes as well as re-election votes) at the expense of longer-term national growth, a sound currency and sustainable economic health. Although such cycles, as Chapter 2 reminds, have been seen throughout history, for convenience and easy memory, we shall begin with the infamous Great Depression and the subsequent 'recovery' model engaged by Franklin Delano Roosevelt (FDR) to solve for the same. As with the French example provided by White's ghost, an eerie pattern becomes easily recognizable.

Long hailed as the President who brought the US out of the Great Depression, the hard and cold math of economics and objective history confirm that FDR's "New Deal" did not rescue America from the arrogant Crash of 1929. Nor was it a local bank run that caused the markets to collapse that same year. Instead, it was the all-too-familiar low-interest rate policy and debt orgy of the prior and roaring 20's that caused markets to grow too hot—a theme repeated to this day in market bust, after market bust... from 1929 to 1987, 2000 to 2008 and then into the current set-up of the 2020's, the perfect backdrop to the greatest financial disaster ever to be witnessed by capital markets.

At the most basic level, FDR helped turn Washington DC into a Ponzi scheme — that is, a fake "income producer" that solves losing old money by stealing, creating or borrowing new money. Today, U.S. policy makers, like others in Europe and Asia, solve old debt problems by, well...taking on even more debt. As for that new debt, it's then "paid for" with currencies created out of thin air.

Sound crazy? Well, it is...

When you run a country or central bank rather than an illegal Ponzi scheme, the template of more debt to solve prior debt disasters is historically and legally achieved by a simple pattern worth understanding early in this book, namely: a) taking your currency off any collateralized controls (i.e. a gold standard) to both inflate and thus debase the currency; b) keeping interest rates low to encourage the oxymoron of more "debt-based growth" and c) simply printing more fiat money whenever you don't have enough on hand to pay the debt. If Bernard Madoff had owned such a money printer, he certainly would have used it, and if the Fed faced the same laws Madoff faced, they too would be behind bars rather than mismanaging our markets and economies.

By 1933, for example, FDR had essentially taken "the Madoff approach" of faking it tell you make it (or get caught). First, he confiscated gold in the US and then embraced the Thomas Amendment, which in the stroke of a pen devalued the gold content of the dollar and thus betrayed global market participants who had hitherto relied on a U.S. currency standard backed by real gold. Without gold acting as a chaperone to the U.S. Dollar to prevent its over-creation, FDR was thus given free reigns to debase the national currency by creating and spending more of the same. By removing the dollar from the gold exchange, FDR, like many other unwise actors to follow, focused on manipulating the US currency rather than addressing US *productivity*—the veritable "P" in the GDP acronym for Gross Domestic Product.

Like so many politicians before and since, FDR's "solution" was a shortsighted and self-serving *political* decision with long-term and highly dangerous *economic* consequences. Specifically, his knee-jerk macro policies interfered with the hard but informative lesson of free markets, namely: Deep recession always follows deep debt. As the saying goes: "There's just no such thing as a free ride." Policy makers, however, like to sell free-rides *to get or stay elected or employed.* That's not heroic—it's self-serving, the placement of the singular above the many. This too, is a psychological and political motive as old as history itself.

Greater yet far less typical leaders such as Dwight Eisenhower or Harry Truman were far more heroic. They acted through restraint, short-term discomfort (and even unpopularity) with a disciplined focus on austerity, the long-term rebuilding of a dollar standard, a sound national balance sheet, open trade, and economic productivity. When Truman led America into the Korean War, for example, he paid for it with taxes rather than more government debt. Sadly, however, such financially disciplined leaders are the exception rather than the rule. More typical, is the myopic quest for quick debt solutions that create longer-term disasters.

Nixon

Of course, short-term self-interest at the expense of long-term distortion found one of its most infamous examples in Richard Nixon, who learned to postpone pain for political gain at the expense of his nation's currency and financial system. Instead of punishing a debt-sick system, he rewarded it. How did this happen? Well, the Austrians provide some answers.

History as well as math confirm that free markets demand periods of heroic qualities, such as policies (and leadership) marked by restraint and humility. This creates the rational setting wherein lessons can be learned from the hangovers of too much debt and diluted currencies. The Austrian School economist, Joseph Schumpeter, described this as "constructive destruction" -- the commonsense as well as mathematically-confirmed recognition that enterprises, individuals and even nations which take debt-based growth too far into unsustainable levels merit some necessary destruction rather than more bailouts, support or debt to continue operations.

By allowing the painful yet well-earned destruction of such weaker, debt-inebriated players and policies, the over-all system cleanses itself of the preceding debt disease and creates a new environment for the survival of more prudent and healthy actors to continue forward. To do otherwise, Schumpeter correctly forewarned, is to create the moral as well as economic hazard of rewarding rather punishing/removing the system's unhealthy and debt-addicted enterprises, leaders and policies. Failing to allow such needed "destruction" places the entire economic organism at far greater risk over the long term. In much the same way parents refrain from giving their children antibiotics for every cough or sniffle in fear of destroying their natural immune systems, Schumpeter and others warned against giving more debt to already debt-broke systems.

Yet somehow in the intoxicated course of events since the days of Adam Smith, policy makers, U.S. Presidents, hedge fund managers, Fed chairs, Wall Street elites, clueless financial "journalists" and Main Street dreamers seem unwilling to allow the debt disease to naturally cure itself through such constructive destruction, selecting instead the nearsighted path of rewarding debt sins with ever more debt which is "paid for" with fake money created out of thin air. In short, they have been historically, financially and politically unwilling to exercise those two key components of *heroic* market courage, namely: Restraint and humility.

And when it comes to lacking restraint and humility, Richard Nixon is an easy target.

In 1971, Nixon was staring down the barrel of an indebted economy on the brink of bad news and not enough dollars to fix it. The gold standard, revived by the *restraint and humility* of the World War II Bretton Woods Accord, meant the dollar was once again tied to a restraining asset (physical gold) upon which global markets and trade partners relied to keep currencies from losing their value through over-creation. So long as currencies were pegged to a fixed and real store of value like physical gold, policy makers like Nixon could not simply create more currencies out of thin air to cover-up or "solve" the debt sins of their past with new dollars, created, literally, out of nowhere.

Nixon, of course, didn't like this. An election was on the horizon and he needed more economically stimulative dollars which he simply didn't otherwise have given the current level of gold in the U.S. reserves. In short, the needed restraint of a gold-standard may have been good for the long-term health of American and global markets and economies, but it could also cost him a renewed seat in the Oval Office. Thus, Nixon was in a pickle. Other nations trusted America's gold-backed currency and were thus buying lots of gold-exchangeable dollars. Unfortunately, the US gold reserves were woefully low compared to the number of dollars in circulation. In order to honestly and *successfully* rectify this imbalance, a heroic leader would have had to initiate a painful yet necessary recalibration of gold to the dollar or otherwise severely tighten the nation's economic belt, which would have meant short-term pain at home, and hence tremendous election-time risk for him.

But Nixon was no hero...

Given the choice between doing the right (and uncomfortable) thing for his country or doing the wrong (and "stimulative") thing to keep him elected, he, alas, did what almost all elected officials before and since have always done, namely: *What was best for him.* In a move similar to FDR in the 1930's, Nixon jettisoned the Bretton Woods gold exchange standard and thus once again welched on US Dollar holders and currency-honest trade partners overseas. With the currency once again untied to any standards, reigns or "chaperones," Nixon was thus free to again devalue the dollar and lower rates to encourage short-term economic activity (i.e., debt) to boost his pre-Watergate election chances on the back of a happy and "re-stimulated" national economy.

He won by a landslide.

Needless to say, the U.S. Dollar slowly began its fall from grace and intrinsic value from that day forward. Measured against a milligram of gold, the U.S. Greenback has lost 97% of its strength since Nixon's infamous decision in 1971 to remove the gold standard.

This "stimulus" mentality (repeated to this day by current policy makers around the world) was tantamount to doping the economy for a quick fix (and political popularity) at the expense of extreme currency debasement and inevitable inflation, which was immediately apparent in the late 1970's when inflation rose to 17% according to a far more honest Consumer Price Index scale to measure inflation than the one used today (*See* Chapter 15). Nixon's policies once again strengthened the template for a now trend-setting perversion of the bad marriage between bad politics and equally accommodating central bankers via a familiar pattern of: 1) debasing the national currency, 2) lowering rates to encourage short-term speculation based on massive debt stimulus which 3) ends in unnaturally large market bubbles and subsequent market collapse.

Look familiar?

Nixon's 1971 decision set the stage for a global perversion of currency exchanges, which haunt markets to this day. By removing gold from the global currency models, we now face the problem attendant to all floating currencies, namely the fact that free markets no longer set exchange rates; instead, national policy makers do, and they do *so selfishly—not heroically.* The U.S. is a poster-child of such economic *self-preservation,* meaning it is able (as the owner and manipulator of the world's reserve currency) to export and monetize its deficits and inflation like an economic virus to the rest of the world (i.e., other nations are forced to import our inflated/devalued dollars) and thus spread and encourage equally reactive inflationary (and currency-debasing) policies overseas. We address this "viral currency disease" in greater detail in Chapter 11.

U.S. currency policies of debasement (which keep anti-heroes popular, and thus in office) have effectively spawned *global* currency policies of debasement, which means the currency in your wallet today is weaker than it was yesterday. Current international "my-nation-first" currency markets are the scene of state sponsored manipulations whereby central banks (from the ECB to the Bank of Japan) can purchase their own sovereign debt pegged to thin air rather than an actual store of value and real money (namely, physical gold) as part of an ongoing and now normalized global policy of debt bubbles and trade battles to punish-thy-neighbor via currency wars. In short, currencies around the world have engaged in a collective race to the bottom ever since 1971.

The Fed—A Bastion of Anti-Heroes

But let's move from easy targets like Presidents and look at even more dangerous folks like central bankers...

The Greenspan Monster

Black Monday, October 19, 1987. In even that pre-CDS and CDO uber-leverage world of derivatives gone mad, markets in the late 1980's, like White's ghost, once again reminded us that any significant degree of easy credit and leverage (by then computerized) leads to equal amounts of greed and then pain, which can come, seemingly, out of nowhere.

The spark which set off the crash of 1987 was the ironic fear/rumor that the new Fed Sheriff in town, Alan Greenspan, might put an end to the Wall Street binge party by raising rates in a "Volcker-like" scenario. And so, in a single day, the nervous stock index dropped 23%–double the 13% declines on the worst day of the 1929 Crash. All this panic came because the markets feared Greenspan would instigate rising rates, and hence higher costs of debt. This terrified the markets, as cheap debt was the rotten wind beneath their otherwise broken wings.

But even more astounding than this Black Monday was the Lazarus-like resurrection of the market recovery on the Magical Tuesday to follow. By 12:30 PM the next day, the markets saw massive buy orders which, in a miraculous swoop, stopped the panic. How did this miracle occur?

Well, it comes down to this: The Greenspan Fed was clearly no "Volcker 2.0" seeking to restrain Wall Street with rising rates. Rather than allow markets their well-deserved moment of "constructive destruction," Greenspan came to the rescue of wayward markets and an over-levered and over-greedy Wall Street by lowering rather than raising rates. Alas, Greenspan was no Volcker. Rather than restrain the excessive leverage and drunken speculation of the late 1980's, Greenspan simply added more spiked, low-rate punch to the already over-flowing punchbowl of easy credit/easy money that is and was the core source of Wall Street excess. In short, if ever there was a "patient zero" for the disastrous Fed policies which have followed since 1987, it would easily be Mr. Greenspan. Full stop.

Rather than punish Wall Street for excessive behavior (i.e., over-leverage), Greenspan tossed his hitherto (and PhD confirmed) reputation for being tough on wayward markets (i.e., by not rewarding bad behavior with low rates) and figuratively got in bed with Wall Street. Unlike Paul Volcker or Bill Martin—true Fed heroes who understood the need for taking away (rather than adding to) the punchbowl of easy credit and low rates from over-heated/indebted markets, Greenspan sold his reputation (and economic views) to Wall Street, a precedent-setting move followed lock-step by other Faustian bet-makers like Bernanke, Yellen and Powell...

That is, rather than allow normalized rates and painful corrections (i.e., a natural market hangover) to teach investors a "constructively destructive" lesson about derivatives, leverage and other speculative landmines dotting the S&P futures pits (which dropped by 29% in a single day) and larger markets, the Greenspan Fed arrived with even more buckets of cheap money and thus destroyed any chance for the cleansing, tough-love of naturally correcting markets. Such policy moves, once again, created the moral hazard of letting Wall Street behave like the spoiled nephews of a rich (and rigged) Uncle Fed: Spending and borrowing with impunity until the next crisis, at which point there would always be an Uncle Fed to bail them out—at least until that uncle (or currency) himself becomes discredited or insolvent (which, ironically, and unknown to most, is precisely where global markets were heading into the 2020's ...)

Modern Wall Street—Almost Nothing but Anti-Heroes

Self-seeking, career-preserving policy makers who create environments wherein: 1) the dollar is unrestrained, 2) credit is easy and 3) regulation is lax (or favors "creativity") stay popular and keep their jobs and prestigious titles, thanks largely in part to Wall Street lobbyists who finance their election campaigns or post selections. They also set a stage wherein clever market players are free to scheme their ways into ever-increasing bubbles for personal wealth at the expense of economic growth.

The Exchange Pits and the Derivatives Cancer

Such self-seeking behavior and financial creativity leads directly to a speculation cancer of over-valuation and lethal risk which metastasizes within every asset class and market corner, including the once humble mercantile exchange of futures contracts (the "MERC"). It was in this former cob-web-modest and Chicago-based exchange where yet another wrongly acclaimed anti-hero, Leo Melamed, applied the fatal (yet near-term profitable) notion of applying *levered* futures contracts (originally and *modestly* created to help humble farmers and suppliers adjust for price volatility) to global currencies, a *greedy* idea which could only have been spawned in the unfettered currency environment created by Nixon's folly in 1971.

Shortly thereafter, Melamed, having conferred with other well-paid "advisors" including a then young and still largely unknown Alan Greenspan, alongside a similar cast of easy-money, self-interested minds (including Milton Friedman), got the green light to open currencies to an entirely new level of speculative alchemy—using bowered money to lever greater risk and profits. Four decades later, the volume of currencies (and risk) traded in *1 hour* on the commodities exchange exceeded an entire year's volume of funds traded on the original **MERC**. Today, like all post-71 markets, the exchange pits have morphed into a casino with an astonishing 50,000X growth based on derivatives, leverage and hi-tech software trades that set up *100:1 ratios of hedging volume to the underlying activity rate.* These modern derivatives are nothing more than levered and profoundly toxic hot potatoes whose degree of risk and *tranched* confusion are so far from the plow of any actual value that whenever a liquidity crisis (i.e. not enough dollars to settle levered trades) arises, this very tall house of cards falls like the others. In Chapter 16, we go into far greater detail on the openly manipulated **COMEX** futures market which literally, and artificially, sets the paper price for gold. Such schemes, of course, have absolutely *nothing* to do with honest supply and demand; as such, they are doomed to eventually implode again, as they did in 1987.

In short, the current future's market is not our grandfather's MERC. It's a ticking timebomb.

By introducing derivatives (i.e., extreme leverage from borrowed money), modern traders (aided later by other falsely acclaimed "geniuses" like Larry Summers) learned to use 20:1 leverage on Treasury-Bill Futures, which soon went to wheat futures. And because the Fed's open market desk was transparently taking the volatility out of the Treasury trade, this was easy money at easy leverage for exchange traders. Yet like all easy money schemes, as White's ghost warned, the party stops at some point, as it did in 1987. In a single day, free market forces stepped in and crushed these guys, as they deserved.

The Fed's heroic reaction? Simple, bail out the bad guys. Not very, well...*heroic*, wouldn't you say?

Greenspan, rather than assume responsibility or learn lessons from "derivatives" speculation and the leveraged time bombs it unleashed upon the Chicago Merc and the S&P futures market between 1971 and 1987, simply blamed the crash on "animal spirits." In doing so, his central bank conveniently (and intentionally) overlooked the fact that those "animal spirits" are never a *cause* of market DUI's, but a *result* of their own FED moonshine (i.e., low rates to use borrowed money for fatal leverage) supplied by deliberate and transparent policies of easy money aimed at boosting Wall Street asset bubbles at the ultimate expense of the real economy on Main Street.

Entering the 2020's, the openly absurd yet publicly ignored nature of the derivatives monster born from the Merc's deliberate and post-

Melamed/Greenspan distortions can be easily seen in the context of precious metal mispricing, manipulation and extreme risk. Again, more on this in Chapter 16.

Enter the Hedge Fund Anti-Hero: Long Term Capital Management

In yet another example of the non-heroic, we saw the 1998 collapse of LTCM—a.k.a: Long Term Capital Management—a hedge fund leveraging over $125B (yes, $125B) at the height of its drunken splendor. This Greenwich, Connecticut-based creation of the not-so-heroic John Meriwether, with a staff of the best and brightest Wall Street algorithm writers and Nobel Laureate advisors, stands out as a telling reminder of three additional yet perennial observations regarding Wall Street's "best," namely: 1) the smart guys really aren't that smart, 2) wherever there is exaggerated debt/leverage, a day of reckoning awaits, and 3) the Fed comes to the aid of Wall Street whenever its misbehaving "elites" gets caught in yet another market DUI on the slippery road of omni liquidity while trading under the influence of easy credit and hence easy leverage.

In 1998, when a Russian default sent the S&P down 12%, this was an acceptable pullback rather than grounds for a "Fed-to-the-rescue" panic. In short, LTCM, along with the markets, were due for some "constructive destruction." This mega hedge fund, whose risk models had no formula for the complexity of black-swans (i.e., "$#!T Happens"), got caught with its hands in the leverage cookie jar and deservedly lost all its fingers. The fund, like the entire French nation of 1793, tanked under the weight of its own vain excess. Nevertheless, the Fed, fearing that the loss of just one mega-hedge fund was too much for *natural* markets to handle, intervened and did what its spoiled nephews on Wall Street had grown to expect: They cut the Fed Funds rate and once again provided artificial stimulus to the markets in the form of more access to cheap debt under the misleading guise of economic "accommodation."

Sadly, this pro-Wall Street, anti-Main Street pattern (and lesson) after LTCM was not headed, it simply continued...

Enter the Dot.Com Anti-Heroes...

Just as the smoke was rising from the Connecticut rubble of LTCM, another classic asset bubble misconstrued as free-market prosperity was playing itself out in the form of a dot.com hysteria.

Co-author, Matthew Piepenburg, remembers this well, as he started his first hedge fund during this crazy period of excess and over-valuation. His hedge fund made an admittedly undeserved fortune. But even at age 28, his common sense already knew that the dot.com NASDAQ was a bubble not a market...

The Fed, as always, misrepresented these rising *stock prices* as proof of a rising *economy*, when in fact, the dot.com mania was just a protracted spring break of speculators gone wild that ended with a memorable hangover and market nosedive. Very few investors or policy makers, of course, saw this coming. They were too busy enjoying the euphoria of low rates, cheap debt and hence easy leverage and rising stock prices. But a NASDAQ trading at 100X earnings at its March 2000 peak should have been warning enough that the market party was nearing an end.

And it was. By April of 2000, a tech bubble inflated by the easy money flowing from DC policies to Wall Street salaries and debt-driven stock bubbles riding a grotesque wave of private (and cheap) credit expansion did what *all* bubbles do: It popped. In retrospect, the dot.com implosion seems obvious. But even at the time it was happening, that market (*precisely like today's*) felt, well: *Unreal.* Consider Dell Inc. It started at $0.05 per share and grew to $54.00/share (a 1,100X multiple) only to slide back to 10.00/share. Does that smack of efficient, fair market price discovery? (There are numerous examples of other roller-coaster mis-pricings of that era, from Cisco, Juniper, Nortel, Yahoo and Lucent to Global Crossing and Commerce One.)

Of course, the markets heading into the 2020's are and were no different. In fact, they are worse. Companies like Tesla and Amazon, despite basement level free cash flows, reached astronomical market cap valuations on the back of euphoria, momentum and access to free debt rather than rational balance-sheet facts. This was largely based upon unfair access to capital and undeniable support from drunken speculation encouraged by an openly Fed-supported stock bubble that allowed their share prices to rise on investor momentum rather than balance sheet profits, all tell-tale signs of a classic bubble. The undeniable as well as massive support by the Fed for such excess was already an open secret by the autumn of 2019, when the Fed bailed out the broken (and bank-favored) repo markets to the tune of trillions while Main Street reeled.

Only a year later, when March stocks sank by 30% in a needed and natural correction, that same central bank unleashed unlimited Quantitative Easing (i.e., money printing) to revive an otherwise dead-on-arrival stock market. As the world held its knees in fear over a lung-destroying COVID virus, the only permanent respirator in sight was the one propping the stock markets from the Eccles Building money printers in DC. Thanks to such Wall Street directed stimulus, otherwise debt-ravaged risk assets climbed to record highs despite a word-wide pandemic marked by record unemployment and the self-inflicted gun-shot wound of a totally locked-down, and increasingly *controlled* global economy.

The pattern by now is fairly clear. Easy Fed leverage (low-rate credit policies) and peak valuations are harbingers of bubble creation and bubble implosion. The dot.com champagne party of the 1990's, like its predecessor in the dapper 1920's, ended in ruins, with the S&P down 45% and the *wild-child NASDAQ off 80% by 2003.* The even larger tech, stock and bond bubbles extending from 2008 into the 2020's would be no different in their eventual fall from grace...

As for the FED and its Wall Street minions, we are correct as well as obligated to pose certain rhetorical questions. Have policy makers learned anything about restraint, humility, "constructive destruction" or the longer-term importance of allowing necessary sacrifice and shorter-term corrections? Have we ever seen policy makers speak plainly of the open debt risks they created or exhibit the personal and professional courage to address and account for the same rather than preserve their posts and reputations by forever telegraphing a message of "be calm, carry on"?

The simple answer is: Nope.

From the rubble of the dot.com bubble, for example, the market-enamored policy makers under Greenspan began the greatest rate reduction policies (and subsequent stock bubble creation) yet seen, resulting in a wide-open spigot for even more easy credit, leverage and hence debt-induced market deformations. That is, they solved one bubble crisis in tech stocks by creating a new bubble in real estate. In the wake of the dot.com collapse of 2001, the subsequent sub-prime mortgage storm was born on the backs of, you guessed it: More access to cheap debt via repressed rates compliments of that oh-so poorly conceived Federal Reserve.

But even as the ominous winds of a mortgage crisis blew across the nation, other currents unleashed by the hot money of the Greenspan rate reduction were churning in a riptide of bad business decisions. A wide and embarrassing swath of wasteful M&A, stock-by-backs and LBO deals took place with alarming speed and drastic results. This new easy/cheap credit (and thus omnipresent hot money) was expressed/deployed in: 1) aggressive stock buy backs (i.e., Cisco, Exxon, Microsoft, Hewlett Packard), 2) M&A mania (Time/AOL, JDS Uniphase/SDL, or the numerous companies WorldCom devoured), and 3) grossly mispriced LBO's (Clear Channel, Alltel, Hilton Hotels). Other highlights of this low point in "American deal making" included General Electric's (GE's) dive from $50 to $10 share prices. Net result? Did GE's Mr. Jeffrey Immelt take his lumps courageously? Did the company learn the necessary ("constructive destruction") lessons of reckless speculation in the fall from its 40X valuation peaks?

Nope. Instead, GE's CEO took a bailout...

Additional examples of executive profiles without courage were plentiful in that pre-08 era of reckless borrowing and spending. The boards and CEOs of countless unprofitable LBOs ("levered buy-outs") funded by cheap debt shared over $300B in a carried interest jackpot while their publicly traded balance sheets stayed permanently red. In short, executives made a windfall just before investors got the wind kicked out of them. The intoxicated and unproductive era which ended in the staggering write-downs on massively overvalued operations were, of course, eerily predictive of the far more pernicious over-valuations seen in the pre and post COVID era of the 2020's, as names like Tesla, Apple, and Amazon followed the same rise and then fall trajectory of their Cisco, Microsoft and GE predecessors.

More Real Estate "Heroes"

Of course, no history of irrational bubbles or over-hyped (and compensated) "anti-heroes" would be complete without a salute to the real estate markets of 2004-2008. And the first name that comes to most minds is Fannie Mae, a GSE ("Government Sponsored Entity") who, along with its GSE cousins Freddie and Ginnie, grew astronomically in the 40 years following their accidental births in FDR's New Deal era. Indeed, the notorious exuberance and balance sheet ballooning of these quasi-governmental operations is now the stuff of legend as a towering example of easy DC money prompting bad, very *anti-heroic* behavior—*and, as always, with horrific economic consequences at the national level.*

Heading toward the Great Financial Crisis of 2008, these real estate entities had completely lost their way and were acting like hedge funds with mortgage pools levered at 200:1. In that all too familiar era of egregious underwriting standards and fast, cheap money, these alleged real estate "caretakers" became dispensers of levered poison, indirectly setting the stage for increasingly bad practices, including the growth of predatory, boiler room mortgage brokers selling non-recourse loans to unqualified buyers whose dangerous mortgages were then consolidated, packaged, *tranched* and syndicated to the world as safe, AAA securities. Of course, these packaged assets were just "pigs in lipstick" whose facade of marketed rather than actual value pushed the Case-Shiller Index up 60% by 2001, and then to a staggering 195% by the housing markets' 2006 peak. Such unprecedented, cheap-debt-based "growth" should have been an obvious sign of trouble ahead, as it had nothing to do with intrinsic value but everything to do with easy credit.

Unfortunately, the real estate market then, like the subsequent real estate, bond and SPAC-heavy equity bubbles heading into the 2020's, was too shortsighted to take its eyes off the immediate prize/profits to consider the longer-term risks ahead for the nation's broader economy. In this all-too-familiar bonfire of greed and self-interest, the stock and option values of Freddie and Fannie skyrocketed. *Like dot.com executives, these horrific GSE managers focused less on national interests and more on the need to keep earnings growing to justify market prices and annual bonuses.*

This meant that these government-sponsored debt-peddlers and fee-seekers had to continually dig deeper into the pigpen of poor credit borrowers (i.e., Main Street suckers) to churn and generate more toxic yet tradable mortgage loans, 80% of which were to be re-syndicated into the growing real estate and sub-prime Wall Street disaster-bubble. (The Chinese, by the way, bought over $1T of this GSE toilet paper). Needless to say, the GSE's, like most of the LBO and M&A deals of the same era (*above*), were not real businesses contributing any actual value to the US *economy*. (As their stock prices roared, US GDP by 2006 was at its worst since the 1930's). In sum, anti-heroes were swarming all over Wall Street and DC and spreading their cancerous consequences across the nation.

The net result of this now familiar pattern of Fed-created, low-rate, easy-money, rogue financed "growth" (from bank "wire-house lines") was, alas, a *massive* housing bubble, followed by an equally massive implosion and national economic collapse. Stated otherwise, a small cadre of short-sighted, self-interested GSE executives accommodated by Wall Street-packaged securities induced by central bank "credit support" helped bring an entire nation (and later global economy) into a recession. As for 2008, all of us remember it well. By the year's close, $5 trillion of stock value had disappeared in the great sucking sound (and whirlpool) of a tanking sub-prime mortgage securities market...

But let us not forget the derivatives market in those same real estate "assets." By 2008, the Fed-supported markets (like Leo Malemud's Merc) had invented even more complex and fatal tools of leverage and speculation –namely an unregulated derivatives market, which gives entirely new meaning to the expression "form over substance" as veritable leverage monsters which Warren Buffet aptly described as "weapons of mass destruction."

The notional value of those derivative instruments exceeded 9X global GDP by the time the 2008 subprime mortgage bubble transitioned into the Great Financial Crisis of the same year. That number alone is simply astounding, openly shameful. Disgraceful. Staggering. But today, that 9X multiple has climbed to almost twice that. This woefully misunderstood, distorted and media-ignored derivatives trade is the off-balance-sheet Ebola market virus (far more dangerous to the world than anyone today wishes to discuss or consider). The implications of such leverage cannot be stressed enough, and yet 9 out of 10 market professionals aren't even aware of such data nor able to explain its horrific implications to the economy at large. In Chapter 10, we address the derivatives trade in more detail in our discussion on current banking risk.

One obvious question, alas, is how did this derivatives disaster happen?

Larry Summers

When it comes to earning blue ribbons for self-interest over national interest, the former Harvard University President and Assistant U.S. Treasury Secretary, Larry Summers, gets an honorable mention alongside Alan Greenspan et al for unleashing the derivatives cancer still quietly spreading within the organs of the U.S. as well as global economy. Like Greenspan, Summers is simply one more surname among so many who confirm Larouchfoucault's observation that the highest offices are rarely, if ever, held by the highest minds.

The equally mis-managed banks, not surprisingly, loved Mr. Summers. He was a handsomely rewarded consultant for Citigroup, did equal "work" for the Nasdaq, D.E. Shaw, Andreessen Horowitz and Alliance Partners. But let's not let credentials get in the way of embarrassing facts, as it's hard not to list Larry Summers among the key architects behind the 2008 financial debacle and the equally obvious debacles to follow. Most veterans of recent market cycles pre and post 2008, for example, would concede that OTC (over-the-counter) derivatives were the heart of the 2008 darkness. These tranches of questionable (and largely misunderstood) asset backed securities (ABS) were passed about the prop desks from Goldman Sachs to Bear Stearns to Joe-trader like hot potatoes until eventually investors discovered this wasn't manna, but levered manure; thereafter: Everyone's hands were collectively burned...

The sordid history of CDO-driven (i.e., derivative) pain is admittedly easy to critique in the 20/20 clarity of hindsight. Michael Lewis and many others have made these levered instruments of mass destruction seem so obvious. In fairness to poor Mr. Summers, perhaps he meant well, perhaps there really was no way for him to know or predict the dangers of those elusive derivatives and the risky collateral beneath (often very, very far beneath) their layers and levered tranches of otherwise crappy credit risks. And perhaps there is no way to know what lies ahead of us going forward in a now much larger derivatives market (*See* Chapter 10).

But then again, perhaps Mr. Summers was just unable to see what other smarter people did see. In fact, at Harvard (where, as its president, Summers ignored repeated warnings by his endowment staff and thus lost the university $2 Billion in funds, half of which were toxic interest rate swaps he helped mid-wife in the 90's), Summers created another scandal when casually observing that women students weren't as mathematically gifted as male students. Ironically, however, one woman in particular, Brooksley Born, then head of the Commodity Futures Trading Commission (CFTC) where these derivative land mines were growing in strength, was a bit smarter and more far-sighted than Mr. Summers when it came to the toxic math of derivatives. Most importantly, she had a ton of common sense, and to her, those derivative markets sure looked toxic... She desperately wanted to detox this poisonous corner of the market and subject it to far greater regulation—i.e., restraint and humility.

But by 1998, then Deputy Treasury Secretary Larry Summers had very little restraint or humility. He telephoned Born's desk at the CFTC and openly bullied her: "I have 13 bankers in my office," he shouted, "who tell me you're going to cause the worst financial crisis since World War II" if she continued moving forward in bringing much needed transparency and reporting requirements to the OTC derivatives market. Summers then went on to attack Born publicly as well, condescendingly assuring Congress that *her* concerns about the potential unwieldiness of these unregulated derivatives instruments were essentially silly, as "the parties to these kinds of contracts are largely sophisticated financial institutions that would appear to be eminently capable of protecting themselves from fraud and counter-party insolvencies." In other words, Summers was telegraphing the now time-worn narrative that extremely well-paid elites knew what they were doing—common sense, math or history be damned.

But fast-forward less than a decade later to 2008 (and an OTC derivatives market which Summers helped take from $95 trillion to $670 trillion via extremely dangerous tools of leverage), and we all learned how those "eminently capable" and "largely sophisticate financial institutions" (Bear, Lehman, Goldman, Morgan Stanley, AIG et al...), of which Summers had previously boasted, did in fact create the worst financial crisis since World War II.

The ironies do abound...

As for the rest of us, is it still prudent to ipso-facto make the comforting assumptions that our esteemed policy leaders (from FDR to Nixon, Summers and Powell to Draghi and Lagarde) are in fact leading us to safety rather than implosion? Should we take false solace in their titles, or should we more bravely take our direction from history, facts, cycles and track records? Toward this end, it's worth remembering that neither Greenspan in 2001, Bernanke in 2008 nor Powell in 2020 ever saw or forewarned of the market crashes which defined those years. In fact, the Fed's record for accurately forewarning dramatic market retracements is 0 for 10.

So much for forward guidance and fiduciary candor...

More Candor—Less Anti-Heroes

Investors heading into the 2020's have been led to the edge of a market cliff built upon inherited patterns of unprecedented levels of post-08 debt and money supply expansion. As of this writing, the current notional value of the global derivatives market is far greater than a *quadrillion*-dollars; the government debt in the US stands at $30+T trillion (more than tripling its 2008 levels) and *government* debt in Japan and the EU respectively stand at $13.1T and $12T, with debt to GDP levels in the US at well beyond 130%, in the EU at 100.5%, and in the appalling case of Japan, at greater than 260%. Global M1 money supply has grown by 10% per year since 2008, representing more money creation in the last decade+ than in the previous century combined; and more money was printed by the Fed in 2020 alone than during all the quantitative easing (QE1 -QE4) produced between 2009 and 2014.

That's a lot of stimulus and central bank support. Unprecedented in fact. Is it any wonder that markets reached record highs in that period?

The recent "binge," of course, is nothing new, just astronomically larger in scope, duration and risk. Though falsely presented as a "recovery," the blatant display of Wall Street socialism disguised as "accommodation" from 2009 into the 2020's was nothing more than an unprecedented expansion of an historically failed template, namely: Cheap and excessive levels of debt and market extravagance "solved" by more debt paid for by an overdose of currency creation and hence currency debasement.

The objective data before us confirms that nothing has changed (or was learned from) nearly a century of artificial market manipulations save for the extent of the asset bubbles created, and hence the extent of the cyclical and natural collapse to follow.

Without taking a political bias or peddling bearish presumptions, we can say with objectivity and candor what most expert policy makers, message-constrained bankers and thirty-something financial "journalists" are afraid (or prevented) to confess. Namely, the markets of the 2020's have inherited a familiar pattern of bad behavior masquerading as policy which predate the warnings of White's ghost by centuries yet are all too familiar in recent eras. From ancient Rome to modern America, the use of extreme debt paid for with over-created and hence debased currencies to alleviate short-term economic pain while ensuring the personal wealth or political survival of a small minority at the expense of the larger majority was never healthy capitalism. It was and remains something empirically far worse. In fact, and more to the point, what we have been tracking for years smacks more of modern feudalism than classical capitalism, as the following chapter confirms.

Chapter 4

Modern Capitalism or Classic Feudalism?

With COVID-inspired central banks unleashed to provide open and unprecedented market support wherein artificially repressed rates and unlimited money creation directly benefited the three largest asset classes in America, namely bonds, real estate and stocks, no one could deny the cause-and-effect powers (as well as beneficiaries) of such emergency "accommodation."

It's an objective fact that greater 80 % of those bubble assets are owned by the top 10% of the nation's wealthiest citizens.

Does that feel like capitalism working at a *national* level, or something far more targeted and far less "free-market" driven? The very concept of central-bank supported (and Congress-lobbied) capitalism is itself a contradiction in terms, and requires on honest re-assessment (and some hard questions) regarding the true meaning of capitalism or the now undeniable wealth transfer for which the Fed and other central banks are directly linked. Can any system, market or sector, for example, that is directly and exclusively supported by trillions in fiat money creation and decades of artificially repressed (and *unnaturally* low) interest rates by definition be labeled "free-market," "natural" or even "capitalistic"?

Be honest.

Had the $8+ trillion in Fed money creation since 2008 truly "trickled down" to the real economy, or had it primarily benefited risk asset markets like stocks on the S&P 500...

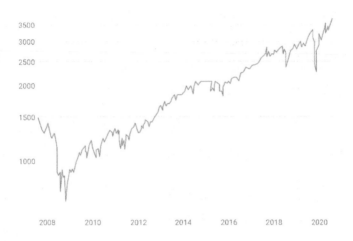

...or real estate owners and their ambitious, commission-focused brokers?

Median Sales Price of Houses Sold for the United States

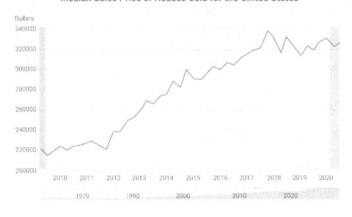

U.S. recessions are shaded, the most recent end date is undecided.   Source: Census, HUD

Again: Be honest.

Whether you be in the top 10% or the bottom 10%, the answer to these rhetorical questions is now *empirically* obvious. Such asset price inflation (i.e., bubbles) in everything from tech stocks to beach front real estate is not symbolic of the lauded and natural "Darwinism" of competitive, free-market capitalism. Instead, such targeted bubbles for the top 10% (and the consequent wealth disparity that followed for the rest of the country) are dangerous indicators of what amounts to nothing less than a kind of post-modern feudalism of the lords and serfs.

That is, the financial world has witnessed a questionable cabal of policy makers subsidizing (aka "accommodating") a distinct minority of beneficiaries who then described the *market* result as an "*economic stimulus*" while the majority of the citizens (using the U.S. example) became poorer by the day.

Source: www.signalsmatter.com/wall-street-disaster/

But again, is *that* capitalism?

Capitalism, whether defined by Adam Smith or abused by fictional Gordon Geckos, is a dynamic, full-body contact sport of almost blood-thirsty competition intended to be played on a *level* playing field of new ideas, equal access to capital and open reward for individual effort. In addition, true capitalism, the kind our fathers believed in, was equally designed to create a *broad* rather than narrow class of winners and prosperity over time.

But do the above charts suggest a broad class of winners or just a narrow sliver of insiders?

Capitalism, moreover, should reward executives. But by how much?

Since 1978, CEO compensation has grown by 940%, whereas employee compensation for the same period has grown by only 12%.

Please: Re-read that last sentence.

In 1965, the average ratio of CEO to median employee salaries was 21:1, today it's over 320:1. For Jeff Bezos at Amazon, the ratio is an openly pathological (i.e., immoral) 1.2 million to 1. Again: Is such objective data a sign of an evolving capitalism or an indicator of something far more disturbing? This too is a rhetorical question. Wealth accumulated at such lopsided levels is not a *reward* of capitalism, but its *distortion*, a signal to something harking back to the aristocratic excess of the Bourbons, Batistas or Romanovs; and we all know how that ended for them...

Fair Competition vs. A Rigged Game

Unfortunately, there are other and increasingly clear signs of rigged policies (from the Fed, Congress, SEC or White House) which have less to do with fair competition and rational compensation—the keystones of healthy capitalism—and far more do with an extended yet media-ignored (complicit?) paradigm of favoritism—i.e., *cheating*. Today, a kind of pseudo capitalism has emerged which is neither empathetic toward (or beneficial to) its host nation. Instead, we have a distorted model of capitalism whose benefits and empathies are uniquely targeted to a singular (parasitic?) minority of companies, individuals and markets. For every member of Congress, for example, there are at least four financial lobbyists (from banks and big-tech) scurrying to influence (i.e., purchase) favorable policy decisions. This too is not fable, but fact, and clearly suggests healthy capitalism is under the influence of legally-sanitized bribery rather than effective policy, and backroom deals rather than fair competition.

Of course, any system that is inherently rigged, like the 1919 World Series, is inherently flawed. Capitalism, when so carefully and deliberately rigged, is no less disgraceful. Such artificial abuses of natural, free market forces will lead, and is leading, to new and far more pernicious systems and policies, including the slow creep of mandated government dependence (i.e. socialism) emerging from, and imposed upon, the understandably angry yet history-ignorant populism that is rising by the day (*See* Chapter 7). As we also discuss at greater length in Chapter 14, the world is turning increasingly toward greater rather than less economic controls and financial repression. We are seeing this rigged game playing out in real time as the weak majority get weaker and the strong minority get stronger in a backdrop that is not a capitalistic "survival of the fittest," but rather a feudalistic survival of the best-connected and most powerful. Those not otherwise included in this "inner circle" are slowly made to become dependent upon it—from handouts to lock-down subservience. In sum, record breaking wealth disparity as well as the open and shameful disconnect between a tanking economy and a rising (Fed-supported) securities market is not an homage to capitalism, but rather open proof of its steady decline.

Tesla, Apple and Amazon—The New Capitalism?

Take Tesla as one example among many. It's a visionary company led by a media darling, but its stock has been skyrocketing on growth projections and historically low borrowing costs, easily managed by exaggerated share price inflation. In March of 2020, it was the 4th most valuable auto company in the world, by Q1 of 2021 it was the most valuable, worth more than Daimler, Toyota and Volkswagen *combined.* Or Apple. It took 12 years for it to arrive at a $1 trillion market cap, but only 5 more months to reach $2 trillion in 2021.

Are such growth stories a consequence of fair, legitimate and natural *free-market* forces, or have they enjoyed an unfair advantage from the policy jocks? And as for unfair advantage, as well as ethically challenged "guidance" from the executive C-suite, Tesla's CEO, Elon Musk, made more money in a single quarter front-running Bitcoin (as well as other penny stocks) with a single Tweet than he did from actual car sales in 2020. Just two years prior in 2018, when his massively bloated/over-valued enterprise was feeling the burn of well-deserved short sellers (i.e., investors betting against Tesla), Musk created his own illegal "short squeeze" (stock surge) by openly tweeting he had "funding secured" to take his public company private. The problem was, this was a total lie, engineered to artificially boost his stock prices, and constituted obvious securities fraud. Rather than jail time, the inveterate liar received a $20M fine from the SEC, little more than a cost of doing business for such a dishonest prince of the new feudalism.

Amazon's rise offers additional, as well as compelling, evidence that the Fed's experiment has led to extraordinary distortions in both the markets and society. Despite years of a *profitless* balance sheet and legal tax avoidance, Amazon's share price bubble, fattened by years of equity market tailwinds of instant liquidity and cheap debt compliments of the Fed, allowed this single enterprise to literally kill, gut and bury small businesses across the nation. Unfair, Fed-induced share price inflation at Amazon allowed it to purchase its own rails and engage in anti-competitive behavior while dumping products and prices due to their access to cheap capital (against which no other companies could compete). As a result, Amazon, an open yet free violator of every anti-trust principle I studied in law school, slaughtered rather than leveled the "fair playing field" upon which true capitalism was designed to be played.

As a result, names like Amazon, Tesla and Apple have prompted openly pro-capitalist thought leaders like Scott Galloway to question whether the pandemic was created, or at least co-opted, for taking the top 10% into the top 1% while sending the remaining 90% downward. This is a fair question.

Two Americas, Zero Capitalism

A recent study by the Robin Hood Foundation, for example, revealed that 32% of the people in the state of New York, the homefield of Wall Street, had been forced to go to a food bank since the onset of the pandemic. That represented more people in the Empire State seeking free food than those who possessed a college degree. By pure math, the U.S. has fallen into a Dickinsonian backdrop marked by the "best of times" for a tiny minority and the "worst of times" for the broader population. Is it truly fair to castigate the majority of real America as "losers" in a so-called capitalistic competition whose rigged rules and policies ensured who the "winners" would be before the game could even start? The rigged game playing right under our noses in the U.S. is not free market capitalism, just as an S&P sitting atop a big, fat, $9+ trillion Fed air-bag, sure as hell ain't a free market.

Natural price discovery, as all honest Wall Street veterans know, died years ago. Nod to Greenspan, Bernanke, Yellen and Powell. The objective truth is that current U.S. markets, competition and politics have nothing to do with fair competition and hence nothing to do with capitalism.

The New Feudalism

As Galloway observed in late 2020, "we are barreling toward a nation wherein 3 million lords are being served by 350 million serfs," simply because US policy decided to favor corporations over populations as capitalism "collapses upon itself." Nor can this modern version of so-called capitalism rely on the "better angel" generosities of billionaires like Gates, Bezos or Musk to save the system. The moral profiles of such overpaid CEO's will not bring the dying middle class back to its glory days.

Frankly, it's up to the citizens themselves to get *informed* rather than *angry*, and *prepared* rather than *bamboozled*. Knowledge, after all, begets better results than pitch forks and knee-jerk tweet-attacks. We wrote this book to both inform and prepare more investors on what to consider, expect and do going forward. Sadly, however, not everyone seeks to be informed or trusts who's informing them. We understand this. Furthermore, we realistically realize that pitchforks require less thinking than reading books and charts. The risk of increased social unrest (*See* Chapter 7) in the U.S. and elsewhere therefore goes up each day as living conditions go down each day for a large swath of the U.S. and global population. America is failing not just because capitalism lost its way or policy-supported CEO's lack the character, ethics and accountabilities of the past. This fall is also due to the hard reality that citizens are losing trust in their lobbied (bribed) leaders (left, right and center). As a result, they are screaming at each other (from left to right, Antifa to QAnon, black to white) rather than opening a single economics, math, ethics, history or anti-trust book. Today, the crowd gets its education from tweets and twits, not informed thoughts, sound leadership, patient knowledge or actual hard facts.

Bread & Circus, Fear & Division

This, of course, makes the mal-informed majority (i.e., the bottom 90%) of "serfs" easier for their "lords" to trick and manipulate. Decision-makers on top, from ancient Rome to Herr Goebbels, have always understood, and hence exploited, such wide-spread ignorance to galvanize their own powers. In short, so-called policy "experts" have been serving a mal-informed population a mixed cocktail of either: 1) *bread & circus* (from Netflix to celebrity virtue-signaling) or 2) *fear* (from "social-distancing" to COVID *infection* rates and omnipresent fear-porn) to keep the crowd ignorant, divided and afraid. In 2021, as pandemic variants spread and more welfare checks were being sent to more households than ever before in history, the headlines were filled with the struggles of Prince Harry and Meghan Markel "slumming it" in Santa Barbara. Most U.S. citizens, meanwhile, were blind to the rudimentary basics of Fed policy, currency debasement, lobbying tricks, or anti-trust principles. Thus, as the middle-class floundered and a new financial feudalism gradually replaced genuine capitalism, the mad crowd had no idea where to place its anger other than at each other in an historically divisive era of *identity* politics replacing anything resembling informed and *unifying* politics.

And in the backdrop of all this profound distortion, fear, anger, mis-information, mis-management, challenged ethics and truth scarcity, the infamous COVID crisis ravaged the citizens and economies of the world. But as we'll discover in the following chapter, even a crisis as massive (and controversial) as COVID served as yet another opportunity for the feudal lords who allegedly "guide" or financial future. In the following chapter, we look more closely at how COVID in fact saved the financial elites.

Chapter 5

How COVID Saved a Rigged Market

Unbelievably, and based upon objective data rather than bewildered bias, the COVID pandemic has only accelerated the speed and depth of the cycles of distortion described in the prior chapters.

Regardless of legitimately debatable views on how individuals and policy makers (from central bankers to health organizations) have handled or mishandled the global pandemic from New York to Sydney, we can all agree that COVID represented a turning point in accelerating an already broken system closer to its own expiration date. But what is perhaps most disturbing, is the fact that COVID was ironically a temporary gift to those already central-bank-spoiled markets. Without obfuscation and fancy terminology, let us make the following (and admittedly ironic) assertion and then support the same with verifiable facts rather than angry adjectives, namely:

COVID-19 was the best thing that ever happened to an otherwise broken global market system.

In case you're concerned that we're suffering from a high fever, let's unpack and support this blunt yet dramatic claim, point by simple point.

The Dollar Crisis—Not Enough of Them Heading into 2020

We begin with the critical issue of the world's reserve currency, namely the U.S. Dollar.

One can't over-emphasize enough how important the supply—or "liquidity"—of U.S. Dollars are to keeping the rigged wheels of the global banks, money markets and inter-bank exchanges greased and turning. In short, dollars (and we mean *trillions* of them) are essential to keeping this massively distorted system running. If the over-levered and hence over-valued banking and trading mechanisms of global securities markets were to ever run low of these needed dollars and thereby suffer dangerous liquidity (i.e., dollar) shortages, demand for those dollars would rise considerably. And if demand for dollars increased too rapidly, interest rates would rise fatally upwards.

Why "fatally"?

Because rapidly rising interest rates (i.e., the cost of money) colliding the with the record-breaking (and rapidly rising) global debt levels described above and elsewhere, would send markets to the floor. Party over. Period. Full stop.

The Fed and other central banks, of course, are trying as hard as they can to keep this artificial, toxic yet all-too lucrative party going. Unfortunately, and heading into the 2020's, it was becoming more and more clear that these clever central bankers were losing artificial control of naturally correcting bond markets and hence rising interest rates.

The First Tremors of Dollar Shortages and the Approaching Shark Fins of Rising Rates

In late 2019, for example, we saw the first deadly symptoms that interest rates were rising beyond the control of the Federal Reserve due to a lack of available dollars. By this, we are referring to the extraordinary, single-day rate spike in the oh-so critical (yet entirely misunderstood and hidden) repo (bank repurchasing) markets which took place in September of 2019. As expected, the Main stream media and Fed deliberately tried to sidestep, hide or downplay this otherwise seminal event for the canyons of Wall Street, but the repo crisis of 2019 was an ominous (and early) warning sign of trouble ahead, signaling a potential end to the post-2008 "recovery" described in Chapter 3. Stated otherwise, the almost hidden 2019 repo disaster (i.e., rate spike) was a glaring, as well as *pre*-COVID, sign that credit markets were running out of *dollars*, a dangerous fact understood by almost no one reading the financial press or income statements from their wealth advisors. But that's how the "lords" like it: Ignorant "serfs."

The Second Tremor of Dollar Shortage Disaster Ahead—The Ignored Euro Dollar Markets

In addition to the dollar-dry repo markets, another media-ignored as well as Fed-downplayed "ticking timebomb" of dollar illiquidity (signaling fatally rising interest rates) had been unfolding in an otherwise esoteric corner of the global financial system known as the Euro Dollar market. Like the repo warnings, those coming from the media-ignored and deliberately confusing Euro Dollar universe were well in play by late 2019, months *before* COVID made its first headline. Without delving into the unpleasant intricacies of this unique market niche, the bottom-line signal from the Euro Dollar system came down to this: Trillions in U.S. Dollars held in non-U.S. banking and financial systems (collectively described as "Euro Dollars") were hopelessly tangled up in highly complex and levered derivatives instruments. Or stated even more simply, because these dollars were all "tangled up," they were not otherwise readily available or "liquid," which meant the global financial systems were fast running out of dollar "grease."

As with the repo markets, if the Euro Dollar market runs out of U.S. Dollars, demand for more pushes interest rates too high, which, in turn, makes the debt markets (the sole wind beneath the wings of our rigged markets) unpayable. That was THE biggest problem for central and commercial banks and financial systems heading into 2020, again: A ticking time bomb of too much debt careening Titanic-like toward an iceberg of rising rates. Or stated more simply: If the cost of paying interest on otherwise unpayable debt obligations becomes impossible due to rising rates, the entire global credit machine (from money markets to bond desks and stock exchanges) begins to smoke, shake and then come crashing down. This makes the "lords" nervous...

Let us therefore repeat: This fear of rising rates was the CENTRAL yet media-ignored fear of all the central banks *prior* to the sudden arrival of COVID. As the architects of the world's greatest debt bubble ever recorded, these bankers knew only too well that rising rates would render their respective economies and disastrous debt experiment insolvent. Thus, they needed a *pretext* for more money, lots and lots of money, to quickly buy otherwise sinking government bonds in order to keep their yields and rates artificially low. But after 2008, the world was tired of hearing about central banks printing money out of thin air to bail out broke countries, greedy bankers and bloated security markets. A far better and optic-friendly excuse was needed, and fast, to justify creating trillions more fake dollars out of thin air as soon as possible...

Pre COVID-19 Rising Dollar Demand—the Ticking Time Bomb

To summarize: The profound signals coming out of the totally media-ignored repo and Euro Dollar markets were flashing red flags (*PRE* COVID) that debt markets were at dramatic risk of unraveling. Given that debt is the sole engine of the current everything-bubble in global markets, if demand for U.S. Dollars (and hence interest rates) continued to climb, it was only a matter of time before central banks would have to concede defeat and witness the inevitable failure of their otherwise desperate money-printing experiment as interest rates rose like an iceberg and hence sank their Titanically debt-bloated markets and economies. But as we've already discovered in Chapter 3, central bankers, like the politicians and markets with whom they collude, don't like to admit to utter failure.

Hence, the *pre* COVID-19 policy makers and media bobbleheads were already prepping the gullible retail serfs by telegraphing hitherto fringe miracle "solutions" such as unlimited money printing (under the euphemistic label of Modern Monetary Theory, or MMT) to keep the global markets "greased" with more fake (i.e., fiat) dollars. But, again, the experts knew this would be a bitter pill for rational minds to swallow. Common sense, as well as the memory of the 2008 Wall Street bailout, suggested that most citizens, as well as voters, would not fall for another massive dose of pro-Wall-Street free money. In sum, a market bailout was needed, but almost impossible to *sell or justify* to a world increasingly tired of handouts to bankers and over-valued risk-asset bubbles which predominantly benefit the top 10%.

Faced with the looming danger of rising dollar demand in the repo and Euro Dollar markets, global policy makers nervously tracked the approaching ice berg of rising interest rates from not enough dollars, the kind of rates that sink bond and stock bubbles and send markets to the bottom of history. In the days *prior* to the COVID crisis, the only hope for global central bankers and debt-soaked economies and markets from DC to Tokyo was some kind of massive *slow-down* in dollar demand as well as a massive influx of dollar supply to keep those fatal interest rates from rising too high. Again, the global markets needed dollars, trillions and trillions of them—as soon as possible.

In short, the problem before them was very clear: How could they sell and hence justify to the masses another market bailout?

But then, and almost as if on cue (?), came the highly fortuitous COVID-19 Pandemic...

Along Comes COVID-19, Fatal Dollar Demand Eases, the Markets are "Saved"

In the wake of a global pandemic (99.636 survival rate...) and hence global economic shut-down, it goes without saying that the global economy came to an historical and unprecedented halt in 2020. Fear, panic and confusion spread faster than the virus itself. The sudden (and forced) collapse of economic activity and commerce in the name of a global "Public Safety Committee" obviously led to an equally massive collapse in demand for U.S. Dollars, which conveniently (some say, too conveniently?) helped justify the needed low-rate environment upon which debt-soaked nations rely to survive. In addition, the Fed's immediate creation of over $4 trillion new dollars in less than a year under the superficial guise of "COVID relief" certainly took the pressure of rising rates off the necks of otherwise broke countries, from the Americas to Europe and Asia. Ironically, then, COVID-19, more than any tool or talking point otherwise available to global market policymakers, helped quell (temporarily) the otherwise *financially fatal* rate hikes on the horizon. All this life-saving liquidity poured into the credit markets, despite the tragic *human costs* to locked-down Main Streets, businesses and psychologically terrified citizens around the world.

Debt Jubilee by Another Name

Not only did COVID-19 take the pressure of fatally rising interest rates off the guilty necks of debt-driven policy makers by justifying never-before seen levels of fiat money creation at the *monetary* level, but it also became the obvious and legitimate backdrop for extreme deficit spending at the *fiscal* policy level. In other words, COVID-19 provided a moral "hall pass" for global governments and central banks to resort to otherwise politically unthinkable levels of money creation and deficit spending to keep markets, individuals and businesses "fed" with massive (just massive!) stimulus packages. The US, for example, saw this play out in the form of SBA loans, congressional CARE packages, $100 billion/day Fed repo financing, rent-abatements, annual mortgage payment forbearances, junk-bond bailouts, and even direct Fed investments in bond ETFs in 2020. By early, 2021, another $1.9T in U.S. relief packages was passed by Congress with funds it did not otherwise have. Much more would and did follow. In short, trillions in new emergency programs were unleashed in record time ostensibly to publicly address a still debatable global health pandemic, measures which would have otherwise never been justified but for a humanitarian emergency.

What most people don't know, however, is that the bulk that monetary policy and fiscal support went into the securities markets, not the real economy or the average, broke and/or "locked-down" John/Jane Doe— i.e. "serf." Alas, as the world endured the omni-present fear porn of rising COVID *infection* rates throughout 2020, a massive Wall Street bailout, greater than anything seen in 2008, snuck in behind the headlines.

With COVID as the perfect and convenient pretext, interest rates were set to near zero, making more cheap debt the official new normal for years to come. Wall Street was thus following Churchill's observation of never letting a good crisis go to waste. As a direct result, massive amounts of more corporate debt were added to a *pre*-COVID debt pyre that was already burning through history at record highs.

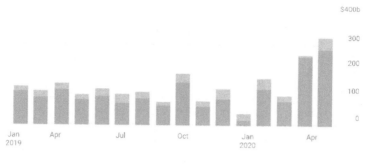

Gorging on Debt

Companies rush to sell new bonds after Fed signals backstop

Source: Bloomberg

Taxes, mortgages, student loans, corporate debt obligations and countless other unpayable and unsustainable "debts" were either (1) expanding, (2) not being paid or (3) radically "re-set" throughout 2020, which indirectly amounted to a radical form of debt extension as well as quasi debt forgiveness by another name—a kind of ersatz "debt jubilee."

But here's the rub: For every pre-COVID debtor who received a nice "break" from the debt noose around its neck, there's a *post*-COVID creditor who is losing money. Debt restructuring, after all, is a zero-sum game: There are winners and there are losers in equal measure. In short: No easy solution.

So, what does this mean going forward for risk assets, the economy, currencies and, as Part II discuss in more detail, gold?

The Stock Markets Are Not Reality

First, even the most novice market participants have begun to see through the obvious disconnect between record-breaking market highs and tanking economic fundamentals in the backdrop of what was perhaps the most surreal economic disaster in modern history. With everything changing so fast, it's difficult to time or perfectly predict what policymakers, central bankers, and investors will do next and when...But one thing is fairly certain: Massive change is on the horizon as central banks around the world will have no choice but to print more fiat currencies (either via direct "money printing" or indirect support from FIMA swap lines and the Standing Repo Facility, or "SRF") in order to monetize the debts of their broken governments and markets. This flood of new money will be used to buy government bonds (IOU's) that the natural markets don't otherwise want. Such artificial bond support (already $120B per month leading into 2021 in the U.S.) would temporarily keep bond prices up and hence yields and rates down, but for how long? And what would such extreme money creation do to the currencies being "printed" at such a staggering pace? In short, the central banks only tool for keeping rates down was to keep money printing or other liquidity spigots high and hence further debase their currencies, hardly an ideal solution for Main Street workers and savers, but an absolute boon to debt-soaked nations needing an excuse to inflate away their unpayable debt with increasingly debased money. Again, one just can't help but wonder how convenient the COVID timing really was for broke policy makers...

In short, the U.S. Dollar (and credit markets) enjoyed a temporary break from rising rates in 2020 and 2021 for all the reasons discussed above. Nevertheless, the sheer (and rapidly increasing) size of the debts and money printing that bought America and the world a precarious "solution" today would and will have far more tragic consequences for tomorrow.

The U.S., like other debt-soaked nations across the EU and Asia, was, in many ways, already experiencing a careful reset—a kind of national restructuring akin to a country wide Chapter 11 filing. Policymakers in this re-set were riding a fine line of keeping the money markets liquid via expanded fiat money creation and repo support while trying to simultaneously and artificially staple interest rates to the basement of history. Again, and worth repeating, walking this fine line required more money creation to purchase otherwise unwanted government debt to keep bond prices high and hence bond yields, and thus interest rates low. But such skyrocketing fiat money creation around the world means that dramatic changes in the global currency system in general, and the role of the U.S. Dollar in particular, are inevitable in the coming years.

As we saw in the examples FDR and Nixon in Chapter 3, the creation of more currencies *mathematically* leads to the *debasement* of those currencies. Without pegging dollars to a fixed supply of gold, currencies no longer have a chaperone to control their over-creation, and hence debasement. Theoretically, and without some calibration of currencies to a gold standard (which we don't expect), the amount of currencies capable of further creation is thus unlimited. This also means, however, that the level of currency debasement and hence the destruction of currency purchasing power is equally unlimited—hence our gold focus in Part II of this book.

In short, an alternative store of value is needed to curtail the abuse of unlimited currency creation—and hence dilution-- to pay for unsustainable debt levels. As we'll discuss in Chapters 12 and 18, some passionately believe that digital currencies like Bitcoin will replace these increasingly debased currencies. Our conviction, supported by millennia as well as current politics, math and *Realpolitik*, however, is that gold will inevitably re-emerge as the only credible and sane player in a room of insane currencies and equally insane, as well as crashing, asset bubbles.

Given the dollar-denominated amount of U.S. *assets* vs. the dollar-denominated levels of US *debt*, a 1-to-1 return to a perfect gold standard (i.e., a gold-backed dollar, destroyed by Nixon in 1971) is implausible, as this would require a peg ratio pricing gold anywhere from $50,000 to $80,000 per ounce.

Instead, gold could potentially be summoned from the lessons and vaults of history to become a kind of middle-ground balancer in the backdrop of a new era which will inevitably marry blockchain modernity with a timeless physical chaperone: Gold. This would involve an intra-central-bank electronic currency (*not* Bitcoin...) backed by something real, rather than fiat, and only redeemable/settled by the central banks themselves. But such a partial gold-backing of a new and global CBDC ("Central Bank Digital Currency) is impossible to predict.

For now, however, we are confident that gold, far from being the "barbaric relic" of the past, will emerge (as it has always done for the past 5,000 years) as the only *reliable relic* to which there is a fixed level of trust and an honest level of valuation for independent and individual investors, regardless of what the central banks do going forward. In short gold will rise, not because gold is so intrinsically powerful, but simply because fiat currencies (be they digital or paper) are so openly weak.

As for traditional gold pricing, it should come as no surprise that fair price discovery in this asset (like every asset class in an over-levered, derivative-distorted and rigged game) is nonexistent. It is an open but undeniable secret, for example, that gold prices have been artificially set by deliberate price fixers within a "un-real" COMEX futures market, as described more openly in Chapter 16. Despite the 2021 Basel III regulations, the *paper* gold price manipulated within an entirely broken derivatives market has absolutely nothing to do with actual supply and demand forces, and thus gold's *paper* price is essentially meaningless. Paper gold traded in the futures markets is not real gold, but merely levered paper contracts theoretically redeemable by the fictional promise of gold delivery. Unfortunately, the number of contracts promising delivery for an ounce of gold outpaced the true supply of available gold by ratios of anywhere from 100:1 to 200:1 pre-Basel III. Going forward, such leverage will be diminished but not outlawed. In short, there's simply more paper contracts for gold than there is actual gold on the planet earth. This creates a wide-open playing field for astounding price distortion and fake valuation schemes.

Explaining gold's continued and future rise involves a myriad of reasons and factors, each addressed in greater detail in Part II of this work. For now, however, it is worth noting that deep down, fewer and fewer informed investors fully trust fiat currencies, mis-reported inflation rates, frothy securities markets or double-speaking politicians and bankers.

No shocker there...

As history and market distortions unfold, genuine forces of supply and demand, as opposed to fictional COMEX futures contracts and truth-challenged policy makers, will determine the genuine value of *physical* gold. Once this occurs, the price for *paper* gold on the nine exchanges in which it trades will have to rapidly catch up with actual supply, which will send gold higher over the coming years. Much further down the road, those patient countries therefore holding the most physical gold will emerge with the strongest economies once currency markets reset after the inevitable as well as disorderly collapse in global credit and equity markets, the architects of which will then place the blame on COVID rather than decades of their own pre-COVID policy failures. This explains why far-sighted nations with much more austere yet experienced histories have been quietly acquiring physical gold with steady consistency—and by that, we're directly referring to China and Russia...

But as this tragic history unfolds, and as White's ghost forewarned, it will do so with patterns all too familiar to those who understand history's warnings and cycles, even if they don't believe in ghosts. Part of this history, as we learned from White's ghost in Chapter 2, involves phases marked by a kind of deliberate insanity or delusional euphoria, one in which common sense is replaced by fantasy, and risk awareness is replaced by an obsession with reward only. In short, the ever-mad crowd enjoys its last-hurrah of self-inflicted and euphoric delusion before the fatal hangover. Stated otherwise, a familiar kind of madness always precedes an equally familiar kind fall. As to such madness, that's a theme and cycle to which we turn next.

Chapter 6

The Madness of Crowds

Crowds, like sheep, are only as safe as the shepherds who guide them. Thus, if the shepherd is mad, so too is the crowd. After more than a decade of artificial support from the unlimited money creation and artificial rate suppression that has increased in speed and depth since 2009, the central bank shepherds of the 2020's have openly led the vast majority of retail investors toward seductively inflating securities markets without mentioning the currency cliff just around the bend. In fact, such temptation-to-disaster sequences are part of that clear yet often ignored template outlined in prior chapters. Understanding this template is critical, for it avoids the dangers of precise forecasting while honoring the predictable lessons of history. The irony, however, lies in the fact that the history of forecasting is also riddled with failed results. With this in mind, what makes our particular diagnosis, as well as prognosis, for the financial future any less subject to doubt?

We think this is a fair question.

The Failure of Predictive Models

Whatever one's view of politics, finance or policy makers, for example, we can all agree that the professional pollsters, pandemic modelers or even market timers armed with advanced algorithms and unlimited data streams have not been very successful in predicting winners and losers in everything from presidential elections to Brexit odds or even vaccine stats. The World Bank, for example, had projected global GDP to increase in 2021 by 4%, despite the obvious damage COVID lockdowns had *already* done to global economies. At the very same time, that very same World Bank had also confessed to a global debt tally of greater than $300 trillion. This meant that total global debt to total GDP was already greater than 3:1, which rendered their own growth projections openly comical from the moment they were "forecasted."

In short: Forecasting is a fool's game.

Which raises a fair question: Are we fools too?

The Fantasy of Central Bank Messaging

Fortunately, however, some forecasting hinges less upon fancy data or even fancier analysts and can boil down to something as basic, timeless and trusted as common sense. As for central banks who print money out of thin air to buy unwanted sovereign debts, they too were projecting miraculous solutions to otherwise staggering debt problems based on, you guessed it again: Creating more debt. And how did they say this debt would be paid? Easy again: With money created by a mouse click at a central bank near you.

But if such "solutions" and predictions seemed a little too good to be true for the economic future, that's because they were. Simple commonsense tells us so. That said, fantasies pitched as solutions have never stopped bankers, derivative traders, virus hawks, political pollsters, central-bank propaganda artists or stock peddlers from making inaccurate and contradictory projections which resemble a kind of open madness. And as for such madness, the maddening double-speak from our central bankers is equally obvious as well as equally comical:

"You will never see another financial crisis in your lifetime."
-Janet Yellen, spring 2018

"I do worry that we could have another financial crisis. "

-Janet Yellen, fall 2018

"There's no reason to think this (bullish) cycle can't continue for quite some time, effectively *indefinitely*."

-Jerome Powell –2018

"The US is on an *unsustainable* fiscal path; there's no hiding from it."

-Jerome Powell–2019

In the post-08 "new abnormal" of deficits without tears and embarrassing new lies like Modern Monetary Theory which pretend that unlimited money creation could never lead to inflation (despite the fact that increased money supply is the very definition of inflation [*See* Chapter 15]), the Fed's fantasy forecasters have been quite busy replacing common sense with madness and omni-bullish hope.

Predicting the End?

And so, we return to our primary question: Can economies, as well as near-term price action in markets, truly be forecasted with results better than a coin toss or Fed double-speak?

Our answer is a clear "yes" and a clear "no."

Why?

Because some things, like the complex movement of a Swiss watch, can in fact be trusted, and hence predicted; while other phenomena, like the madness of crowds and their understandable preference for fantasy, cannot.

Trust Can Not be Forecasted

The vast majority of investors, for example, traditionally have an almost blind faith in central banks housed in impressive buildings with highly-educated folks running them. Measuring that faith, as well as the inevitable loss of that faith, is harder than a Rolex repair. In fact, it's impossible to time, even when objective evidence suggests that the experts are and were indulging in open madness while markets for nearly every asset class passed the Rubicon of disaster long before their price tickers evidenced the same.

As outlined in Chapters 3 & 4 above, for example, we already know that since 2009, central banks and policy makers have done nothing but put lipstick on an economic pig by using artificial money to buy unwanted IOU's/bonds and then telegraph the asset-bubble result as "free market capitalism," or even worse, a "recovery." To ignore such madness in favor of blind faith in fantasy and "expertise" is itself a kind of madness, and madness, like COVID-19, spreads best in crowds.

Since the so-called "recovery" from the Great Financial Crisis of 2008, the vast majority of investors had gone financially mad, yet most didn't even know this as they marched into the 2020's with rising (central-bank-supported) markets justifying their delirium. Alas, the crowd had become openly euphoric as fundamentals left the scene and risk assets skyrocketed. The set-up which followed was not impossible to predict, as crowds are in fact quite predictable when it comes to madness.

Some Market Forces Can be Forecasted

Informed investors, as well as students of history, math and common sense, have long since stood outside of the crowd. They accept that natural market laws, like the natural laws of physics, are actually quite predictive. For example, *not once* in the history of nations, markets or exchanges, has any empire, system or economy ever successfully prevented an economic, currency or market collapse by simply printing gobs and gobs of fake new money to pay for gobs and gobs of real and record-breaking debt.

Not once. Not ever. White's ghost, and the example of 18th century France, are just two reminders among countless others.

The Austrian school of economists, unlike the Keynesian school of debt madness taken too far by global central banks in the 20th and 21st centuries, long ago understood that an economic keg-party sustained by extreme debt *always* ends with a brutal hangover caused by that same debt. Just as physicists long ago understood that for every action there is an equal and opposite reaction, Austrian economists like von Mises similarly understood that market forces are no different: For every exaggerated debt rise there is an equal and opposite debt fall. Given that the global economy of the 21st century has been supported exclusively by the greatest debt levels ever recorded in the history of capital markets, can we not therefore be confident in forecasting one helluva a day of reckoning for the global markets and currencies which marked that era?

As von Mises so bluntly warned in the first half of the 20th century:

"There is no means of avoiding the final collapse of a boom brought about by credit expansion. The alternative is only whether the crisis should come sooner as the result of voluntary abandonment of further credit

expansion, or later as a final and total catastrophe of the currency system involved."

The short answer, then is yes, some things *are* foreseeable. 1+1 still equals 2, and exaggerated debt-based "recoveries" *always* fail, along with their inflated currencies. Despite such cold facts, the fantasy pushed by the MMT crowd (as well as increasingly desperate and discredited politicians and central bankers from Japan to the U.S.) maintains that such economic reckonings (including inflation) could be outlawed by a money printer.

But as White's ghost reminds from Chapter 2, and as 7% year-over-year inflation spikes in 2021 confirm: That's madness in a nutshell.

Such short-term fantasy explains how economies right outside our front doors were tanking while stock markets (enjoying artificial, low-rate debt rollovers paid for with printed currencies) in the U.S. and elsewhere approached new highs with each passing week. We already know, however, that those highs were, of course, quantifiably correlated to global money printing like this:

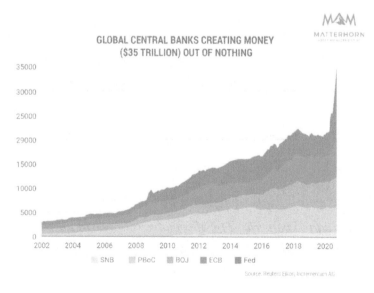

...and artificial rate and yield suppression like this:

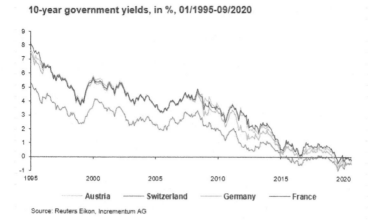

10-year government yields, in %, 01/1995-09/2020

Austria ——— Switzerland ——— Germany ——— France

Source: Reuters Eikon, Incrementum AG

Such money creation and yield behavior are, well...signs of staggering madness.

The foregoing charts are appalling, and should have been a universal wake-up call to any sane observer of global markets. Again, to believe otherwise, frankly, smacked of a kind of madness, just as ignoring the obvious warnings of prior market bubbles compared against the size of the latest bubble was an open madness. Does the following graph, for example, look like an obvious stock bubble to you?

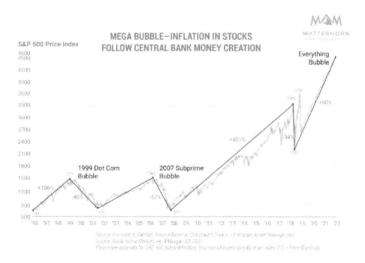

But as Mark Twain again warned, crowds often prefer a comforting fantasy (like the rising bubbles above) over a hard fact, and are thus easy to fool. He also said that lies can travel around the world faster than it takes for the truth to put its boots on. In other words, common sense is not as common as we'd like to believe when reason can be tempted away by the sweet, siren-like voices of a rigged yet rising stock market. In such a seductive backdrop, economic policy makers continued to dishonestly lead a starry-eyed crowd of investors and ordinary citizens toward a cliff of unsustainable debt paid for with diluted currencies that destroyed their hard-earned wealth with each drunken step. The *inherent* purchasing power of all major currencies had been tanking by the second when compared against timeless measurements of value like gold.

The following and oft repeated graph, which measures the decline in global currencies against a milligram of gold, is perhaps the most important one you will ever see, and is worth repeating throughout these pages:

Purchasing power of main currencies valued in gold (log), 01/1971-09/2020

Source: Reuters Eikon, Nick Laird, goldchartsrus.com, Incrementum AG

In short, global currencies are among the first dominos to fall in an artificial global economy sustained by grotesque levels of debt paid for by equally grotesque levels of fiat money creation, which is nothing more than an open and deliberate policy of fiat currency debasement as well as open insult, again, to common sense. Inevitably, economies and markets fall in succession with their currencies. And as Part II confirms in more detail, the historical cure for such currency madness is physical gold, which far from being a "barbarous relic" of the past, is a timeless and common-sense solution for the present and future.

Again: This *is* predictable. This *is* forecastable.

To consider such evidence yet burry one's head is merely a form of self-inflicted madness. To ignore the evidence of negative bond yields, rising stock bubbles and dying currencies, or worse yet, to hide or downplay it (as the Fed does with inflation, *see* Chapter 15), was even more maddening, in addition to being flat out dishonest. Most "financial journalists," unfortunately, studied marketing rather than markets and were hardly reliable warning bells. They understood click-bait techniques and key words, and received the bulk of their data from a Google search rather than a basic grasp of core economic forces. Sadly, not 1 in 10 average investors (or 1 in 100 of average "financial journalists") had ever paused to consider simple charts like those above or throughout these pages. This largely explains the easy and wide-spread fantasy as well as madness of crowds who believed that their currencies, stocks, and bonds were otherwise in the safe hands of rational experts and rational markets. But as White's ghost and informed historians, mathematicians and even market insiders have always known, those experts (as revealed in Chapters

3 and 4) are predominantly paper tigers of consensus-think, private avarice and job-security, not financial lions. Stated otherwise: Our emperors have no clothes.

Nevertheless, a mad faith in their mad policies continues.

Timing the Impossible, Preparing for the Inevitable

But for how long?

Timing human emotion, blind faith or even collective madness is, again, a fool's errand. The emotional as well as attendant irrational element of the global economy and markets are far too complex for easy modeling and precise timing, providing further explanation as to why the vast majority of market participants trusted the "experts" in general and the central banks in particular. Comforting speeches from the FOMC and empty headlines from the sell-side press owned by a handful of corporate boards on the latest tech stock easily replaced basic economics, math and history. Stated more simply: Fantasy replaced facts.

No one, including us, however, can time the precise expiration dates of misguided yet ephemeral trust in fantasy. But as both history and natural market forces confirm, that trust ends once currencies lose their value and the madness of crowds turns simply into mad crowds. As we saw in the example of France in the 1790's (Chapter 2), euphoric and irrational optimism inevitably evolves into anger when the paper money in one's pocket becomes worthless. In the following chapter, we address how this gradual shift from mad-crazy to just plain mad-angry slowly and similarly began to unfold in the U.S. by the early 2020's.

Chapter 7

The Anger of Crowds

Long before the storming of the U.S. Capital in January of 2021, the evidence of increasingly angry crowds and social unrest within the U.S. had been making headlines by the day. Journalists, of course, spent the bulk of their time, tweets and ink linking such unrest to political and social events centering around increasingly topical racial divides, police violence and ongoing political polarizations between the left and right, all of which made for tantalizing as well as inflamed popular engagement.

But as White's ghost again reminds, when economic stress and wealth disparity slowly rises from an ignored concern to an open reality, social unrest *always* follows, even if otherwise draped in political division, identity politics and all the social tensions (and divisions) which flow in their wake. Without discounting the significance of sociological forces, racial inequality or political polarization, we contend that the *core source* of the many open symptoms of social unrest today lies within the often hidden but much more fatal cancer of *financial* unrest. Stated even more simply: As more people go broke while a few folks are getting richer, social fracturing of many forms always follows.

The Chapter 2 warnings from White's ghost, for example, tracked the slow evolution of extreme debt and currency debasement in France which culminated in violence and the rise of a totalitarian/autocratic regime—the worst, but all too common culmination of financially-driven social unrest. Today, as COVID narratives justify ever-increasing control over our financial and personal lives, this trend toward declining personal liberties and rising autocracies is self-evident and by no means a coincidence. Instead, it's merely a familiar cycle understood by those who can read and think critically and independently. What Professor White saw in the extreme French example may seem far way and of another time and dusty past, but its paradigm and warnings have pressing relevance to what has been unfolding in the 2020's, despite no presence, yet, of pitchforks in DC or Brussels.

That said, the January 2021 storming of the U.S. Capital came pretty close... Angry American crowds, most notably, are making headlines themselves, and although social and financial conditions may appear far better in the modern USA than those of 1789 France, one might want to pause and think a bit deeper. The facts, as well as irony, actually indicate that the staggering levels of global debt, market distortions and wealth disparity which mark the 2020's are eerily similar to (and in many ways worse than) the conditions which stimulated the pitchforks of 1789 France.

Historical Correlations—From Markets to Main Street

Investors like to track correlations. Historians as well. Stocks follow the Fed and social unrest follows rigged and deteriorating financial schemes. In trying to understand what makes stocks "tick," for example, there's always an analyst somewhere tracking everything from oil prices and money supply levels to the number of Presidential tweets in order to find some pattern of correlated cause and effect.

Needless to say, we are no different. For decades, we've been carefully tracking the correlation of mis-information coming out of the Fed (in everything from dishonest inflation reporting to equally rigged employment and GDP data) to rising securities markets. Equally correlated is the incontrovertible relationship between rising money printing and inflating stock indexes, which have led directly to rising wealth inequality--despite Powell's staggeringly dishonest declaration that monetary policy has no impact on the same. In short, one "cause" had a clear "effect" regardless of open denials by the so-called financial and political "leadership." One can easily track, for example, how trillions in bonds bought with trillions in printed dollars by a central bank make those bonds go up rather than down in price, allowing for an easy bond front-run based upon the simple reason that the two forces are openly, well: *Correlated.* In short: What (and who) the Fed supports, enjoys a considerable tailwind. Similarly, one can equally track the far sadder fates of those economic sectors and individuals whom the central banks have traditionally ignored, which includes most of those angry faces we see on TV and across the daily headlines, namely: The broader population of the real economy.

Today, the open inequality of access to cheap capital, which is so essential to enterprise success, yet which so clearly favors large, publicly traded enterprises over smaller businesses, is an open and obvious shame, as well as direct result of Fed policy. Many of those ignored and smaller businesses (and their employees) have been permanently shut down, and this, of course, creates anger, and hence the angry crowds.

Market Forces Affect Social Forces Too...

Heading into the 2020's, the U.S. witnessed wave after wave of social unrest, from the rioting streets of Minnesota to the burned out, retail-fleeing neighborhoods and tent cities cropping up seemingly overnight, from Portland to Seattle, San Francisco to Los Angeles. Many have understandably attributed such growing unrest to racial tensions, others to pent-up lock-down "hysteria" unleashed by unpopular COVID restrictions; still others attribute this social unrest to the extreme political partisanship which tracked the steps of a controversial Trump presidency into an equally controversial Biden White House. But whether one attributes the growing social unrest which unfolded in the U.S. to increasingly polarized debates over race, gender, sexual orientation or headlines on police brutality or partisan politics, it's fairly undeniable that 2020 and beyond were not stellar years for "uniting" the states of America.

So, what happened?

Why so much social divisions? Why were statues tumbling, cultures "cancelled," cities rioting, politicians scrambling and media bobbleheads fighting like hungry wolves to signal virtue (left or right) at every opportunity? Did all this open anger and fracturing of societies really boil down to an obviously bad cop doing an obviously horrific thing in Minnesota? Was the January 6th storming of the Senate exclusively a Trump aberration conducted by "domestic terrorists," or was there a larger, deeper anxiety and hence anger at play here?

Financial Unrest Equals Social Unrest

With history as a guide (from the Rome under Pompey, the France of the 1790's, the Russia of 1917, the Europe of the 1930's, or even the Cuba of the late 50's) our take on this rising frustration and social unrest is fairly blunt. It boils down to a simple correlation seen and studied throughout history, again, from the ancient Romans to modern Wall Street and an increasingly ignored Main Street. Namely: When openly rigged financial conditions begin to fall apart and *ressentiment* from the have-nots boils from the bottom-up, the natives get understandably restless. Stated even more simply, social unrest always follows economic inequality and weakness, and our economies, riddled by debt and sustained by policies of ever-more debt, have been growing weaker and more unequal by the day.

In this turbulent and distorted economic backdrop, the historical reality as well as cycle of cause and effect has been mostly ignored by the prompt readers and Hollywood celebrities scrambling to appear racially, sexually or politically progressive (or even victimized) from the highest tax brackets, despite *knowing almost nothing* about history, economics or basic math. As always, they were missing one key reality, and that's the *economic* correlation between financial insecurity and social instability. As the former increases, the later expands equally. That's why understanding markets, central banks, and yield curves is so critical today, as these forces are more important than just predictors of price movement in risk assets. They are also predictors of history and the very stability beneath our feet.

In short: Economics matter. Debt matters. Policies matter.

For years, we've tracked and warned about the disgraceful wealth gap in the U.S. We've tracked and warned that the shamelessly obvious and rigged game played between the Fed and Wall Street had been devastating to a dying middle class. And this was occurring in what was otherwise described as the "richest country in the world," despite dispositive evidence that a critical swath of that country was broke, with over 50% of its children under the age of 18 living within some form of social assistance. We had also warned that such a rigged game ends badly, causing social unrest and a recession from the bottom-up while Wall Street enjoyed bailout after bailout from the top-down. With each new market high after new market high, an increasingly ignored and restless core of that system and society rotted from within.

Such blatant disconnects between what families, individuals and employees felt in their wallets and dinner table conversations and what we heard from Wall Street seemed openly absurd. This was because most individuals would agree that regardless of one's politics or individual take on objective rather than inflamed data on everything from police shootings to transgender bathrooms and vaccine efficacy, trust in leadership and policy making was dying. That is, regardless of what the media prompt readers and Wall Street sell-siders were saying, the vast bulk of their pablum was not nearly as relevant to one's daily reality as to whether or not one could pay his/her mortgage, make a car payment or send their kids to school in the fall.

And given that markets tanked in early 2020 and jobs were lost (including 1/3 of African American businesses), was there really any surprise that social unrest—inflamed by COVID fears, distractions, frustrations and policy debates—rose in direct step with economic pain and increased political controls, one following the other? In sum, people were worried about money, not just the color of one's skin or the election sign in one's yard. It's just that basic. And when those financial worries peak, so too does social unrest and finger-pointing in every compass direction for almost any reason and any trigger, from race, to gender to politics.

The financial policy makers, of course, forever seek to stay above the social fray. Fed Chairman Powell, again, continued his open lie (self-delusion) that Fed policy had nothing to do with wealth inequality or economic pain on Main Street. Across the board, policy makers sought to hide, ignore or repress their direct responsibility for decades of excessive debt policies, blaming their failures on the COVID crisis rather than on the reflection in their mirror. But as most informed investors already knew (Chapter 5), the fatal weaknesses in these markets and economies existed long *before* COVID made its first headline.

Financial Cause & Effect Is Global, Historical and Inevitable

Nor is this link between financial disaster and social unrest just a U.S. problem. It's a human problem, and as such, it's a global problem. Take the biggest pension fund in the world—the Japanese Government Pension Investment Fund. It lost over $160 billion in the first quarter of 2020. Needless to say, that represented a genuine moment of "Uh-oh."

But as we'll discover in the following chapter, pension funds in the US were and are in no better shape, and are equally broke, too broke, in fact, to pay all those school teachers, firemen and other hard-working yet debt-saddled Americans who were otherwise promised a safe retirement for years. Such unspoken disasters and deeply rooted fears lurking within our rigged markets make people legitimately upset. They are angry, frustrated and looking for someone, something—*anything*—to blame. Ironically, and at many points in this evolving social unrest, there was serious policy of limiting the police forces as armed and broke crowds took over an entire section of Seattle, Washington.

Our opinion is that limiting the Fed would have been a far better solution for America. Does that seem revolutionary? Reactionary? Anti-capitalist?

In fact, we are proud capitalists with an admitted sweet tooth for the good things in life. We like financial success, freedom and gains. We've never denied nor apologized for this. But when three US billionaires have more wealth than 50% of the entire nation, or when the average executive to wage earner salary ratio skyrockets from 21:1 to 320:1 in just four decades, one has to wonder, as we have in Chapter 4, just how free such free-market capitalism truly is? One has to wonder if the current system is even one of capitalism at all. As importantly, one has to wonder just how long social unrest like the kind germinating in the 2020's can be contained without the further incursions of a more totalitarian control system, made all the more possible by COVID control measures cleverly masquerading as humanitarian health concerns.

As we'll discuss at greater length in Chapter 14, the end-game for increasingly cornered policy makers will boil down to either watching their entire system implode, or resorting instead to command-controlling the same with even greater desperation and financial repressions. For now, we can only assert that as the market and policy distortions explained in prior chapters confirm, genuine capitalism and free market price discovery died long ago. It has been replaced instead by the open secret of an odd flavor of Wall Street socialism, the kind that ruins rather than builds nations, the kind that fans rather than quells economic inequality and social unrest. For this, we can recall Chapters 3 and 4 and once again thank a long history of anti-heroes, from FDR to Nixon, Greenspan to Summers.

With: 1) over $300 trillion in global debt, 2) GDP lagging and 3) other hard-fact indicators pointing toward an obvious moment of current and future "uh-oh," one cannot ignore the lessons of history nor the ever-increasing need to protect one's wealth in such a fragile and distorted backdrop. The sad, but undeniable fact is that the U.S. in particular, and the larger economies of the world in general, have been living beyond their means for far too long, and at levels of decadence too deep to sustain. Spending has simply outpaced income at extreme levels. The ongoing needs of the economy can thus no longer be met by globally sagging productivity. As mentioned above, one clear warning sign of such unmet needs comes directly from the growing weaknesses within the American pension system, another embarrassing yet media-ignored theme to which we turn next.

Chapter 8

Pension Fund Risk

Heading into the 2020's, pension funds across the U.S. were massively underfunded yet massively over-allocated to puffed stocks and junky bonds, and, hence... massively at risk. This trio of facts represented a ticking time bomb of demographic and market risk set to explode.

In prior chapters, we've touched upon historically (record) high and mathematically-confirmed overvaluations in stock and bond markets, all converging amidst a barometric, low-pressure front of investors entering the 2020's with topping exposure levels in topping markets colliding with the largest debt bubble in recorded history, a bubble set to implode (or come under extreme governmental controls) the moment the Fed loses control of interest rates. In short – a truly perfect storm.

And as these converging wind speeds increased, the fatally flawed U.S. pension fund system had set itself up as among the first to drown. In fact, dying pension funds, temporarily "saved" by central-bank driven asset bubbles post March 2021, could very well become the singular gust of wind that ultimately pushes the U.S. economy to the basement of history. When this large class of pension investors sees their dangerously overweight credit and equity holdings tank, the economy will face years of systemic stress as retirees find themselves with increasingly less income than otherwise anticipated. The evidence of such risk was already overwhelming as we entered the 2020's. Toward this end, let's look more carefully at how this increased risk plays out and how we got to such a tragic crossroads.

The Baby Boomers

At the close of World War II, a new generation was born that comprised the largest population surge in U.S. history: Baby boomers. Like most kids, this generation didn't want to be like their parents, a prior generation psychologically marred by two world wars which induced a genuine instinct to expect the worst and thus do nothing more than save, save, and save. The free-spirited baby boomers who followed this generation, however, wanted to spend, spend, and spend rather than save, save, save. Sure, they worked hard too, but the key components of the baby boomer's generational story were work, spend, and consume.

But other than generational rebellion, what caused these baby boomers to be so optimistic, carefree and potentially reckless?

The answer is simple...

Wall Street Led Them Astray

The new Wall Street that grew up alongside the baby boomers had convinced themselves and each other that there was no need to save and worry anymore. Coming out of a victorious war and leading the world in credit, manufacturing and infrastructure, this new generation of Americans followed their financial leaders' warm promises: "Just let our expertise and the ever-rising stock markets make you safe." This was, of course, a great theme and tailwind for the wealth advisors, fund managers, and bankers who could exploit such optimism to cash in on the fees that accompanied a constant inflow of dollars pouring into Wall Street from the paychecks and retirement funds of Main Street's largest investment class – the post-war baby boomers and their growing faith in the post-war future.

Of course, the pension funds and trustees to which this generation trusted their money drank the same Kool Aid from the Wall Street crowd. Nearly every penny that went into these pension funds (as well as 401(k)s and IRAs "advised" by so-called "retirement planners") went directly into stocks or other equity-related risk vehicles, i.e., private equity, venture capital, and hedge fund strategies hired out by the notoriously not-so-savvy pension fund advisors and allocators. This, of course, was an absolute boon for Wall Street salesmen (who saw the poorly experienced managers of these pension funds as easy "suckers"/buyers of their products and services). Very quickly, large allocations from these fattening pension funds helped push markets to all-time highs in the 1980s and 1990s. But Wall Street didn't stop there; it added an extra twist in the 1980s, namely easy credit – otherwise known as debt. Baby boomers soon went crazy for stocks and even crazier for borrowing. Pension funds effectively became casinos for speculation while many baby boomers went into debt rather than saving.

Big Promises, Little Returns

But hey, why worry? The stock market only goes up, right? The pension funds had your backs, right? Well, that's what the experts (i.e., the Wall Street sell-side) were telling investors year after year. Unfortunately, however, reality set in. By 2000, and then again in 2008, the foregoing system of "speculate and borrow" blew apart. Pension funds (and the workers they represented) lost massive amounts of money in these epic market crashes, which meant the baby boomers looking to retire in the future were in a pickle. Despite the raging bull ride that soon followed the Fed-driven 2009 "recovery," the prior losses of 2000 and 2008 were deep enough to gut most U.S. pension funds and prevent them from meeting target returns. Apparently, all those fund advisors forgot the first rule of wealth management, namely: The key to success is to *avoid losses*, not chase gains.

Unfortunately, the pension funds didn't avoid those two seminal market crashes. As a result, as 2020 rolled into view, their collective assets didn't come even close to matching their collective liabilities, which meant the pension funds couldn't pay out what was otherwise owed to *all* of their would-be retirees. That is, they had more liabilities (top line) than assets (bottom line). In other words: "Uh-oh."

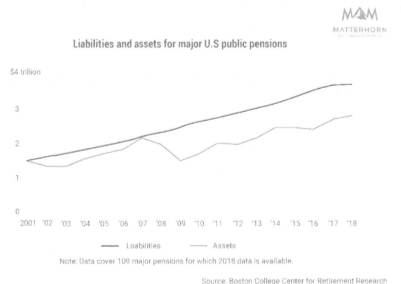

Liabilities and assets for major U.S public pensions

Note: Data cover 109 major pensions for which 2018 data is available.

Source: Boston College Center for Retirement Research

By 2019, the average age of a baby boomer was 64 years, and the average retirement age is 64, which meant many baby boomers wanted to retire and were thus beginning to ask the pension funds for their promised money...

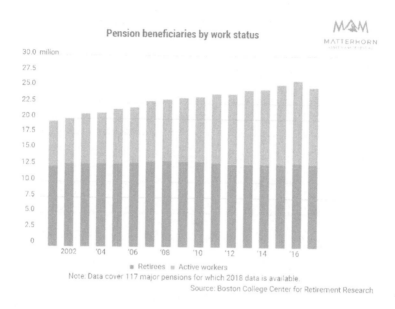

Pension beneficiaries by work status

■ Retirees ■ Active workers

Note: Data cover 117 major pensions for which 2018 data is available.

Source: Boston College Center for Retirement Research

But here's another rub: Many of those retirees couldn't afford to retire because retirees, like pension funds, were not flush with the monies that Wall Street had promised them during the better times. This explains why the labor force participation rate for those *over* 65 was skyrocketing past 20% by 2020. Again: *Many folks simply couldn't afford to retire.* A systemic and structural shift was occurring in the U.S. retirement population.

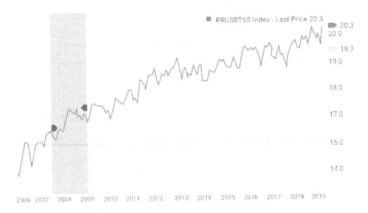

Source: Critical Signals Report/Bureau of Labor Statistics

But how could this be? After all, D.C. and its statisticians (as well as Wall Street and their media minions) kept telling the world that the *average* household net worth in the U.S. was off the charts positive, with the average 65-year-old owning $24K in bonds, $269K in stocks, $300K in real estate, $100K in savings, $150K in pension funds, and another $200K in "other assets." However, and for many of you reading these statistics today (and past the age of 65), you might be thinking that such numbers may not resemble *your own* personal experience or personal wealth.

Well, you're not alone...

The above statistics, like so many optimistic data points produced by the number crunchers on Wall Street and DC, are not what they seem. The foregoing account summaries use an *average* rather than *median* metric, which means their overly-optimistic data includes the top 1% of U.S. wealth, which *massively skews the data*. If one stripped out the absurdly skewed wealth of the top 1% of Americans, the *median* household net worth data came much closer to earth. That is, rather than the skewed data above, the truer median retiree wealth is composed of $4K in bonds, $45K in stocks, $54K in real estate, savings of $18K, pension assets of $40K, and other assets of around $20K.

Quite a difference, no?

But by now, you should no longer be surprised by how D.C. statisticians effectively lie to make reality seem better than it is. In short, there is a massive difference between *average* household wealth and *median* household wealth.

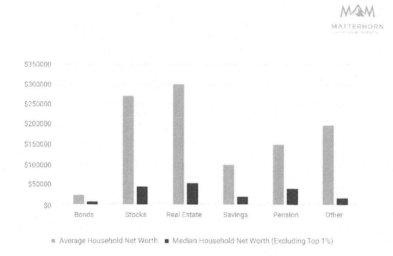

Source: Critical Signals Report

Of course, many folks have far less than even this "median" level of wealth to rely upon in the future. In short, and given the increased life expectancies of modern times, most baby boomers simply can't afford to stop working or worrying.

The Solution for Crazy? More Crazy…

So, what have baby boomers and their pension advisors done to make up for the losses rather than windfalls that Wall Street had promised? Well, the *real* data is in, and the answer is as obvious as it is both predictable and maddening, namely: Wall Street had 'em "suckered" again. Everyone, including the under-funded pension funds, went into the 2020's hog-wild chasing even more of the highest risk securities, namely more equities and equity like vehicles, pushing up stock prices while simultaneously increasing their risk profile. In short, Wall Street and pension fund trustees simply asked more hard-working, trusting and financially tapped-out citizens to double down on the greatest asset bubble (and hence risk profile) in history rather than exit, hedge or truly diversify their high-risk stock recommendations, thus adding to both market and pension fund risk.

Yet once again, history warns and reminds that such conventional, high-risk advice will get this massive class of baby boomers slaughtered the moment the greatest securities bubble in U.S. history does what all bubbles do: Pop. It's either sadness of euphoria…

And given the immense size of the baby boomer generation, the fallout from a pending market crisis will have devastating consequences for the larger markets and economy in general. Heading into the 2020's, investors and broken, under-funded pension managers were going "all-in," collectively chasing dangerously overvalued markets and hence doubling (even tripling) down on stocks (and therefore stock and pension fund risk) to try and close the gap between what they needed to retire and what was otherwise absent in their actual wealth. Such optimism and "retirement planning" works great when markets are melting up, but would and will become a life changing disaster when those asset bubbles implode. Despite such risk, pension funds and Wall Street continued to induce investors to go further and deeper into "miraculous" stocks, while their pension fund trustees were quietly muting their promised "return expectations."

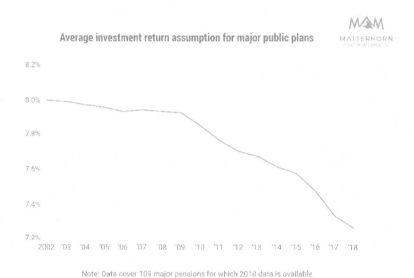

Note: Data cover 109 major pensions for which 2018 data is available.

Source: Boston College Center for Retirement Research

Many households and pension funds, like their very own government, simply didn't have enough money. In order to stay afloat (and keep retirees afloat), this meant pension funds had to take on even crazier levels of risk in an even crazier/riskier stock and bond market.

Not a Safe Bet–Pension Fund Risk Ahead

It's crazy because by *every metric* - be it standard PE multiples, median PE multiples, cyclically adjusted PE multiples, or even market cap to GDP ratios – *the U.S. stock market was at all-time record highs of overvaluation heading into the 2020's.* In short – not the safest bet, especially for wannabe retirees. Of course, no one wanted to see such risks or warnings while stocks ripped northward on the back of a seemingly immortal and omni-supportive central bank forever pushing liquidity (i.e., printed money) into the financial markets.

Not only were retirement funds taking their client assets further and further into stock market risk to gain larger returns, they were also taking those same clients further and further out on the risk branch of grossly overvalued bonds in a desperate search for that otherwise elusive and Fed-destroyed concept known as "yield." Rather than risk-free return, pension funds were chasing return-free risk.

As explained previously, bonds had become so over-bought and over-valued due to central bank support (i.e., purchasing) of the same, that bond yields (which move inversely to inflated bond prices) had all but disappeared in traditional corporate and governmental bond markets. In the 1990's for example, the typical yield for a 10-Year Treasury bond was 7%, buy 2021, that yield had sunk to 1.4%, not enough to beat inflation rates skyrocketing to 7+%. As a result, pension fund managers looked for more and more yield in the worst places, namely that fowl-smelling corner of the credit market known as junk bonds, the veritable D- students of the otherwise bloated bond market class.

"Junk bonds," of course, get this title for a reason: Their risk of default is extremely high. As a result, investors traditionally expect much greater return (i.e., "yield") for the much greater risk they are assuming with "junky" bonds. And once upon time, they were at least allowed this greater reward for greater risk. But fast-forward past 2008 (and the great deformation of the bond market due to Fed "accommodation"), and even the junk bond sector of the bond market had become so overbought in the thirst for any kind of yield at all that yields sank even in the riskiest of all bonds. In the 1980's, for example, investors were seeing 18+% yields for taking junk bond risk, by 2021, those yields had fallen to 3-4%. In short, miniscule return for massive risk, and, as of this writing, not even beating 7% inflation.

That's distortion in a nutshell.

But pension managers, as a class, ignored such risk in their desperate search for return--any kind of return--to expand their so-called performance reporting. With increasing speed and desperation, they began piling up their investments in those riskiest of all risk assets: The junk bond market.

Pension Funds, A Ponzi Scheme?

Meanwhile, and as already described, we also saw a record-high number of baby boomers seeking to retire and draw upon assets held in state pension funds and defined benefit plans *that did not have the money to pay them.* As with a Ponzi scheme, only those who are and were able to get their money out first and fastest could be certain of full benefits. Sadly, these Ponzi-like pension funds will have even less money going forward when massively over-valued markets inevitably implode and market bubbles turn into market busts, which central banks desperately seek to postpone, but by no means outlaw.

Such implosions are inevitable rather than theoretical given that pension funds have been speculating, gambling, and going deeper into the riskiest assets to *appear* successful in good times. What they have entirely ignored, however, is the reality of the inevitable bad times, which is a sign of reckless mismanagement and broken fiduciary ethics. Apparently, pension funds want to believe that the Fed will outlaw falling markets, which is like Newton trying to outlaw gravity. But as all sophisticated market veterans know, one of the most important characteristics of markets is that they always revert to their mean—like a stretched rubber band pulled from one's finger, market highs "revert" back with a sting. Based upon prior resistance and support lines, such mean reversions can and will result in losses like those plotted below.

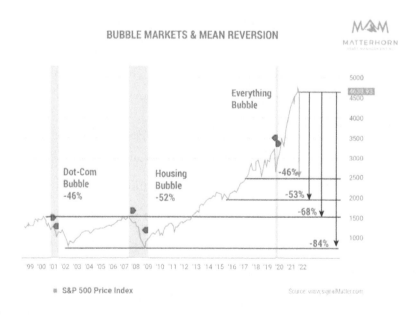

Furthermore, and despite such a willful disregard for the lessons of risk, history and mean-reversion, the average U.S. pension fund by late

2019 was already falling well short of their promises and performance. Returns among 36 pensions tracked that year were already down by 26% over the last fiscal year.

Faced with such objective data as well as risk, what does Wall Street, the pension funds, and the broader "retirement advisory complex" still advise future and current retirees to do in the backdrop of this obvious yet non-disclosed pension fund risk? It's no big surprise, and it's the same thing that all Ponzi scheme managers, including Bernie Madoff, would say: "Show me more of your money!"

In short, Pension funds are telling participants to buy even more bubbled stocks and crappy bonds. But with stocks and bonds heading into the 2020's at record high-risk levels, this meant the "experts" were literally inviting retirees to walk ever closer to an ignored market cliff. When such a pension scam system sees major losses, it, like any Ponzi scheme, will only have enough funds to pay out the early withdrawals, not the later ones, which means baby boomers and markets are facing a demographic time bomb colliding with a recessionary storm front.

As for state pension fund risk and defined benefit plans, which have been collectively trillions of dollars in the red, we cannot break this devastating data down state by state or pension by pension in these pages. What we can say here is that these desperate, broken, and frankly unethical pension strategies were at a point in history where the only solution they were "promising" in 2019 for their duped baby boomers was that an ever-rising stock market or junk bond sector would save them from then until at least 2027 without any downside risk. Of course, by 2020, when markets tanked by greater than 30%, those same pension managers could only sulk and wait for the Fed to "re-stimulate" the markets higher on the backs of (you guessed it) more currency-killing money printing and more postponing of the inevitable mean-reversions and market losses ahead. Admittedly, the massive market returns of the surreal stimulus provided post-March of 2020 helped these funds, but only as a *provisional* illusion not a long-term solution.

Time for a Reality Check on Pension Fund Risk

Entering the 2020's, the U.S. saw millions of baby boomers massively overweight in high-risk equities and even junkier junk bonds (yielding almost nothing for their insane risk levels) and yet seeking to survive on a stock and bond market entering both an acme of record highs (and hence record risk) as the longest business cycle and bull market ever recorded neared its approaching end.

That is a perfect storm.

Meanwhile, Wall Street and grossly underfunded pensions (as well as fee-seeking advisors and clueless "business developers") ducked in the corner pretending not to worry about tomorrow's pension fund risk because stock markets, as they assured one and all, would *never* fall. As we discuss in Chapters 6 and 18, such optimistic thinking is little more than madness bordering upon the criminally-negligent and dishonest. In fact, and notwithstanding the Fed's monetary "doping" since 2008, normal business cycles contract once every 4-8 years, which means recessions and market crashes were and are as inevitable as thunderstorms and hurricanes, even without the added and insane levels of *postponed* risk which the Fed had added to credit and equity securities.

Always Sunny in Wall Street?

By 2019, however, 10 years into the most hated (and artificial) bull cycle in recorded history, the majority of retirees were still being told that market thunderstorms or hurricanes no longer existed. As such promises were being peddled, Hurricane Dorian was wreaking havoc on the Bahamas and Carolinas. Of course, the Bahamas and Carolinas, like the stock markets, are known for their mostly sunny days. But as both Dorian and the above facts confirm, it's not sunny *every* day in the Bahamas – nor in the stock and bond markets.

Despite such common sense and facts, Wall Street and its cadre of gambling pension advisors would still have investors believe it never rains in Fed-supported markets. Unfortunately, the gathering market storm is all too real, and as White's ghost reminds, the dishonesty and hope-peddling from the so-called "experts" (including pension fund managers) always reaches its acme of greed, dishonesty and madness just *before* the markets fall under their own weight. And as White's ghost further reminds, history is equally full of those minority, yet blunt, voices seeking to warn (rather than scare) the majority of investors about debt cycles, currency risks and safe-havens in a financial world gone mad.

This book, of course, is *our* effort to provide such a blunt voice and warning. Part II, moreover, offers an equally blunt solution to the artificially-postponed yet cyclical risks facing stocks, bonds and currencies around the globe, namely *physical* gold held *outside* of a fractured financial and banking system.

Toward this end, it is critical to consider the management of risk and certain critical tools of wealth preservation, including precious metal ownership, *before* rather than *after* the storm hits. Recessions, for example, are always date-stamped in *arrears*, which means it takes two down quarters of GDP (plus a month or so to figure that out) before the National Bureau of Economic Research (NBER) even lets investors "officially" know when a severe recession has actually begun, which is effectively *too late*. Many, of course, can make a reasonable claim that any economic or market catastrophe can be quickly remedied by more money printing and cheap debt compliments of a command-control government or complicit central bank near you (*See* Chapter 14).

In the fully distorted and central-bank-supported "New Abnormal" within which the financial world now spins, bad news is ironically seen as good news by markets. This is because it is expected and assumed that central banks will always add more steroids (i.e., fiat currencies) to perpetually "recover" otherwise debt-soaked and overbought markets and economies. Again, that is the New Abnormal. Unfortunately, and worth repeating over, and over and over, this can only mean one thing: As more artificial currencies are created to solve for otherwise unsolvable debt crises and naturally required market recalibrations (i.e., "constructive destruction"), those expanding currency levels are automatically and mathematically headed for further and continual *debasement*, which means the currency by which you measure your wealth is getting weaker by the day.

Fortunately, Part II confirms that there is an historically-confirmed path to ensure against such obvious currency risks. Before we get there, however, it is important to look at other examples of market risk against which investors need to be *insured* and for which investors need to be *informed*. Specifically, we will examine the open yet largely ignored risks which lie within the dramatically rising ETF, or "Exchange Traded Fund" universe, described next.

Chapter 9

ETF Risk

As recently as November of 2019, the *Wall Street Journal* came out with an article heralding the massive growth, as well as consolidation within, the then $4 trillion passive ETF (Exchange-Traded Fund) industry, which had grown by over 90% in the prior five years. That was all very impressive, but the same *WSJ* article conveniently left out key risks hidden beneath this industry's otherwise massive growth story. In fact, if one digs deeper and looks at the opportunities as well as risks lurking beneath this ETF market growth, a clear and present danger emerges.

The Best of Times, The Worst of Times

ETFs remind us a lot of the opening line of Dickens's novel, *A Tale of Two Cities*: "It was the best of times, it was the worst of times..." In other words, there are some aspects to admire and some things to greatly dislike about the rise of passive ETF products. They can, for example, be the wind beneath a market's astronomical rise; but they can quite quickly become the anchor that takes securities markets, and your money, to the basement of history.

A Friend in the Best of Times...

As for the "best of" characteristics of passive index ETFs, there are many:

(1) Certain ETFs act as proxies for over-all indexes/markets like the S&P or the NASDAQ, and thus one can trade an entire Index, long or short, with a simple "click" on a single ETF ticker.

(2) ETFs can be great sources of risk and reward "diversifiers" for broad sectors, i.e., "baskets" of tech stocks (Investco's QQQ Trust ETF –

QQQ) or commodity exposure in the energy sector (Energy Select Sector SPDR ETF - XLE), thus allowing investors instant exposure to a range of "like-minded" securities within a single ETF vehicle/trade.

(3) In addition to allowing investors to trade (and spread risk exposure) across many stock and/or bond "marbles in one bag," ETFs also give investors easy, as well as inexpensive, access to *specific* assets like gold (SPDR Gold Shares ETF - GLD) and Silver (iShares Silver Trust ETF - SLV), all with minimal headache—at least on the surface. (More on the risk of gold ETFs in Chapter 16.)

(4) ETFs also allow investors to bet *against* (i.e., "short") the market without having to go through all the complex administrative and counter-party borrowing maneuvers otherwise required to borrow stocks when entering into a short trade or option strategy (i.e., "put-buying") to bet *against* a certain market or sector. That is, by going "long" (i.e., simply buying) an *inverse* ETF, investors can bet against (i.e., "short") a market, sector, or specific asset class (from oil and precious metals to the overall market itself) with one simple ETF purchase.

(5) By and large, passive index ETFs involve no active management, and thus, unlike mutual funds, are far less expensive and, in *the right conditions*, highly liquid, and thus easy to enter and exit.

Such qualities may explain why the ETF industry has grown so remarkably in the last decade, especially in the post-08 market surge. Indeed, exchange-traded products (ETPs) overall are projected by

ETF.com to continue to grow exponentially in the years to come, raising assets to $15 trillion in 10 years, topping mutual funds.

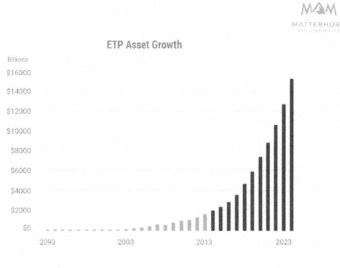

And as the same 2019 *WSJ* article revealed, all of this astronomical growth was being led by two big players in the passive index ETF space, namely Blackrock's iShares and the Vanguard Group. Together, Blackrock and Vanguard have quashed other competitors whose ETF's often have less than the minimal $50-$100 million asset size needed to ensure safer liquidity for investors. In short, the big boys were and are winning the ETF war for subscribers, and thus more and more investors are piling into the same ETFs, the growing size of which is pushing securities markets even higher.

And that *is precisely where the hidden danger lies in the passive ETF universe.*

Your Enemy in the Worst of Times...

Ironically, embedded within the very growth success of the most popular ETF's lies the seeds of their ultimate risk – as well as the ultimate risk in the overall markets and sectors they track. In fact, the sheer size and passive nature of these bloated ETF products is why market legend Michael Burry (made infamous in the book/film *The Big Short* for predicting the mortgage catastrophe way ahead of Wall Street) now considers passive index ETFs as *the greatest threat* to modern investors since the sub-prime crisis.

Why?

Because similar to the build-up of the 2008 market crisis in which investors were piling into otherwise toxic but highly popular mortgage-backed securities, investors heading into the 2020's were blindly herding into passive ETF instruments without paying any regard to the massive risks (i.e., overvaluation and illiquidity) embedded within them. The extreme growth of, and over-dependence upon, the most popular ETF's means that too many dollars were pouring into them from hedge funds, pension funds, retail investors, sovereign wealth funds, and other institutional players. This allocation over-inflow caused the ETFs to gain *un-natural* price valuation by the sheer *volume* of their inflows rather than the actual *quality* of the underlying assets (stocks, bonds etc.) within the ETFs themselves.

In other words, ETFs in general, and the securities within them in particular, were rising on inflow momentum (trade volume) rather than the fundamentals of their underlying balance sheets. Or stated even more simply, many otherwise rotten boats were able to rise on a rising tide of one-way-flowing dollars. Take the popular tech FANGs for example – an acronym for Facebook Inc. (FB), Amazon.com Inc. (AMZN), Netflix Inc. (NFLX), and Alphabet Inc. (GOOGL). To gain exposure to such stocks, there are choices here, either investing conservatively in tech ETFs with considerable FANG exposure, or investing in more concentrated (but much smaller) *leveraged* ETFs like MicroSectors FANG+ Index 3X leveraged ETN (FNGU, $125 million). Leverage (borrowing to enhance exposure), we remind, can be a very dangerous thing. In fact, there are three flavors of leverage offered by MicroSectors ETFs (1X, 2X, and 3X leverage), and not surprisingly, the majority of investors herded into the riskiest, 3X levered ETF, exemplified by the greed and fear-of-missing-out (FOMO) mentality that was prevailing as markets raced upwards into the 2020's. Such 3X leverage can mean 3X returns in good times, but greater than 3X losses in bad times.

See the risk?

These tech and other ETF products have enjoyed massive inflows over the years, inflows which partly explain why tech names that were otherwise showing no actual profits (think Amazon) could nevertheless be trading at equally massive 85X multiples of price to earnings by 2019. The good, the bad, and the ugly were thus rising together within a tide of passive investor flows pouring into the ETF's that held them. The same "rising tide effect" also took place in the broader market indexes like the SPY and QQQ mentioned above. That is, massive inflows into these popular ETF's trickled down into *all of the stocks* which comprised these exchange-proxy ETFs, thus pushing *all* the S&P and *all* the NASDAQ stocks up together, despite the fact, again, that many of those stocks were absolute lemons. Index ETFs were thus directly responsible for creating dangerous over-valuation (and hence price distortion and inflation) in the broadest markets as well as across the sector-specific corners of the market, like tech.

In other words: Dangerous bubbles were forming.

No One's Looking

Of course, during the good times (such as the absolute abomination/euphoria that became the Fed-driven, Twilight Zone of the post-08 stimulus), no one wanted to see these risks. Remember White's ghost and the example of the French? Such euphoria and risk blindness are nothing new. All that investors saw were markets rising, ETF's growing fatter, and hence the stocks within them hitting record highs, despite the fact that most of the stocks within these ETF baskets were largely profitless and high risk. In short, ETFs were morphing into momentum creators rather than baskets of fair value. We (and Michael Burry, cited above) saw the same willful ignorance during the rise of subprime mortgage-backed securities (MBS), which everyone was piling into before that market suddenly tanked in late 2008.

But here's the rub: As those massive *inflows* inevitably and eventually turn into massive *outflows* whenever and however a market trigger pops the undeniable asset bubble in risk assets like stocks and bonds, those same ETF vehicles, along with all the equities and or credits piled up inside them, begin to fall in price rapidly and deeply, going down (way down) far faster than they rose upwards.

That is what has informed investors (including us and Michael Burry...) so concerned.

The Fall Is Faster Than the Rise

All market veterans know that markets fall faster than they rise, and that when assets grow too fat on momentum, popularity, institutional inflows, central-bank "accommodation" and herd ignorance masquerading as collective confidence (as we saw with the subprime MBS bubble of 2008 or the dot.com bubble of the late 90's), the size, scope, and speed of the subsequent fall can be (and always has been) devastating. Stated otherwise, the bigger the bubble, the greater the subsequent fall. And folks, the ETF bubble heading into the 2020's was a doozy...

The size, scope, and speed of the *WSJ*-heralded ETF rise thus highlighted, yet failed to address, an equally obvious (but largely unspoken) risk of an equally devastating fall. This ETF ticking timebomb posed a particularly devastating threat to the pension fund industry described in Chapter 8, already *way too top-heavy* in its exposure to passive, broad-based index ETFs. When, not if, sell-offs rather than inflows hit this grossly bloated ETF industry and someone yells "fire!" – the exit doors (i.e., ability to sell) in those once "favored ETFs" become the size of mouse holes. In other words – investors and markets get fatally burned as ETF's sink faster than investors can escape them.

Such third-degree burns, of course, stem from the gasoline-and-match dangers represented by extreme market risk (directly resulting from extreme central bank policy/liquidity) whose symptoms, as well as triggers, are openly apparent within the openly distorted (yet openly ignored) pension fund system and ETF industry. Adding to such extreme market risks, is the obvious currency risk (*See* Chapter 11) which follows from the extreme monetary policies discussed throughout these pages. Finally, no discussion of global financial risk (and hence personal wealth preservation) would be complete without addressing the equally critical topic of banking risk, to which we turn next.

Chapter 10

Banking Risk

When it comes to the topic of banking risk, well...one can only lean back in a chair, sigh and exclaim: "Where to begin?"

A Rich and Deep History of Risk

Banks, and hence banking risk, come in so many flavors, because bank mismanagement and short-sighted ignorance and greed comes in so many packages. As such, a thorough discussion on banking risk would necessitate hundreds of pages and examples.

From the woefully arrogant and even more woefully mismanaged central banks, to the equally arrogant and mismanaged commercial banks, the history of almost unbelievable avarice, risk, and over-paid (and over-touted) bank hubris is almost endless.

Perhaps this is what prompted Henry Ford to observe that if ordinary citizens actually knew how banks operated (from fractional reserve banking to special derivative deals with over-levered hedge funds), there would be immediate revolution in the streets.

Although such observations may seem like an exaggeration bordering upon the sensational, one only needs to look beneath the surface of those otherwise impressive buildings to realize that reality (and banking risk) is indeed stranger than fiction.

In prior pages, we've touched broadly upon extreme banking policies and risks that date back centuries, even millennia.

In short, it's never difficult to put a finger on the map of history, locate any major moment of financial crisis and then find a banker (be he clad in a toga, French silk ruffles or an Armani suit) sulking in a corner somewhere, head down and hoping not to be recognized or caught.

This is simply because global history, as well as the history of bankers and major financial disasters, from the money lenders of the Old Testament to the S&L Crisis of the 1980's or the Lehman Moments of 2008, are, sadly, all too common, all too familiar, all too inevitable and all too predictable.

Again, entire books can be, and have been, written on such a sordid, yet easily confirmed, trail of complex banking practices leading to horrific consequences for nations, financial systems and of course, individual investors. The current chapter, therefore, is merely a sliver of the full story on global and historical banking risk.

Modern Banking Risk: No Less Real

Today's level of complex banking practices, and hence banking risk, is in fact higher than ever. The amount of non-performing loans (NPL's) sure to stream out of the post-COVID (and self-inflicted) gunshot wound (Chapter 5) due to lockdowns and failing small businesses and commercial real estate owners and tenants is just one among many risks facing the current banking system, which, as we'll cover in Chapter 14, is quietly coming under greater and greater governmental command control. In fact, the level of banking risk which lies beneath the so-called bank "recovery" from the Great Financial Crisis of 2008 is higher than most pundits, sell-siders and media pablum-pushers would otherwise have the vast majority of investors believe. After all, good news, even artificial news and artificial bubbles, sell stocks and make investors (and bankers) happy. The spin behind so-called "healthy" banking news is no different, which is to say, no less mis-reported and bullishly comforting. As all bankers wishing to remain employed know, the financial world spins on optimistic projections, optimistic data and optimistic delusion. Today, such market delusion (in everything from Tesla stocks to negative yielding bonds), as well as banking risk, has never been higher.

As markets distorted by desperate central bank policies reach record highs on balance-sheet challenged, debt-soaked corporate securities, the mad crowds continue to chase return, completely blind to all manner of risks, including banking risk, otherwise hiding in plain sight. In fact, and due to modern uses of leverage and equally modern weapons of mass destruction in the form of financial derivatives colliding with a central-bank-created debt tsunami the likes of which the world has never seen, banking risk has never, *not ever* been this high. And yet the vast majority of TikTok savvy and Tweet-educated investors have *zero* idea of the rocks lurking beneath the market wave of the early 2020's. Market sentiment, despite a global pandemic and historically unprecedented debt crisis, had never been higher.

As we like to say: The ironies do abound.

But rather than pen hundreds of pages of this banking history here, let's just consider one flashing, neon-red symbol of banking risk that was hiding in plain sight as investors marched into the 2020's. That is, let's toe-dip into that clever, banker-invented timebomb otherwise known as the global derivatives market.

The OTC Derivatives Trade: The Real Killer Virus

One does not need to pass a FINRA exam or spend years working the prop desks at a major commercial bank to understand the broad strokes of the otherwise extremely (and intentionally) complex, opaque and non-reported world of derivative instruments circulating like an Ebola virus throughout the modern banking system. The fancy lads call this the OTC market—or "over the counter" derivatives trade. "Over the Counter," by the way, is just a euphemistic way of saying a highly *illiquid* arms-length trade, one not executed on a public exchange, but conducted instead among over-paid bankers and other institutional counter parties on a daily basis. You know, the so-called "experts" ...

The gross value of this OTC derivatives market is nearly impossible to define, as the various contracts, swaps and options that compose this tangled web of levered obfuscation and arbitraged assets are in fact valued (marked) by the banks and counterparties themselves, not the open market—akin to letting students rather than teachers assign their own grades in school. That's clever, but it doesn't make it safe or accurate. But the banks and counterparties engaged in derivative trading understood long ago that if you're going to be guarding (i.e., valuing) your own hen house, it helps to be a clever fox, and bankers are certainly clever.

Keeping Derivatives Simple

Conservatively, however, it's fair to say that the current OTC derivatives market is in the neighborhood of $1.5 *quadrillion* in size, a number we're not even sure how to type on this page. Yet despite such an almost fantastical valuation and size, none of these many zeroes (and hence risks) are reported on the balance sheets of the fancy banks who trade them. Like we said, bankers are clever little foxes.

So, how do these foxes get away with guarding (valuing) their own hen house? How do they hide the risk and size of these trades from their own books? This too, involves a bit of complicated banker (and book-keeping) lingo which would make both your eyes (and ours) glaze over if entirely unpacked here. But as Einstein liked to say, if you can't explain even the most complex concepts to a child, you aren't a very good teacher. Hopefully, therefore, we can make the otherwise intentionally complex and hence opaque derivatives trade more understandable here.

Simple Arbitrage, Simple Leverage, Simply Crazy

Toward that end, we need to address that fancy little banking term known as "arbitrage," which basically boils down to buying and selling the same asset simultaneously and pocketing the difference—hopefully, at a profit. Recently, for example, I purchased a special horse saddle on line, and then decided to sell it to another buyer hours later for more than I originally contracted/paid. Voila: *arbitrage*. In that brief period, however, between when I bought the saddle for $X and then contracted to sell it for $X + $100, I was in what the fancy lads at places like Deutsche Bank or Goldman Sachs call an "open position"—or stated otherwise: I was between trapezes. Stated even more simply, if I didn't get delivery of the saddle when I needed it, I'd fail on its subsequent delivery to the next buyer, who would be angry to say the least, having already paid money for non-delivery of his saddle.

Such failure to perform is what those same fancy lad bankers call "counter-party risk." Fortunately, I delivered the saddle as contracted and the counter-party risk was minimal. Easy, right? It's the same for banks buying and selling futures contracts, swaps, call options, put options and all those other fancy derivative instruments they arbitrage to the tune of billions every second...but with one minor exception: Unlike the example of the simple horse saddle purchase, those fancy lad bankers use 100:1 to 300:1 leverage to buy and sell their clever little contracts. And this, we soon discover, is a very risky way to bank.

A Market Premised on Only Good Times

In normal market conditions, counterparties to these grossly levered derivatives perform as expected. Like the horse saddle example, all goes well, and trillions pass between computer screens on arbitrage desks from London to New York, Frankfurt to Tokyo. But derivative trades are a lot like water skiers being dragged behind a speeding boat: If the boat rides straight and steady, and the water has no ripples, the skiers (i.e., counterparties) glide blissfully, rapidly and safely across a sea of easy money.

But this, of course, is where the entire concept as well as reality of the derivatives trade gets scary, and frankly, just plain absurd, for its entire survival and risk-less existence assumes that speed boats never turn sharply, seas never get rough and accidents never happen. In short, the derivatives trade depends on a perpetual scenario (delusion) of smooth riding and smooth markets to avoid fatal risk among counterparties. But as anyone, and we mean *anyone*, who has traded or studied markets for more than an hour knows, nothing about financial markets is a perpetually smooth ride free of frequent ripples or an occasional tidal wave.

Despite such obvious common sense, the entire derivatives market (and its buying and selling of premiums, counterparty-spreads etc.) is premised upon the complacent fantasy that seas are always smooth and water skiers never fall.

Does this seem a bit absurd to you?

A Ticking Timebomb

Thus, despite massive amounts of leverage, massively low "OTC" liquidity (every market crisis, by the way, is at heart a *liquidity* crisis), massive counterparty risk, and massively obvious macro risks (as evidenced in everything from broken central bank policies, supply chain disruptions, and geopolitical risks to zombie credit markets marching daily toward default), the un-noticed and un-reported ($1.5 *quadrillion+*) derivative trade just keeps ticking away at a major commercial bank near you—ticking, that is, like a financial timebomb.

Timebomb?

Yes. Time. Bomb.

But if this seems sensational, once again, let's just do the math and resort to numbers not adjectives.

Take the example of Deutsche Bank, that oh-so notorious bad boy of the otherwise media-ignored derivatives sand lot. Like all major commercial banks trading in home-made derivative instruments, Deutsche Bank does not value its derivative exposure based upon the actual leverage used or the true dollar amounts at risk, but rather based upon derivative contracts whose value, as well as risk, is not "marked" (i.e., placed on the bank's balance sheet) until the contracts themselves are *safely* exercised. Using the horse saddle example above, this would be the equivalent of not mentioning (or booking and valuing) the entire transaction until *after* it is successfully completed. The book keepers at banks like Deutsche Bank call this the "net" value of their derivative trade. In the case of Deutsche Bank, whose overall balance sheet asset valuation in 2020 was around $800B, the ledger regarding its "net" derivative exposure was reported at a measly and innocuous $1B. In short, not the least bit scary at all for a mega-bank's otherwise strong, $800B balance sheet or risk profile.

But here's the rub: The "net" value of derivative exposure reported on the books by banks like Deutsche Bank deliberately and completely ignores the truer derivative exposure and valuation known among the fancy lads as the "gross" derivative value, which more accurately accounts for the actual amount of leverage, premium spreads and counterparty obligations behind their trades and currently *at risk*. Again, this more accurate "gross" valuation (and risk exposure) is not "marked" on the balance sheets of these water-skiing banks...

Turning back to the Deutsche Bank example, we discover that this bank, with a total balance sheet asset value of $800B, marks its "net" derivative value down at only $1B, yet neglects to report its "gross" derivative exposure of $40 *trillion*.

Please: Read that last line again. It's not a typo.

That right; the "gross" (yet legally *unreported*) derivative risk exposure at Deutsche Bank is $40T, despite an enterprise asset value of just $800B for the entire bank itself. The risks they are taking are infinitely greater than the bank's actual value by unheard of multiples.

That's Banking Risk

So, do you still think there's no banking risk out there? The staggering, yet entirely ignored reality is that the current banking system is literally nothing more than a balance-sheet chicken roosting on a nuclear bomb of levered derivatives exposure set to explode the moment any number of potential and "nuclear" red buttons go off in an otherwise completely distorted global market. In fact, the list of potential "red-button" moments behind this derivative mega-bomb is so long, that the odds of a derivatives implosion (i.e., the "saddles" bought with borrowed dollars not showing up when needed), and hence banking implosion, is not just high, it's closer to 100%.

For the sake of brevity, just consider the following potential red-button triggers:

-Counter-party risk, mere hints of which we've seen at Long Term Capital Management, Lehman Brothers, AIG or Bear Sterns in the past, or more recently in headline-making leverage places like Archegos Capital, whose derivative swap trade (co-authored by commercial banks) lost over $30B in shareholder money almost overnight in 2021.

-Supply Chain interruptions (as already hinted by oil futures trading negative, or actual gold deliveries failing in the COMEX market);

-Central Banks imploding under the weight of their own balance sheets and losing control of interest rates, which turn zombie bond pits into cemeteries;

-Any black swan, happening at any time—think Ukraine and beyond...

In short, if there is any counter-party error (ripple or tidal wave wherein buyers don't buy) of any genuine and collective magnitude in this over-levered minefield known as the global derivatives market, the seemingly harmless *net* derivatives exposures on the seemingly yet *deceptively* "safe" balance sheets of the major commercial banks could morph into a *gross* exposure, and hence a gross *loss*, of greater than 50X the total valuation of the banks themselves. After all, the Deutsche Bank example is hardly the only example or bank playing this dangerous game of derivative-roulette.

Needless to say, the cost of bailing out these Too Big to Fail (TBTF) banks in such a derivative implosion would dwarf the TBTF bailouts of 2008, and force central banks to create even more currency-destroying dollars out of thin air to save the banking sinners while leading to even more centralized, government control of our banking system, a dangerous trend already in motion (*See* Chapter 14). This means that when, not if, a crisis occurs in this toxic commercial banking system sitting above a home-made derivatives time bomb, do you want to hold your gold, or any asset, in such falsely esteemed, globally recognized and balance-sheet savvy commercial banks?

Chapter 11

Currency Risk

As of this writing, current public (or government) debt in the U.S. is climbing past $30T. By 2030, we believe that figure could nearly double to levels of $50 to $60 trillion. Given the condition of our broken financial system and the fragility-accelerator of COVID, informed investors must bluntly accept galloping deficits ahead and more fiat money creation to "pay" for (and inflate way) the same. Needless to say, few politicians or policy makers of any party, postal code or title have consistently and openly confronted this massive debt issue, nor confessed that tax increases alone will not solve the problem. And please don't hold your breath for enough economic growth to pull the global economy out of a debt hole infinitely deeper than anything ever seen before in the history of capital markets.

As most have come to know and accept, the only policy going forward, left, right or Martian, is more borrowing, and the only way to "pay" for that borrowing is more magical fiat money creation to allegedly absolve sovereign debt sins. Nine decades of running deficits by the left and the right in the U.S., as an obvious example and proxy for other developed economies, has consequences—social, economic and political, all themes we've addressed throughout these pages.

Similarly, creating fiat money out of thin air also has consequences for the U.S. Dollar in your pocket or levered in your local bank. The open threat to the inherent purchasing power of the U.S. Dollar is equally important to those whose currencies and banks lie *outside* of the U.S., as we discuss below. As the world's reserve currency, the U.S. Dollar, alas, impacts the world, and understanding its role is therefore critical to understanding currencies in general and gold in particular, themes we address in far greater detail in Part II.

For now, however, let's stick to currency risk in general, and the U.S. Dollar in particular.

Nearly every U.S. President, of course, boasts about the "strong U.S. Dollar," but none of these lofty office holders told those who voted for or against them that their U.S. Dollar was getting closer and closer to worthless by the second. This can be seen in something as simple as the Big Mac indicator. In 1970, for example, one could buy this edible symbol of Americana for 65 pennies; but as of 2018, that same cheap burger would cost you $5.51 American Dollars. Compared to the comical inflation measure used by the U.S. Consumer Price Index, or CPI, the cost of a hamburger can tell you a lot more about actual inflation than a government agency...

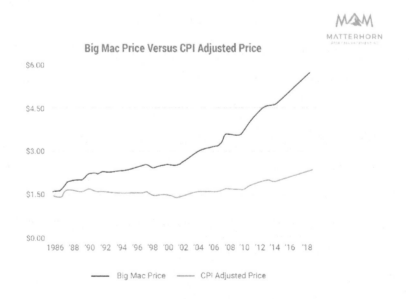

Despite the fantasy of unlimited money printing without inflation (which Big Mac consumers apparently understand better than central bankers) and openly Keynesian policy makers ignoring the risks of too much debt (which even J.M. Keynes himself warned against), no economy ever achieves lasting prosperity via unlimited money creation. If it were really that easy, the entire planet could simply retire and wait for a handout, printed at a nearby central bank. Even better, we could just outlaw taxes and make Big Macs universally free...

Golden Voices

For precious metal owners and informed investors, the only honest voice in a world of fiat currencies is a golden voice. Gold bluntly speaks to what is actually happening to the *value* and *purchasing power* of the U.S. Dollar, not its *relative* strength against other equally and grossly debased currencies like the euro or yen. And by gold, we are referring to the kind you can hold and touch, not the paper version which the future's markets leverage, or the kind that banks allegedly "store" for you in non-segregated, unallocated accounts which essentially gives you a second priority lien-interest rather than actual ownership of the gold, all of which we discuss at greater depth in Part II of this book.

The current gold price doesn't even reflect the cancerous ramifications of the foregoing debt levels and nearly $5 trillion of currency creation at the Fed in just the last 2 years. Despite such facts, many argued that gold was rising too high in price in 2020, but such arguments completely ignored the implications of price action and rising money supply. Again, the following graph shows that gold, when placed alongside the U.S. money supply, was as cheap at its 2020 highs ($2070/ounce) as it was in 1970 (when gold was $35/ounce, or in 2000, when gold was $288/ounce).

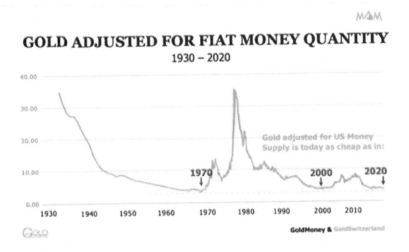

For those looking to speculate on gold price (which always sees pullbacks), a longer-play is more worthy of consideration. Savvy investors exploited price pullbacks because they understood that gold would go much higher for no other reason that the currency creation (and hence debasement) needed to pay those higher debt levels would grow much higher in the coming years. We, however, have never looked at gold as speculation, but rather as simple currency insurance. In short, gold will strengthen not because gold is getting stronger; rather, gold will strengthen because the U.S. Dollar, like every other fiat currency in a central-bank distorted world, is getting weaker. *Folks: gold is a wealth preservation tool –an insurance policy for currencies already burning to the ground.*

It's just that simple. That clear. That obvious. But as we hinted above, the fate of the all-mighty U.S. Dollar is intricately linked to the fate of *all currencies.* Sadly, however, the U.S. Dollar is now walking a very fine line between the sublime and the ridiculous, which means the same is true for all the major fiat currencies.

A Little Napoleon…

While retreating from a burning Moscow after a great military victory at Borodino, Napoleon's once unstoppable "Grande Armée" later disintegrated into the snows of a brutal Russian winter. Watching this epic disaster unfold, Napoleon quipped to his shivering aid: "Indeed, it is only a very small step from the sublime to the ridiculous." The staggering chart below shows the death rate of Napoleon's army as it retreated from Russia after otherwise "conquering" Moscow in 1812. 450,000 soldiers went in; only 10,000 came out.

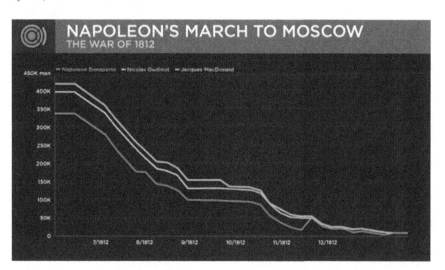

Ironically, the chart of Napoleon's dying army in 1812 looks a lot like the dying purchasing power of the U.S. Dollar since 1971.

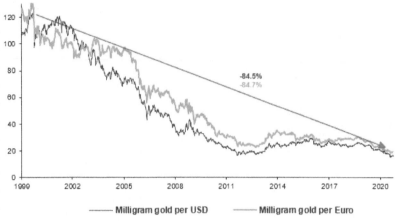

Milligramm Gold per USD & EUR, 01/1999-09/2020

-84.5%
-84.7%

Milligram gold per USD   Milligram gold per Euro

Source: Reuters Eikon, Incrementum AG

Fast-forwarding to the 2020's, as the Fed's power (and the markets over which it ruled) reached equally historic and "sublime" heights, we witnessed the first signs of its equally slow, small step toward the "ridiculous." In order to track this embarrassing trajectory and Fed experiment, we must first understand how the Fed, like Napoleon's army, was able to wield such initial and admittedly extraordinary power over the rest of the world's currencies.

The Power of the U.S. Dollar

The bulk of this power boils down to the fact that the Fed controls the supply of U.S. Dollars, which became the world reserve currency following the Second World War. This is critical, because the U.S. Dollar comprises 60% of the global currency reserves, 80% of the global banking payment system, and (since the 1970's) effectively 100% of the global oil exchange under the Petro-Dollar system. In short: That's a VERY powerful currency ("army") to have under its control. In 2008, for example, when U.S. banks tanked and the Fed created money to bail them out, we saw the immense, *Napoleonic* power of this central bank money-printer at work to save their failing commercial banks/primary dealers. But when those extremely mismanaged commercial banks got caught swimming naked with toxic mortgage debt in 2008, the problem was in fact much bigger than just rotten mortgage-backed securities on their balance sheets. Trillions in market value were also lost across entire sectors within the U.S. as well as global securities markets.

Why?

It's called the "contagion effect."

Hedge funds and other big institutional players trapped in one large and toxic asset class of bad mortgage-backed securities had to cover their margin calls and losses by selling their "good stuff" to pay for the bleeding losses in their "bad" trades, causing massive sell-offs in otherwise "blameless" assets and players. (As alluded in Chapter 9, a similar pattern is in play within the current ETF system.) When the Fed began printing trillions of U.S. Dollars in its panicked Fed experiment to save their spoiled banking nephews on Wall Street in 2008, other central banks around the world were forced to swap their currencies with the U.S. Central Banks. This is because all banks (and hence economies) must essentially bow to the Fed's powerful, i.e., "Napoleonic," U.S. Dollar just to keep international banking and currency systems precariously aligned. In short, most of the world's central banks literally had (and have) no choice but to follow the Fed's dollar and hence the Fed's bumbling yet powerful monetary lead in the current global experiment of ever-increasing centralized controls.

Alas, the U.S. Dollar and the Fed are not only "KING" – they're a veritable Napoleon. But then again, we all know what happened to Napoleon...

At some point down the road (which we are seeing with ever-increasing clarity), the Fed and even its U.S. Dollar will similarly fall from its majestic throne – that is, take that "small step from the sublime to the ridiculous" in which the dollar, especially when faced against gold, inevitably suffers its final "Waterloo moment." We're not there yet. But getting closer. Until then, it's *essential* that investors understand and respect the twisted but nevertheless *immense power* of the Fed and the dollar it commands.

The Fed's Napoleon Complex – Wanting More Until It Crashes Under Its Own Power

In 2008, when banks like Goldman Sachs, Citibank, and Morgan Stanley should have been allowed to die on the field for their fatal over-exposure to toxic mortgage bonds, the Fed resurrected them with Lazarus-like effect using a magical money printer. Of course, the name given to this money-printing "miracle" was Quantitative Easing, or "QE1." Like Napoleon at Borodino, the Fed should have stopped "sublimely" there, as it originally promised. Instead, it kept marching forward toward the "ridiculous," printing trillions more fiat dollars than anyone thought possible back in 2009. Slowly, the Fed experiment grew stronger and bolder, and was driven by Napoleonic hubris and addiction rather than sober reality.

After QE1, the Fed, like a greedy Napoleon, wanted even more printed money, and QE2, QE3 and QE4 followed with trillions more dollars printed from 2008-2014. Interest rates, as importantly, were artificially kept at or near 0% all the way to 2015. Of course, by 2020, the COVID crisis (Chapter 5) gave these desperate financial field marshals another excuse to simply run wild with even more printed currency ammunition and repressed low rates—the veritable infantry and artillery divisions of the Fed's two-pronged army.

The media, banks, and politicos called this victorious march of printed dollars through Wall Street a "recovery." But the more honest word is "experiment" – and years ahead (or sooner) it will be a *failed* Fed experiment. Again: A true "Waterloo." This is because all that experimental Fed "support" (i.e., money) went primarily into the banks and markets, not into the real economy or GDP, which has seen a textbook depression in growth, averaging at just 2.2% since 2008. In fact, the key definition of a depression is a decline in the inflation adjusted rate of GDP growth per capita. Based upon this definition, the U.S., and many major global economies, have *already* been in an economic depression for years, as GDP per capita growth rates for the last 14 years are *lower* than those seen during the Great Depression of the 1930's or the Long Depression of 1873-1896.

United States Comparing
The Three Global Economic Depressions of the past 150 Years
(REAL GDP PER CAPITA GROWTH, IN 2011 US DOLLARS)

——— The Long Depression(1873-96)   ----- The Great Depression(1929-47)   ----- The Silent Depression(2007-??)
Source: Madison Project Database (1872-2016), International Monetary Fund Estimates (2019)

Meanwhile, as the world slipped into a media-ignored yet data-confirmed depression, the **S&P** skyrocketed ("re-inflated") by 300+% while **U.S. GDP** was freezing in the snow even pre-COVID.

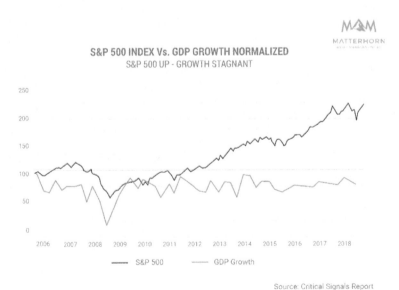

S&P 500 INDEX Vs. GDP GROWTH NORMALIZED
S&P 500 UP - GROWTH STAGNANT

——— S&P 500   ——— GDP Growth

Source: Critical Signals Report

Markets, swooning before the Fed experiment, like Napoleon, simply got addicted to their own Fed "power," namely the capacity to print U.S. Dollars and keep interest rates stapled to the floor and send risk assets rising toward Mars as economic growth tanked.

The Fed Is Fighting a Two-Front Conundrum: A Bloated Stock Market and a Dying Economy

But the Fed experiment, like Napoleon fighting a two-front war with Russia and England, found itself in a losing, two-front war between the real economy and a dangerously bloated stock market. The Fed's biggest fear today is to be in a scenario in which a panic in this inflated stock market occurs *at the same time* as an economic recession. In the past, for example, we've had business cycle recessions without market panics (like in 1989) or market panics (like that of 1987) without a business cycle recession. In 2020, with the world on its knees in a global pandemic and controversial lock-down policy, markets hit record highs despite a global recession/depression.

Go figure?

In fact, the Fed is not against declining markets – such as a market losing even 15%-20% over a period of 12 months. However, what the Fed experiment and its Wall Street field marshals can't stomach are such market declines (as occurred in *sudden and steep panics* in September of 2015, December of 2018 or March of 2020) at *the same time* as an economic recession. Again, their great fear is losing the war on both fronts. Stated otherwise, a sudden market panic in the backdrop of a GDP depressed global economy would be a true disaster—the ultimate "Waterloo."

This is because such sudden panics quickly lead to a contagion - i.e., a rapid and widening fall across all asset classes and markets. This is precisely why immediately after each and every market panic subsequent to 2008, the Fed instantly "paused" or reduced further rate hikes in order to quell contagion fears and hence re-inflate already grotesquely bloated markets on even more cheap/low-rate debt paid for with printed "liquidity." The Fed after all, serves risk assets, not Main Street. Sadly, however, the Fed experiment was running out of credibility (and dollars) heading into the 2020's—especially with regard to interest rate reserves. By 2019, it had to lower rates even further, thus depleting what little ammunition it had left with regard to normalized rates. After all, once rates get nearer to zero, there are no rates left to "cut" when the next market crisis emerges.

The Fed Can't Raise Rates to a Meaningful Level

By 2018, for example, Powell's Fed desperately wanted to *raise* rates to a level of at least 4%, as it fully understood that such a rate level was the minimum amount historically needed to later *cut* rates in order to be an effective policy tool in a future recession. It is precisely for this reason that ever since 2015, the Fed experiment had desperately tried to forward-guide or even annually raise rates by quarterly, pre-announced increments of 25 basis points. But as we all remember too well, our totally QE-doped and debt-soaked markets couldn't handle even such minimal rate hikes.

In late 2018, a pre-announced rate hike of just ¼ of 1% (i.e., 25 basis points) sent markets to their knees.

Such market reactions were open warnings that the Fed experiment was clearly starting to fail. Drowning in debt, U.S. companies in late 2018 couldn't bear even small and "forward-guided" rate hikes. Instead, as rates rose, we saw those two dramatic panics in which our markets tanked by greater than 11%-15% in less than 30 days heading into New Year's Day of 2019. As expected, the Fed experiment immediately shifted, as the Fed stepped back and "paused" further rate hikes. In fact, after the December 2018 panic, things got so bad that the Fed promised not to raise rates at all for the entire year of 2019. Needless to say, COVID conveniently created even more reasons (as well as excuses) to further *lower* rates to the basement of time going forward.

Trapped in a Conundrum of Its Own Making: Running Out of Recession-Fighting Ammo

So, there you have it folks, the ultimate Fed conundrum: In trying to prepare for the next recession by gently raising rates, the Fed ran the risk of actually triggering a market implosion. If it raises rates, the markets puke; if it doesn't raise rates, the Fed has nothing to "cut" in the next recession and hence the only weapon left in its arsenal is more inflationary money printing—which kills currencies with no regard for their flag of origin. Stated otherwise, the Fed has effectively made itself increasingly more impotent. Once rates are repressed to the zero-bound, the only weapon it has left is more money creation, and hence money debasement. In short, the Fed, like all the major central banks, has no choice going forward but to engage in pure auto-pilot monetary expansion, printing unlimited money month after month into the 2020's via QE or QE by another name—i.e., extreme liquidity via FIMA swap lines and the Standing Repo Facility.

Alas, the Fed is marching blindly like Napoleon's army from Borodino into a burning Moscow and utter disaster.

The Most Critical Market Signal Is the Fed Itself

Like it or not, the Fed is the primary force nervously guiding current markets and currencies. By extension then, the Fed and its policies are the most critical signals to track market and currency behavior/direction in this tragic, post-2008 crawl from the sublime to the ridiculous. This is openly, well, appalling, for such a "Fed experiment" has nothing at all to do with capitalism or free-market pricing, as discussed elsewhere. It's nothing but centralized economic planning, which, like Napoleon's thinning army (or Lance Armstrong's steroids), works for years until it simply and ultimately ends in disgrace.

Despite our open criticism for this Fed experiment, we are nevertheless forced to listen to Fed policy meetings as much as we look at market data. But when it comes to Fed policies, as well as U.S. Dollars impacting (and infecting) the rest of the world's currencies, one needs to look deeper into the subject of forced dollar-demand.

Forced Dollar Demand

Ever since the U.S. Dollar acquired its global reserve currency status, trillions and trillions in U.S. Dollar-denominated *debt* have been imposed upon the rest of the world in the form a global reserve currency forced into the global banking system. These dollars and debt levels are now colliding with the forces of supply and demand. Greater than $1.5 trillion, for example, is required each year *just to pay the interest* in U.S. Dollars within this massive debt storm. Such a forced debt system, all by itself, acts as a powerful source of U.S. Dollar demand and hence *relative* U.S. Dollar strength. We've already seen the sickening levels of near $30 trillion in U.S. government debt, up nearly *3X* from the Great Recession of 2008.

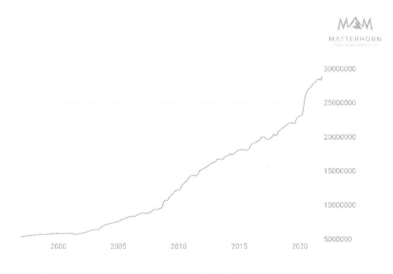

Source: TRADINGECONOMICS.COM | U.S. DEPARTMENT OF THE TREASURY

But *outside* our borders, there is another $4.2+ trillion of US dollars held by *foreign* entities and governments that owe the U.S. money in U.S. *Dollars*, not local currencies. Again: This creates massive U.S. Dollar demand.

U.S. DEBT HELD BY FOREIGN ENTITIES
TEN LARGEST FOREIGN HOLDERS OF U.S. DEBT, IN BILLIONS

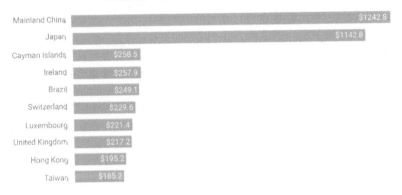

Mainland China	$1242.8
Japan	$1142.8
Cayman Islands	$258.5
Ireland	$257.9
Brazil	$249.1
Switzerland	$229.6
Luxembourg	$221.4
United Kingdom	$217.2
Hong Kong	$195.2
Taiwan	$185.2

Source: Heritage.org

In order to pay all this dollar-based debt, there's going to be an *increasing U.S. Dollar demand*, and as all high-school economics students know, the *more* the *demand*, the *higher* the *price* of any widget. In the case of U.S. Dollar demand, it is currently supported by international banking systems, and with it the *relative* strength of an otherwise grotesquely diluted U.S. Dollar is assured, at least for now. This means the price of already grossly overvalued U.S. stocks can also rise with the dollar, until of course, even that bubble pops...

This tragic debt reality is especially apparent in the emerging markets, which have been saddled with years of toxic loans from U.S. lenders which these nations can't repay in U.S. Dollars unless they dramatically crush their own local currencies via equally inflationary policies in order to buy more increasingly debased Greenbacks. This is how the U.S. essentially exports its inflationary policies to the rest of the world.

DEBT BOOM

FOREIGN-EXCHANGE RESERVES OF EMERGING-MARKET ECONOMIES
AS A PERCENT OF EXTERNAL DEBT

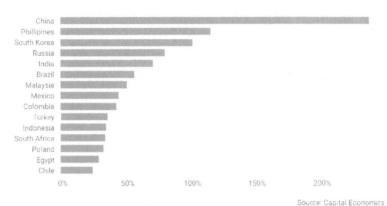

Source: Capital Economics

Take the example of Argentina. It's in debt up to its ears and debasing its currency via inflationary death traps to pay back dollar-denominated debts. In 2000, one Argentinean peso could buy one U.S. dollar. By 2020, that same peso could only buy *two* U.S. pennies.

Yep: two pennies.

But the sad fact is that the U.S. Fed has exported U.S. inflation (via sickening money-printing "solutions") to the emerging markets for years, and now those countries are increasingly broke, de-stabilized and increasingly devaluing their local currencies in order to pay back U.S. Dollar-denominated debt. The interest rates in Argentina alone were at 60% in 2020...Does that seem like a benevolent global monetary system? Orderly? Fair? Sustainable?

Given how desperate the Fed is to keep interest rates compressed, we can expect the Fed to print more money in the years ahead, and as discussed in Part II, inflate away the U.S.' own staggering debt levels with increasingly debased U.S. Dollars.

The Rest of the World Is Rotting First – and Fleeing to U.S. Markets

Argentina in particular, and Latin America in general, are by no means the only regions of the world rotting from within and desperately seeking U.S. Dollars to repay record-breaking debts. As authors who know the European Union quite well, let us bluntly say that the European Union is facing a blender of its own astronomical political, regulatory, and financial woes as well. Italy is effectively bankrupt, and Spain and Portugal are close behind. Even Germany is a small breath away from that fine line between the sublime and the ridiculous. Of course, Brexit was only further proof of the first signs of a *disintegrating* EU at worst, or a *bankrupt* EU at best.

In such a backdrop, investors and institutions in Europe saw the debt and currency writing on the wall and were thus increasingly sending their currencies into the relative "safety" of U.S. markets, which meant there was an epic conversion of euros into dollars taking place heading into the 2020's, which would only increase until conditions (and debt) worsened in Europe to such unsustainable levels that a new "Bretton Woods" takes place and all the policy-making professionals who put us into this debt trap attempt to invent a new debt solution, likely one involving Central Bank Digital Currencies as part of an expected and already well-telegraphed "global re-set." The IMF (International Monetary Fund) and BIS (Bank of International Settlements) were already telegraphing a "New Bretton Woods" by the summer of 2020. This will simply replace pathetic fiat "dollars" with equally pathetic fiat digital currencies, known, again, as

Central Bank Digital Currencies, or CBDC. In short, same music, different band.

Until then, this currency flow toward the U.S. Dollar can further push up demand for dollars and hence the price and *relative* strength of the Greenback – along with U.S. stocks. Unfortunately, however, such "dollar strength" totally ignores the larger counter-force of the dollar's increasingly *debased purchasing power* due to the extreme money printing at the Fed going into the 2020's.

In short, the "currency crisis" in *emerging* markets is already spreading to *European* markets; meanwhile the U.S. Dollar, increasingly debased with each passing second of broad money expansion, is itself getting weaker and weaker when measured by the declines in its *inherent* strength—or even the cost of a Big Mac. This of course raises the key question: Where to hide from ever-weakening global currencies? We shall tackle that question in Part II with full and blunt clarity.

Unhappy Endings

In the interim, a *relatively* "strong" U.S. Dollar may sound sexy, but in fact, it leads to a very unhappy ending. First, a strong Dollar crushes U.S. exports, as U.S. goods increasingly become *more expensive* and thus *less competitive* internationally. Secondly, as U.S. Dollar demand rises and the U.S. Dollar increases in *relative* strength only, all those other countries, from Turkey and Argentina or India to Italy, go deeper into recession by trying to repay debts with increasingly *unpayable* U.S. Dollars.

The Ironic Short-Term Boom for U.S. Markets in a World of Chaos

All this currency strife, ironically, nevertheless sent U.S. markets rising into the early 2020's for the simple reason that its already pathetically over-indebted, distorted, and dishonest markets were still considered a "safe haven" by the rest of the world. In short: U.S. markets and Dollars were still seen as *the best horse in the global glue factory.*

Some argue, however, that all this terrifying global debt – and hence dollar demand – will just end as countries, banks, and companies simply begin to default *en masse*, i.e., as they rub their hands and walk away from their debt obligations, and by extension, the U.S. Dollars needed to pay them. We accept that such an epic and deflationary debt "reset" or global default could easily happen. But if it does, once the debt disappears, *the electronic dollars behind that debt also vanish* – straight to "money heaven." If the dollars disappear alongside defaulting loans writ large, then the *supply* of dollars goes *down* – and hence the relative *value* of dollars against other currencies just continues to *rise*. Meanwhile, however, the purchasing power of even that sacred U.S. currency will have already been gutted.

See the vicious circle? There's just no way of avoiding the debt-induced disasters facing global markets and hence the increasingly dangerous *overvaluation* of the world's openly debased yet *relatively* stronger reserve currency: The U.S. Dollar.

In such a grossly distorted setting, what can investors do to protect themselves from the consequences to come?

Part II

The Golden Solution to Distorted Financial Markets

Chapter 12

Why Gold, Why Now?

In Part I, we addressed the myriad cracks (market risk, currency risk, banking risk) in the ever-thinning ice of a global financial system distorted by decades of extreme debt expansion supported by desperate central bank policies which directly impacted securities markets, money supply, and even social division. The consequences of such unprecedented intervention by the world's major central banks are no mystery. Inflation, which is defined by an increase in the broad money supply, became an inevitable outcome, one which terrifies traditional policy makers while simultaneously setting up the perfect backdrop for rising gold prices. Speculators, of course, can track and trade such price moves, but as we discuss throughout Part II, the daily *price* of gold measured by dying currencies is far less important than the *role* of gold as purchasing power insurance against such increasingly debased currencies. As each of the major world currencies compete in a race to the bottom, gold, as a genuine rather than digital or paper store of value, will serve as a primary and highly viable insurance policy against the declining purchasing power (as opposed to relative strength) of these increasingly discredited global currencies.

In short, gold matters.

Candidly, with the nearly endless stream of gold bugs spinning "MUST BUY GOLD NOW" messages for years, we recognize that many investors misunderstand and even distrust this precious metal. The pawn shops of the world, often located in the less desirable parts of town, have created an image of gold as some kind of scammer's asset bought and sold by questionable retailers within unscrupulous settings and unfair premiums. To some extent this is true of the highly unregulated and often shady practices of the consumer gold coin market. But physical gold as an historically significant commodity circulating within and among the global markets or in select private vaults, is of the highest importance. In short, gold is a critical, scarce and serious asset, watched carefully by the global policy makers whose failed fiscal and monetary experiments are nearing their end. Gold, alas, holds massive amounts of power and influence over these markets and decision makers, and for that reason is no stranger to equally massive amounts of intentional price manipulations by the bullion and central banks, the broader details of which will be described in the pages to follow. Despite such open yet often unspoken manipulations, gold's future as well as historical role is unstoppable, for the simple reason that its natural value, like a submerged cork, always rises to the surface whenever the obvious failure of unnatural market policies, extreme debt levels, rising inflation and increasingly debased currencies becomes self-evident to all.

Thus, as macro conditions (from global political tensions to central bank desperations) continue to deteriorate into the 2020's, now is a critical time to directly and thoroughly address the role of gold in every sound investment portfolio and risk management strategy.

Getting Emotional

Perhaps more than anything, gold is an emotional issue. Some swear gold is the only asset worth owning while others maintain that this metal is a "barbaric relic" of an ancient system, no longer relevant to the modern world of complex monetary engineering by which recessions have been increasingly promoted as extinct creatures by central bankers with their hands on the switch of global money printers. Even the great Oracle of

Omaha, Warren Buffett, doesn't see any value in gold, and no reason to buy it. For him, gold (unlike silver of which he owned over $1 billion) has no technical or other identifiable inherent value or use. As he famously said: "It doesn't do anything but sit there and look at you." Well, despite all due respect owed to Mr. Buffett, we take a different view.

Thinking Swiss

Based out of Europe, we sit in the capital of Switzerland, a country where 70% of the world's gold bars are refined and wherein some of the most sophisticated and patient minds in the precious metals space are gathered, most of whom are officed in Zurich. The Swiss are part of a continent that has seen (as well as avoided) generations of economic cycles, horrific wars, and market moves that pre-date the birth of the U.S. (and Warren Buffett) by centuries. In sum, the Swiss are not "gold bugs," they are prudent and patient realists who speak from a history, math, and a country code which provides the rest of the world with an intelligent perspective on (and comfort with) the essential importance of owning physical gold.

In terms of purely technical jargon and data, gold broke through $1,500 in the summer of 2019, which was $150 above the long $1,350 resistance line that had been in play for the previous five years, what Egon famously described then as gold's "Maginot line." Furthermore, even on the inevitable pullbacks which we foresaw, including the dramatic moves seen in 2018 (when gold opened the year at $1,400, sank to $1,180 in August, and then closed the year at $1,300), gold had been increasingly making higher "new lows" since bottoming in 2015. In short, a rising trend pattern had been set for gold, and we argued then (as well as now) that gold was entering the first stages of a gold bull market, despite, again, the inevitable kind of price swings we foresaw as recently as 2021.

The Not-So-Technical: TRUST

Technical trend lines and vacillating price points are one thing, yet market instincts and historical facts are another. Ultimately, and as we'll unpack in detail below, gold is about trust, and makes its greatest moves higher when trust in everything else – from markets, central bankers, media bubbleheads, big bankers, and politicians – make their greatest moves lower. Toward this end, we can all agree that "the times they are a chang'n," as evidenced throughout the chapters of Part I. Trust in monetary policies, economic stewardship, Wall Street trading practices, desperate pension funds, media reporting, social and economic sustainability and even vaccine science itself had already fallen to record lows by the early 2021. As the previous chapters have made mathematically clear, investors have been conned for years by what is little more than a debt-driven "recovery" emboldened by half-truths from policy makers and bankers on everything from employment and inflation data to GDP, earnings and net derivative "safety."

This trend of distrust and distortion is global rather than just regional, from New York to Beijing, Tokyo to Sydney. Italy, for example, has seen periods of open rebellion, Brexit served as a glaring vote of no confidence for the Eurozone and its central bank, and the yellow vested protestors cropping up in 2018 France were just the opening symptoms as social unrest, coupled with a lack of confidence in markets and politicians, made its penultimate political and social expression in the Bastille-like storming of the U.S. Capital in early 2021. In many other corners of the world (from Poland to Hungary or Spain to Belgium), political, populist, and economic tensions have been palpably rising as European markets, overwhelmed by immigrant waves, declining GDP, autocratic vaccine policies and growing debt levels neared their inevitable breaking points. Even Germany, the European Union's economic centerpiece and export-dependent heartbeat, was already approaching a recession pre-COVID, a decline only made worse by an unresolved trade war between the U.S. and China.

In the U.S., again *pre-Covid*, markets were already gyrating around record (yet increasingly volatile) highs as retail investors continued to drink the Fed Kool-Aid that all was fine and would forever be fine – as if the seemingly immortal (i.e., liquidity-supported) stock market was the real economy, which it is not. For years, the post-08 market highs had been purchased on pure debt, not productivity, as cancerous U.S. debt levels raced toward levels twice that of the Eurozone and Japan.

Public debt: euro area, USA, Japan, in USD bn, 2002-2023

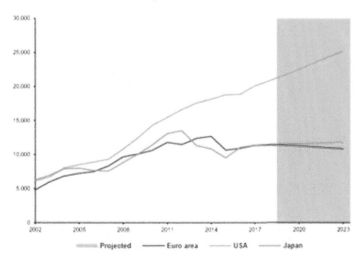

Source: IMF, OECD, Incrementum AG

This debt, of course, bought a small percentage of the population with access to inflated securities markets great wealth, using U.S. markets as proxy for all developed economies. However, graphs like those below on record-breaking wealth disparity were all the confirmation one needed to confess that the alleged "great recovery" since 2008 was little more than a veiled yet historic wealth transfer benefiting only a small percentage of that once robust nation. Such wealth disparity, meanwhile, was pushing the rest of America toward the bottom – and hence extreme left and right tensions and rising populism. In sum, trust was eroding and emotions were rising. As for who has the bucks and who has the debt in the U.S.A., the data is now undeniable:

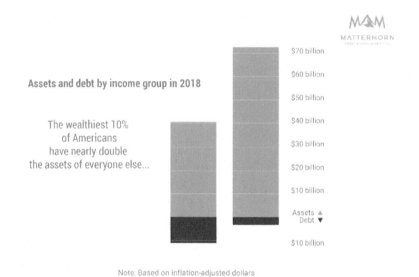

Note: Based on inflation-adjusted dollars

Source: Wall Street Journal analysis of the Federal Reserve distributional financial accounts

Who's winning, who's losing? The above data makes it obvious.

Such social and political trust was crumbling all around us while markets were approaching their last hurrahs and record-breaking highs before the long yet inevitable march south.

Gold and Recessions

Those who have done even the most rudimentary gold research know already that gold traditionally acts as a hedge against falling stocks and as a countermeasure to aggressive, yet failing monetary policies (i.e., debt-crazy, money-printing central banks). As for the Fed, there's no debate any more that they have been in full-on desperation mode for years, artificially cranking rates to the floor and giving up any pretense to genuine balance sheet tightening as they prepare for the inevitable (yet increasingly less effective) money printing "solution" whenever and however markets take yet another nosedive, like the kind we saw in March of 2020. Such policy reactions were (and remain) as easy to foresee as a cavity to a dentist. But the policy moves (i.e., money expansion) we saw in Q4 of 2018 or Q2 of 2020 were just tremors, not the big quake. As early as 2017, we warned our clients that markets would tank massively in October of 2018 and into the Christmas holidays.

Were we psychic? Not at all. It was easier than that. The Fed literally told the world in October of 2017 that they'd be dumping big chunks of their bond holdings starting in October of 2018 as part of a monetary "taper." This meant higher bond supplies into the market, lower bond prices, and hence higher yields, which meant higher rates.

As we warned then, higher yields/rates would immediately create an "uh-oh" market sell-off in a debt-driven market bubble, which is precisely what occurred. We all remember the market bloodbath of Q4 2018 in the U.S. By early 2019, the Fed immediately back-peddled on its rate-hiking (i.e., "tapering") policies of late 2018. Of course, with COVID at their backs in 2020, the rate suppression continued into the 2020's and a policy of "unlimited money printing" to the tune of $120B per month came back into full swing into 2021. Even the much-headlined "taper" of Q4 2021 and into 2022 was a bogus taper, as QE reductions were simply offset by more hidden yet currency-killing liquidity from the repo facility and FIMA swaps. In short, central banks post-COVID went into full "emergency mode," which the Fed falsely calls "accommodation" to keep retail suckers fully invested in a dangerously topping, yet once again Fed-supported, market careening toward an over-valued collapse by every honest indicator in conventional (and non-conventional) analysis. As such critical market signals (from PE ratios to negative sovereign bond yields) pointed toward increasingly unacceptable risk in the securities markets, faith in policy "experts" waned as concerns over an obvious day of reckoning went from the theoretical to the inevitable.

Such inevitable falls meant more countries, institutional players, and individual investors were turning toward gold as a protective asset in times of global economic pain.

ETF gold holdings, in tonnes, and gold price, in USD, 01/2003-04/2019

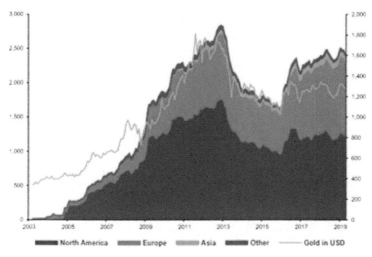

Source: World Gold Council, Bloomberg, Incrementum AG

For years we have been tracking massive waves of gold buying at every dip in its price. Flows into gold ETFs and gold mining stocks skyrocketed in Q4 of 2018, and dramatically outperformed falling stocks in every major market as stocks tanked:

Gold in local currency, and domestic stock index, annual performance in %, 2018

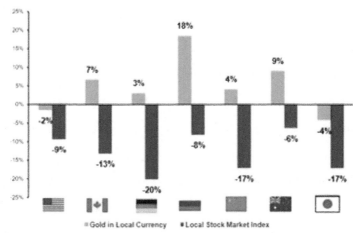

Source: Bloomberg, Incrementum AG

Quite simply, gold loves a bear market – it always has and always will. Investors buy gold when that bear begins to growl and investor fear-levels rise with great *emotional* speed:

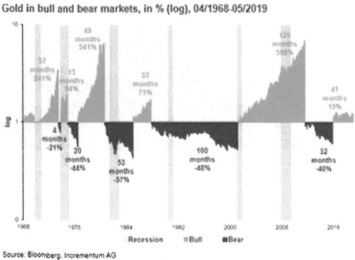

Gold in bull and bear markets, in % (log), 04/1968-05/2019

Source: Bloomberg, Incrementum AG

Countries Losing Trust

It's not just that more investors were and are catching on to the deteriorating economic signals all around them. Countries and central banks, the very skunks who rigged the financial woodpile into a powerfully dangerous complacency, were themselves running for the safety of gold and gold-backed securities, frantically adding to their gold positions. In 2018, for example, they bought over 650 tons of this precious metal. In 2019, that number exceeded 750 tons. By early 2022, as markets began to tremor again on talks of "tapering" liquidity, inflows into gold ETF's surged and central bank gold purchases reached an all-time high.

Gold's Naysayers

Despite all these otherwise objective indicators of trouble ahead, there remain headwinds as well as common counterarguments to gold. Let's consider the most popular and traditional of the anti-gold arguments.

The Rising Dollar is Bad for Gold?

Consensus thinking has always maintained that as the USD goes up, gold prices go down. In prior markets (before central banks distorted the entire playing field, including currencies, in 2008), this thesis was confirmed by both history and math: A strong dollar meant weaker gold pricing. But in the backdrop of the tremendous post-08 distortions in the money supply and international currency systems discussed in Part I, the global patterns have changed, and a rising U.S. Dollar didn't keep gold from rising as well.

Why?

Part of this rise can be attributed to the fact that demand for gold from Emerging Markets (EM) countries had skyrocketed. Countries like China, India, Russia, Turkey, Poland, and Vietnam were playing the long game and didn't give much concern or attention to gold's daily price fluctuations. They had increasingly become major buyers of gold. In many ways, this is because the EM zip codes had no choice. With over $11 trillion in USD-denominated debt owed around the world by 2019, EM countries had been forced to devalue their currencies to pay back this USD-based debt, which meant on a *relative* basis, the U.S. Dollar was in higher demand and hence growing stronger despite the fact that its inherent purchasing power was falling by the second due to extreme money creation (Chapter 11). As a result, EM countries caught in this dollar-debt-trap and local currency devaluation strategy had to increasingly buy gold as "insurance" against their own weakening currencies. In 2000, for example, 19% of world GDP came from EM countries. Today, that percentage has climbed to greater than 50%. With such countries showing high affinities for gold as a local currency hedge, the rising demand for gold will, in turn, push its price higher over time. Such global scenarios explain gold's rise, rather than fall, even as the U.S. Dollar grew stronger.

It's also worth noting that the U.S. Dollar's relative rise is under longer-term threat, as more countries (including the big players in Europe) increasingly seek ways to de-dollarize by getting away from the stranglehold of dollar-denominated banking regulations and SWIFT transfer systems. The 2022 war in the Ukraine only accelerated this trend. Over the coming years, the U.S. Dollar is poised to lose its coveted dominance as a global reserve currency, hitherto weaponized in the oil and banking industries to control foreign policy. This shift, however, will take years, not days or weeks.

Bonds Are a Safer Hedge in A Recession?

Traditional risk-parity portfolio thinking had always advised that bonds are a safe haven for falling stocks in a recession. But given the staggering distortion in overbought credit markets due to the extreme monetary policies discussed in Part I, traditional portfolio thinking is not only outdated, but extremely dangerous. More investors are seeing greater safety in "zero-yielding" gold rather than *negative*-yielding bonds. This is because the post-08 bond market has completely lost its way into over-valuation thanks to central banks artificially propping (i.e., purchasing) otherwise unloved sovereign bonds with trillions in printed money while global interest rates fell to the basement of a 5,000-year history.

Bond markets are so incredibly inflated and distorted by central banks pumping up prices to such unnatural levels that by late 2021, over $19 trillion in global bonds were trading at *negative-yielding* levels for the first time in world history. (Remember: Bond prices and bond yields move *inversely.*) As bond *prices* skyrocketed, bond *yields* plummeted. These negative-yielding bonds served as open proof of a camouflaged sovereign bond default playing out, for by pure definition, a negative yielding bond is effectively a *defaulting* bond. When such bond bubbles pop under their own weight – gold prices soar as more investors pour into this far safer safe-haven.

In the United States, over 60% of U.S. corporate bonds are designated as junk, high-yield, or levered loans – in other words, they're crap. As credit conditions worsen, many of those credit instruments will default. And when adjusted for inflation, *half of the world's bonds are now yielding negative returns* – meaning you are *guaranteed* to lose money the moment you acquire them.

Crazy? Absolutely.

Thus, if you think bonds are a safe hedge in a recession, think again. In the nearer-term, however, U.S. Treasuries heading into the 2020's continued to rise in price as real rates and yields fell to zero (or below) in a desperate attempt by central banks to postpone the inevitable rising rate disaster in the global securities markets.

Low Inflation Means Low Gold Prices?

Another common/consensus view in the gold space is that low inflation, dis-inflation or even deflation means low gold prices. Once again, however, the paradigm has shifted since the central banks took over global markets in 2008. Everything is now topsy-turvy.

So how could gold rise in a low inflation world? First, inflation, as reported by the U.S. CPI is a blatant and now confirmed lie. As discussed in greater detail in Chapter 15 below, actual inflation as mis-measured by the Consumer Price Index, or CPI, heading into the 2020's was closer to 10+%, not the falsely reported 2%, which skyrocketed to 6% in 2021 even under the bogus CPI measurement. But even if you chose to believe the fictional inflation numbers at the Bureau of Labor Statistics in D.C., their so-called "low inflation data" did not prevent gold from hitting $1,500 in 2019 or $2070 in 2020, despite low inflation in those years.

Why?

Because the smart money understood that the big players (institutions, central banks, funds, family offices, informed investors and wealthy families) were going to buy gold despite the "low inflation data."

Furthermore, long-term investors understood that the growing popularity of fantasy solutions like the unlimited money printing of Modern Monetary Theory (MMT), heralded by the left, would result in even more ghastly money printing to "solve" a sovereign debt problem.

Unfortunately, this debt "problem" isn't a problem, it's a fatal illness, and more money printing to cover that debt would inevitably debase global currencies, for which gold emerged as a wise countermeasure and real store of monetary value regardless of the so-called "low inflation" backdrop.

Realism

The foregoing signals all converge on what we consider to be *the* single most important long-term asset to protect investors from a market implosion and economic depression while also favoring significant returns over the next decade, with gold passing well beyond the $4,000 level in the coming years.

Does this mean gold will only go up? Of course not. In fact, we anticipate pull-backs in gold when commodities lag stocks in "opportunity costs" during QE-driven melt-ups, or whenever yields on sovereign bonds are temporarily higher than dishonest (i.e., downplayed) inflation rates, a relationship we explain with plain-speak in Chapter 13. As discussed above, gold can experience violent moves as markets change, and we are not recommending gold as a *speculative* trade, but as a long-term play/investment – that is: Life insurance for *already* (and openly) dying currencies.

The Real Reason to Buy Gold

Notwithstanding all that has been revealed above as to recessions, trust, the Fed, inflation, bond decay, etc., perhaps the most important and obvious reason for considering physical gold boils down to these simple but compelling images, which plainly reveal that every dollar (euro, pound, yen, etc.) you own is losing purchasing power by the year, month, day, and second.

Purchasing power of main currencies valued in gold (log), 01/1971-09/2020

Source: Reuters Eikon, Nick Laird, goldchartsrus.com, Incrementum AG

Gold is not merely recession insurance or a portfolio and volatility hedge against declining stocks and bonds in a rigged market distorted by years of central bank over-intervention. Nor is gold merely a tactical countermeasure to fluctuating inflation and interest rate moves. Far more importantly, gold is simply the ultimate and historically-confirmed antidote for nations, banks, and currencies who have lost their way in the backdrop of inconceivably high debt traps that have sent sovereign currencies (and trust in them) to the floor of history.

Regardless of your level of wealth, we know you've worked a lifetime to amass it while your central bank and economists (including the delusional dreamers behind MMT or the current Fed mouthpieces at the Eccles Building) have been crushing the purchasing punch of every dollar, euro, peso, lira, yen etc. you've earned, saved, and invested. In the case of the United States, its former Fed Chairman, Ben Bernanke promised as far back as 2009 that the emergency money printing he helped unleash then would be at "no cost" to the larger economy or to individual wellbeing. He also promised that such emergency measures would fade out by 2010. Well over a decade later, we now see how openly wrong (dishonest?) this so-called "expert" prognosis was. Does the following graph of the U.S. Dollar's decline in purchasing power truly appear as if there was "no cost" to extreme money printing?

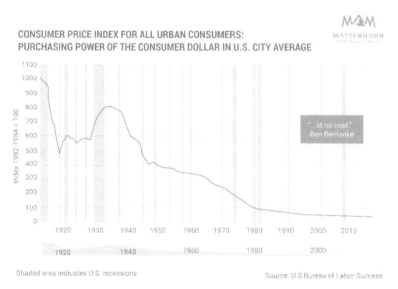

Yet look how gold's purchasing power relative to the U.S. dollar has performed for the same period...

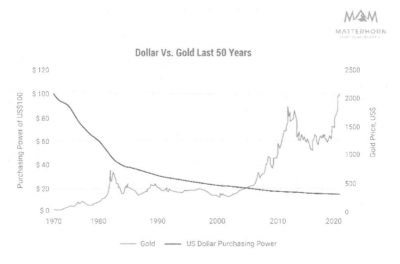

Dollar Vs. Gold Last 50 Years

Source: Bureau of Labor Statistics, KE benchmark Administration (IBA)

Bitcoin?

Many who understand the weakened purchasing power (as opposed to relative strength) of our openly broken currency system might choose the Bitcoin or crypto path as another alternative currency option.

We get this. As a speculative trade, cryptocurrencies can offer incredible upside (and volatile downsides) which gold simply can't beat in terms of speed or range. But cryptos like Bitcoin are far too volatile to serve as a protective asset and thus, to our mind, will be a speculative rather than preservation asset for decades to come--assuming they are not otherwise impacted in the interim by severe legislative restrictions, which we'll discuss elsewhere. "Digital gold," by its very name, is a deceptive oxymoron and represents no intrinsic value; as such, these "digital coins" are effectively just another, albeit popular and profitable, fiat currency, despite their fixed supply. Crypto's have been "trusted" for 13 years or less, whereas gold's track record for saving farsighted investors from dying currency regimes goes back millennia to the very origins of market exchanges, from the first merchants of Persia, the dynasties of ancient China and the Empire of Rome to the once steady economic leadership of the once powerful United States – that is, before Nixon left the gold standard in 1971.

In the chapters to follow, we will look deeper into the forces which will not only send the price of gold higher as a speculative trade, but far, far more importantly, make gold the ultimate long-term investment as much needed insurance in a world of increased money supply, increased inflation and hence increased currency destruction. In addition to these obvious tailwinds for gold, we will also address the equally important headwinds facing gold in the near-term, including the arguments from those in the deflationary camp, those touting the rising popularity of crypto currencies as the "new gold," and the ever-powerful yet increasingly discredited attempts by commercial and central banks to distort honest gold pricing in the futures market.

Chapter 13

Gold's Tailwinds: Rising Money Supply &
Inflation Outpacing Bond Yields

We've often joked that fretting over daily price moves in individual stock names in a grossly distorted market bubble is akin to fretting over the tempting desert choices on the Titanic's final dinner menu.

In short, the critical issue is not chocolate vs. vanilla eclairs, Amazon vs. Tesla or even Bitcoin vs. gold; instead, the critical issue of obvious concern is the massive debt-iceberg off our bow. Today, the big questions, and the big variables (as well as icebergs) impacting one's wealth preservation, all hinge upon the "macros"—you know, boring things like historically unprecedented (as well as unpayable) debt levels, openly absurd risk-asset bubbles and the artificial measures central bankers and politicos will and must employ to postpone the inevitable sinking of the global financial ship.

What to Watch

Toward this end, central banks and fiscal deficits are the big forces/variables to watch, as are rising or falling bond yields and inflation rates. Whatever one's view, for example, of the COVID pandemic and the questionable relief policies which followed, there were 10 million less folks employed in the U.S. in 2021 than in 2020, despite massive fiscal support from the government, and even more massive money printing from the central bank. This also means we can expect even more aid, and hence more debt ahead, as the deficit levels incurred in recent years can *never* be repaid without issuing even more debt and printing even more fiat currencies to pay interest on the same.

Of course, such a "solution" is both delusional and unsustainable. Debt cancers cannot be cured by more debt. More money supply creation to service more debt also means more money supply inflation ahead, as inflation is literally defined and measured by an increase in the money supply. It's thus rational to anticipate a base case of increased government deficit spending ahead and hence a Fed continuing to create dollars to purchase the bonds issued to pay for that spending, recently at a rate as high as $120B per month, which means we can expect *at least* another $2-4T in deficits per year.

Why Deficits Matter

Deficits, of course, matter. They are like credit ice cubes which turn into debt icebergs. We can thus predict, quite confidently, that the money expansion needed to purchase those otherwise unloved sovereign bonds (governmental IOU's) will continue in the near term at staggering levels.

Why?

The answer is as simple as it is tragic: If the Fed didn't buy those Treasuries, no one else would. In such a scenario, their yields would rise, which means interest rates (i.e., the cost of debt) would rise too.

But here's the rub: Our cornered Fed and Treasury Department (like their peers around the world) can't afford rising rates. Not even one tiny bit of them. Thus, to keep rates and yields artificially low, desperate measures to cap and control bond yields are inevitable rather than debatable. The Fed, like every other major central bank in the world, literally has NO CHOICE but to continue its pattern (think Q4 of 2018 & 2019 or Q2 of 2020) of rushing to the rescue and creating new liquidity whenever markets tank in order to purchase otherwise unwanted bonds and thus artificially repress yields and interest rates. Alas: More "Uh-Oh" moments are inevitable, as is more broad money expansion and artificial rate suppression--at least until even that rigged game implodes and a *disorderly* reset, marked by more fiat money and more debt (i.e., massive fiscal policy, deficit spending etc.), becomes unavoidable.

Revisiting Inflation

So, what can we rationally expect going forward? What key indicator, as well as key asset, are the logical choices? History, as usual, gives us some credible maps to follow. As always, this involves a deeper dive into seemingly "boring" topics like inflation, Treasury yields and desperate bankers. Toward that end, we need to revisit key macro themes, which include, you guessed it: Inflation forces. Fortunately, the 20th century gives us two inflationary case studies—the 1940's and 1970's—to make the future clearer, with no need for tarot cards.

1940's Inflation

The 1940's, very much like today, saw inflation in the backdrop of massive fiscal deficits (coming out of the Second World War). In the 1940's, as today, government debt to GDP had climbed above the critical 100% marker. Of course, that's a lot of debt, too much debt for any realistic chance at economic growth. And if the cost of that debt measured by interest rates (or Treasury yields) ever climbed too high, Uncle Sam would have become instantly insolvent, as the interest on its staggering debt balance would be unpayable. In order to cover those staggering debt obligations, the Fed in the late 1940's, just like today, opted to buy lots and lots of U.S. Treasuries to keep their prices high and hence their yields and rates artificially low. That is, the rich Uncle Fed of the 1940's deliberately kept yields (and hence interest rates) no higher than 2.5% across the entire duration of the yield curve, from short-term to long-term Treasuries. This was a classic case (as well as mix) of massive debt, high inflation and low rates compliments of what the fancy lads call "Yield Curve Control," which is just a polite way of saying central bankers will print gobs of dollars to buy government bonds in order to keep their yields and interest rates artificially stapled to the basement of history.

1970's Inflation

The 1970's period of inflation, however, offered an entirely different inflationary flavor and "solution." Unlike the 1940's, the nation's debt to GDP ratio (at the government, corporate and household level) in the 1970's was much smaller. Thus, when inflation reared its ugly and predictable (and post-Nixon) head, Paul Volcker's Fed was able (unlike today) to allow yields and rates to skyrocket at double-digit levels in order to stem the inflation that followed the decoupling of gold from the US Dollar in 1971.

2020's Inflation

Needless to say, we are entering into a debt setting and hence inflationary period far more like the 1940's than the 1970's. In short, *we will never see an intentional Fed rate hike akin to Volcker anytime soon.* Why? Because today, as in the 1940's, debt levels are factually too high to withstand rising interest rates. Today, if real (i.e., inflation-adjusted)

Treasury yields and/or interest rates were allowed to naturally rise to even 4% or 5%, the debt cost to Uncle Sam would be fatal. The U.S. and her markets of Titanic debt would hit a rising-rate iceberg. Party over.

That's why more Yield Curve Control (i.e., artificially repressed rates and yields) and *deliberate* inflation was as inevitable to foresee as a fibbing politician, despite the fact that very few heeded our warnings of inflation, even in 2021, as inflation began to surge. But as for inflation in the 2020's, it didn't just happen overnight, especially since the U.S. government, as discussed more in Chapter 15, made every effort to misreport the actual levels of US inflation. In 2020, when CPI-reported inflation was below 2%, we wrote countless articles warning of coming inflation. Again: Very few believed us. By the end of 2021, the year-over-year inflation rate had climbed above 6%, which the Fed tried to downplay (i.e., lie) as "transitory," despite our incessant warnings that it was anything but that.

Thus, many were rightly asking us, as recently as early 2021, why we'd compare the 2020's to the inflationary 1940's? After all: Where was the inflation?

Well, inflation, as we warned for years, came—and more is coming. Here's why.

Inflation & the Velocity of Money?

Many deflationary proponents say there can't be inflation without an increase in the velocity (i.e., circulation) of money within the real, "Main Street," economy. But inflation, of course, is more nuanced than just rising money velocity. History, in fact, confirms that inflation doesn't require the velocity of money to *increase*; rather, inflation can occur so long as velocity simply keeps from falling. During the *inflationary* period of the 1970's, for example, the velocity of money was significantly lower than the *non-inflationary* decade of the 1950's. That said, increasing fiscal stimulus, direct security purchases by central banks, and the growing trend of government hand-out checks will and did greatly spur money velocity (circulation) and M1 and M2 money supply, despite the grotesque efforts by central banks to curb the reporting of that skyrocketing US money supply (see below). Thus, despite the importance of money *velocity*, the safest and surest measure of inflation has always been its correlation to *an increase in the broad money supply,* discussed at greater length below. Simply stated: When broad money supply increases, that, by definition, *is* inflation.

Inflation & Rising Commodity Prices

Inflation has other measurements and indicators, most notably as measured by consumer prices for goods, which typically rise when commodity prices rise. In order for our current era to see rising consumer price inflation (i.e., *CPI* inflation), we'd have to see two forces in motion, namely 1) non-falling money velocity alongside broad money supply increases and 2) a scarcity (and hence price increase) in commodities. And guess what? These forces were already converging as early as late 2020. Notwithstanding the over-supplied energy sector (which eventually and politically rose anyway in price), the early 2020's witnessed this commodity scarcity (and hence price rise) in the broader commodities market—from copper and lumber to beef and corn. This cyclical shift toward a super cycle in commodity price inflation was a neon-flashing sign of consumer price inflation felt in the wallet and measured by the **CPI** scale, however broken that entirely fictitious indicator may otherwise be.

Prior to the commodity boom, the broader money supply of printed dollars went straight into grossly *inflated* stocks, bonds and real estate, each of which were already in classic bubble territory by 2020. But as we moved forward into 2021, such commodity scarcity (and hence commodity driven inflation in the CPI) became more apparent, and will increase in the coming years to such obvious levels that even the openly fraudulent **CPI** inflation scale will have no choice but to move noticeably upwards, as it already began to do in late 2021—precisely as we warned it would. In the meantime, the evidence of a commodity super cycle, so critical to rising **CPI** inflation levels was fairly hard to ignore by as early late 2020.

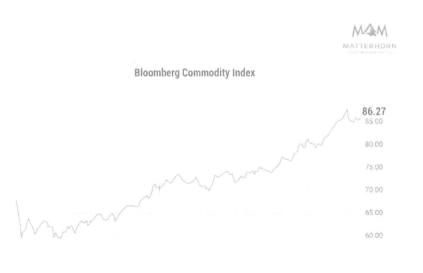

Bloomberg Commodity Index

Source: Bloomberg Markets

Inflation and Precious Metal Direction

Of course, the common response of most precious metal owners is that such inflation signals are always a tailwind for gold. This is largely true, but the inflation-to-gold correlation, like all things, is not always that direct or that simple. Many inflationary forces are at play now, yet need to be understood at the most basic levels. Gold, for example, had been rising throughout 2019 and 2020 in openly *deflationary* conditions, so the gold discussion is not simply one of inflation alone, but inflation when measured against yields/rates. This is a very critical relationship to understand, so we'll keep this simple and blunt.

One of the most important and accurate forecasters of gold price (and not ordinarily making the headlines or reading lists of retail investors), boils down to this: *Gold rises when inflation rates significantly outpace interest rates as measured by the yield on the 10-Year US Treasury.* The fancy lads call this "the inverse relationship between negative real yields and gold pricing." This may sound complex, or even boring, but a key variable for gold forecasting is *negative real yields* —that is, the 10-Year Treasury yield *minus* the official CPI inflation rate. Again, and more simply stated: Gold's price rises as *real* (i.e., inflation-adjusted) yields fall deeper and faster into *negative* territory; or to repeat: When inflation rates significantly out pace interest rates, gold shines.

In the 1970's, for example, we saw this interplay of sinking negative real yields and rising gold prices; the compelling gold surges during that decade occurred when negative real yields sank to as low as -4%. More recently, from mid-2018 to mid-2020, gold was once again rising dramatically because real yields were collapsing from +1% to -1%. In short: Inflation rates were outpacing bond yields. This rapid rate of change toward negative real yields (red line) was a clear tailwind for gold (yellow line).

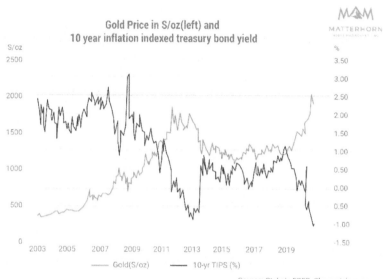

Gold Price in S/oz(left) and
10 year inflation indexed treasury bond yield

Source: St. Luis FRED, Cherrypickers.org

By late 2020, however, the nominal yields on the 10Y Treasury began to rise faster than the official (and then still anemic and dishonest) CPI inflation rate. As a result, the real yields (that is: inflation-adjusted yields) weren't as dramatically *negative* as in the prior year. Not surprisingly, gold's dramatic price rise came to a temporary and expected halt by early 2021 as inflation no longer outpaced bond yields at a significant level. Such lackluster price action in gold was no surprise, because yields were rising as *reported* inflation stayed artificially dormant/repressed in the early days of 2021. Consequently, gold prices were forced to bide their time, yawning in the short term, but stretching their legs for a sprint upward as soon as inflation made its inevitable move upwards. By the close of 2021, for example, inflation was once again outpacing yields and hence *real* yields were once again falling past -1% as gold consolidated to continue its inevitable trend north, which began again in 2022.

We knew then, as well as now, that real yields would again break below -1% as rising inflation began to outpace artificially repressed yields, and thus gold and silver would revisit their price climb to much, much higher valuations in the coming 5+ years. How could we be so confident that negative real yields would sink further and gold would rise higher? That is, how we could we know that inflation would outpace interest rates?

History and math told us so.

Back to the Future—or At Least the 1940's

Lessons of the past, as well as embarrassingly fat debt levels and openly desperate central bankers, are key indicators. In other words, we knew rates (and bond yields) would stay repressed/capped as inflation crawled upwards. Again, debt-soaked nations and markets are driven by policy makers and pro-market central bankers who are terrified of rising rates. Like most informed investors, we could also be fairly certain of this fact: *U.S. Government debt to GDP would increase rather than decrease over the coming years.* For this reason, rates had to stay "controlled-low" to service this expanding debt. And toward this end, the inflationary case study of the 1940's was a helpful guide. As commodity-driven CPI inflation increased, alongside the obvious and text-book money supply definition of inflation, the central banks, politicos and nervous markets started to get scared. Real scared–just like in the 1940's. In other words, policy makers would become increasingly allergic to rising bond yields and hence interest rates.

Again, this is because rising rates would make their debt *impossible* to repay and would force their debt bubbles to come to an abrupt end. Given the open fact that the post-08 markets as well as government "recoveries" have been nothing but a debt party, any hint of rising rates was a career-ending omen to the central bankers of a "party-over" scenario. We thus knew that *central banks would have NO CHOICE but to artificially control/repress bond yields and rates* at the same time that CPI inflation pushed inexorably northward for all the reasons discussed here and in subsequent chapters. Quite simply, the bankers didn't want to end the debt party and experience the hangover to come.

Furthermore, and despite public promises to "combat" inflation, policy makers secretly and *deliberately* promoted more inflation to do what all broke regimes have always done: Inflate away their debt with increasingly debased money. This meant inflation rates would eventually rise higher than artificially repressed/controlled bond yields—at least for as long as the Fed (and other central banks) could print enough money to control rates and yields. And hence, by pure high-school math, we knew that the gap between Treasury yields (falling/repressed) and inflation rates (rising/mis-reported) would increase—a confirmed tailwind for gold.

History Lessons

Why else were and are we so confident that inflation would and will rise? Again, and just like in the 1940's, the money-printing Fed of the 2020's wanted to "solve" their otherwise unsustainable debt nightmare by devaluing the currency to partially *inflate* their way out of debt. In the 1940's, for example, cash lost 1/3 of its purchasing power and debt levels in that era only went "down" because inflation and *devalued* dollars pushed it down with debased Greenbacks. Again, debt was not really *paid* back, it was *inflated* away with *more* and hence *weaker* dollars. We knew that an identical policy of deliberate (but mis-reported) inflation was already in play for the 2020's simply because, and again: The Fed had no choice but to inflate away its self-inflicted debt and hence debase its own currency.

Such policies, of course, are great for debt-soaked leaders but a disaster for Main Street citizens, whose money was being secretly "taxed" and stolen by rising inflation. But remember: Central banks serve the markets, not the guy on the street.

Putting It All Together

The golden case for gold boils down to this: *Gold rises when inflation rates are greater than interest rates, as measured by yields on the 10-Year government bonds.* This is because gold loves scenarios wherein rising (and deliberately encouraged yet *misreported*) inflation collides with deliberately suppressed bond yields. Given that central banks needed to both inflate away debt via more money creation while simultaneously suppressing rates to make their debt payments more affordable, we saw the near and longer-term conditions as ideal for gold rising alongside rising inflation measured by rising money supply (as opposed to a rigged CPI scale).

As for inflation, other forces beyond just increased money supply and commodity super cycles had us convinced of its rise. The sudden structural shift wherein governments began guaranteeing the loans of commercial banks was another massive yet largely (if not completely) overlooked indicator of greater inflation ahead, a topic we address in more detail in Chapter 14.

But What About the Case for Spiking Yields?

Many, of course, can make an equally valid case for rising rather than sinking or "controlled" bond yields when (not if) the extreme fantasy and experiment of unlimited money creation and massive debt expansion to support otherwise unloved bonds simply collapses under its own weight. In such a scenario, the Fed loses control of its yield-control policies, and thus suddenly un-supported bond prices would tank in price, sending Treasury yields and interest rates to the moon rather than below the waterline. Although impossible to time such an implosion within the bond market, we see such a scenario as equally inevitable *in the long term.*

But haven't we just said that low yields and rates, as opposed to spiking yields and rates, were good for gold? In fact, the good news for gold is that even such a spiking rate scenario doesn't change the end result for precious metals or the aforementioned case for negative real yields. What investors need to understand is that the actual level of yields and interest rates is not the key issue. Yields and interest rates can be as low as 1% or as high as 17%. The percentage makes no difference to gold, *so long as the inflation rate is higher than the prevailing interest rate.* Thus, if central bank yield suppression fails or collapses under its own weight and yields abruptly spike rather than sink, the gold-favoring scenario of inflation outpacing yields just expands rather than unwinds. Stated otherwise, if the Fed were to ever lose control of Yield Curve Control and thus those previously *suppressed* yields became *spiking* yields, interest rates and inflation would also spike up to and including a setting for hyper-inflation.

Thus, whether continued central bank suppression of yields succeeds or fails, we still get the same result: *negative real yields* and an ideal setting for gold to shine. Such a setting makes inflation forces an absolutely critical component of the price narrative for gold.

Yet perhaps most importantly, and worth repeating, is the critical and historical definition of inflation, which hinges on rising money supply. This rise heading into the 2020's is no longer open for debate. As for the inflationary tailwinds of increased money supply, the data is so clearly in gold's favor that policy makers are finding it more difficult than ever to hide the obvious weakness of their own currencies as the money supply skyrockets. The reaction from central bankers is neither surprising nor ethical and boils down to this: Policy makers are resorting to disinformation to keep their currency-debasing schemes of a rapidly-rising money supply off the radar of public knowledge.

US Money Supply: More Lies from On High

Upton Sinclair famously observed that, "it is difficult to get a man to understand something, when his salary depends on his not understanding it." After decades navigating among Wall Street sell-siders or reading the pablum that passes for financial journalism in the retail space, we always knew it was an open secret in the big banks that if you wanted to move up the ladder, don't rock the boat.

In short: Keep the message bullish, as bears get fired and bulls stay hired.

Such *Realpolitik* is nothing new; employees, be they working for the *New York Times*, the Federal Reserve or Goldman Sachs, have a vested interest in staying employed and hence staying bullish, regardless of the bearish evidence staring them straight in the eyes. This does not necessarily make these self-preserving fiduciaries cowards, but it certainly doesn't make such professionals helpful to those trying to make sense of that oh-so elusive chimera otherwise known as objective facts and hard truths. In the halls of financial power, and by extension financial messaging, such self-preservation and job security often entail a bit of open dishonesty, which frequently takes the form of concealing rather than just misreporting the facts. As the expressions goes: "A man does not sin by commission only, but often by omission."

The U.S. Fed, like the vast majority of central bankers, has a long history of messaging fantasy over reality (i.e., lying) in the name of self-preservation and/or maintaining "market order." (Chapter 3). Their most effective lies are typically characterized not just by what they *say* overtly, but sadly, and far more often, in what they *conceal* covertly.

Lies of Distortion

The open charade, for example, of low inflation fictionally published under the U.S. CPI scale is a classic example of omitting certain facts in order to derive a comforting fiction. Again, we discuss this topic of dishonest inflation reporting at greater length in Chapter 15. Such clever distortions of reality are not mere exceptions to Fed reporting and/or Fed speak, but a way of life for policy makers with an Orwellian capacity to be "ministers of truth" despite hiding truth from the masses on a daily basis.

Lies of Omission

As for hiding facts, the Fed recently decided in the Spring of 2021 to suspend the *weekly* reporting of the M1 and M2 money supply data which typically came out every Thursday at 4:30 PM. And if you want to know why they did this, the answer is as simple as it was predictable: *When policy makers don't like the facts, they just bury them.* Like a child who tries to hide a bad report card from his parents, the Fed likes to hide bad facts from the masses. Take, for example, the following graph of the rise in the M1 supply, which tracks the level of current hard cash notes, coins, paper money and checking account deposits.

By April of 2021, the M1 supply had gone from $4.5T to $18.1, a rise of 450%.

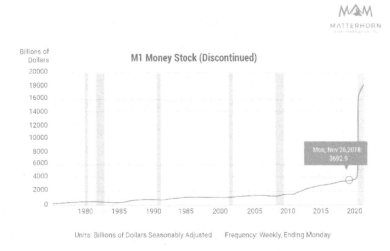

Needless to say, such data represented a pretty poor report card for the Fed's failed monetary experiment of unlimited QE. Staggering M1 data like this has many embarrassing and undeniable implications regarding inflationary risk, currency risk, social risk and hence political risk.

The Fed's solution to the problem?

Hide it.

In 2021, we saw the same suspension of *weekly* M2 data, which comprises the M1 money supply plus "near money," namely: money market securities, mutual funds and other time deposits. As the graph below confirms, the M2 levels had surged by 30% from $15T to just under $20T by mid-2021:

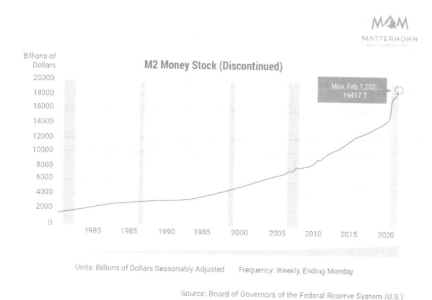

Units: Billions of Dollars Seasonably Adjusted   Frequency: Weekly, Ending Monday

Source: Board of Governors of the Federal Reserve System (U.S.)

Given that such a dramatic rise in the money supply points directly to the consequences of extreme money creation which leads to extreme inflation (which, again, is *defined* by money supply) and hence extreme currency debasement, the Fed naturally chose to discontinue (i.e., hide) such weekly reporting of the same.

Yes. Really. They did this.

A Foundation of Lies

Again, such lies of distortion and omission are nothing new for a *private* bank whose very name "*Federal* Reserve" is itself an open lie, as is the irony of it being headquartered on *Constitution* Ave., despite our founding father's clear and Jeffersonian intent to *never* allow such a bank within our Constitution...

To repeat: The ironies do abound.

The Same Ol' Same Ol'

Be reminded, for example, that just as the U.S. was marching straight into the Great Financial Crisis of 2008, (unleashed by Fed Chairman Alan Greenspan's pre-08 rate cuts), an embarrassed yet truth-challenged Fed decided to *fully* discontinue M3 reporting in 2006. Two years later, of course, the markets tanked in the Great Financial Crisis of 2008. In short, we see a familiar pattern: When the data is bad, hide it. M3 money supply was the measure of M2 money supply *plus* institutional money market funds, larger deposits and larger liquid assets. It too was a screaming indicator of trouble ahead, and thus the Fed simply chose to cancel the truth; M3 reporting by the Fed vanished and has *never* come back.

Yes. Really. They did this too.

Cancelling truths, alas, appears to have become a national pastime in a country where even Dr. Seuss had become a cultural threat by 2021...The sad truth, however, for those who are willing to report, share and face it, is no great mystery: Grotesque elevations in the money supply mathematically destroys the purchasing power of the underlying currency. And as for grotesque levels of money printing, just use your own two eyes. The Fed, along with all the major central banks, are trigger happy, fake-money creators. As such, they are literally killing all the major currencies with the same monetary bullet, Again, just consider the facts (printed currencies) below:

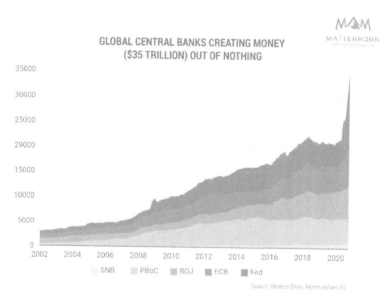

The trillions of U.S. dollars created out of thin air in 2020, as well as the trillions which preceded this printing-frenzy between 2009-2014 (QE1-QE4), have mathematically dire consequences on the purchasing power of America's once sacred but now totally inflated, and hence *debased*, currency. (Again, this is true for all developed economies and currencies, not just the U.S. or its Dollar.) By debasing the dollar in your checking account, wallet or portfolio report, this *private* bank otherwise mis-labeled as the *Federal*

Reserve is literally stealing money from you by the second, which, of course, is a compelling motive for them to hide the evidence (M1, M2 and M3) of their crime.

Anyone who took a basic econ class in college, for example, knows that exaggerated growth in the money supply is a currency killer. But apparently the very chairman of our Federal Reserve at the inception of "QE gone wild" must have skipped that class. Recall that at the opening hours of what is now a money printing nightmare on auto-pilot, former Fed Chairman Ben Bernanke made two promises and two lies in the same breath. First, he said the money printing that began in 2009 would only be *temporary*; second, he promised it would be "at no cost" to the overall strength of our economy. But as the following (and now familiar) graph of the declining US Dollar confirmed (while Mr. Bernanke was still in office and preparing for a self-congratulatory book tour), our Fed Chairman was literally lying.

There was a cost to his "solution," namely the dollar's purchasing power:

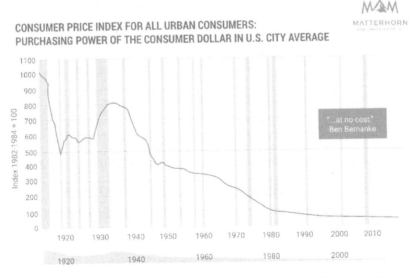

CONSUMER PRICE INDEX FOR ALL URBAN CONSUMERS:
PURCHASING POWER OF THE CONSUMER DOLLAR IN U.S. CITY AVERAGE

MATTERHORN

Shaded area indicates U.S. recessions   Source: U.S Bureau of Labor Success

But such lies from on high are sadly no surprise to anyone who can fog a mirror and read a graph at the same time. With the foregoing facts before you, are you still struggling with trusting the Fed? Do you still think their 0 in 10 record for properly forecasting and avoiding recessions is grounds for confidence? Do you still think the Fed has or had your back as risk assets rose to bubble levels never seen before in the history of capital markets? Do you still think markets never mean-revert and crash? Do you still think this *private* bank masquerading as a *public* office and public servant is indeed serving the ever-debasing dollar in your pocket?

As the pages throughout this book confirm, we ask you to think again.

In the following chapter, we will look at another key inflation factor that is rising to the surface in the 2020's and, for which, again, the vast majority of investors are not informed, namely: Increased governmental involvement in commercial banking, which means increased money creation and circulation—all of which are inflationary forces, and all of which favor gold's steady rise as currency strength continues its steady decline in the near and distant future.

Chapter 14

Government Command Controls & More
Inflationary Tailwinds

It was often said from Plato to Schopenhauer that the only certainty in life is uncertainty. Philosophy majors thus warn us to be weary of anyone who says anything is certain. That said, we are now arguing (as we've been arguing for some time) that inflation is certain.

Hmmm.

Why?

Well, we've spent years (as well as pages herein) tracking the many factors which make inflation inevitable rather than theoretical as we embark upon the 2020's. Specifically:

Inflation, based on the hitherto honest rather than current CPI scale (*See* Chapter 15 below), is factually (as of this writing) at 14% to 15%, not the farcically misreported 2+% of weighted-average range of 2020 or even the 6+% year-over-year numbers of 2021. In short, inflation is *already* here. By 2021 year-end, even the U.S. Fed altered it's meme of "transitory" inflation to "persistent" inflation.

Unlimited QE, regardless of optic "tapers," by definition, means greater money supply, and inflation, by definition, is about precisely that: Increased money supply.

QE for Wall Street (and the embarrassing new reputation of Modern Monetary Theory) is slowly being joined by "QE for the people" in the form of an unprecedented and "COVID-justified" surge in the broad money supply in the form of *fiscal* spending and hence fiscal deficits which are directing money (and the velocity of the same) straight into Main Street, a classic tailwind for rising inflation.

The now openly felt winds of a commodity super cycle are driving commodity prices higher in everything from corn to plywood, and gas prices, all undeniable tailwinds of increasing inflation.

Finally, and perhaps most importantly, governments around the world have never, *not ever*, been as deep in debt as they are today, and the only way to dig themselves out of the Grand Canyon of debt in which they and their central banks put themselves (and us) is to now *inflate their way out of it*. In fact, in early 2021, the ECB openly confessed as much.

But in case none of the foregoing objective realities discussed in prior chapters has you convinced of inflation's arrival and growing windspeed, we have another key reason to expect, its, well...*certainty*.

The Structural Shift Toward Open Inflation: Government Credit Guarantees

Unknown to many, inflationary forces far stronger than just monetary and fiscal stimulus have been in open and deliberate play by the world's major governments in the form of government credit guarantees to commercial banks. This is a critical structural shift.

Why?

As we touched upon in Part I, central banks have been in bed with commercial banks and broke governments since they're not-so immaculate conceptions. Toward this end, governments are all too aware that commercial banks (who like to charge high rates) couldn't thrive or create credit (and hence profitably loan/distribute money) at the artificially repressed rates otherwise so crucial to keeping massive sovereign debt obligations affordable. Thus, by early 2021, governments began to stimulate the commercial banking sector (and hence money circulation) by guaranteeing bank credit risk in everything from business loans to mortgages.

Although such moves went largely unnoticed by the almost comically complicit (or just market ignorant) financial media, governments were not only quietly aiding and abetting bank survival in a low-rate new abnormal, but were and are effectively (and slowly) *taking greater control* over the commercial banking sector. Such credit guarantees from governments ensured further bank money creation to increase spending and borrowing in everything from housing and the green agenda to consumer and corporate debt needs.

This new direction represented *a permanent structural change* in the banking system which, despite being overlooked or misunderstood by the average citizen or financial journalist, mathematically leads to an even greater expansion in broad money growth, and hence, by definition, a deliberate and now structural as well as *global* expansion in the inflation rate. In short, *global* governments are permanently taking a more centralized role not only in our travel rights, health choices and public gatherings, but in the *global* banking system and hence the financial system in which you now sit, wide-eyed to be sure. By early 2021, the major global markets had already witnessed undeniable and intentional broad money growth—tripling the rate of growth in a period of just 6 months by the end of the first fiscal quarter.

But What About Interest Rates? Well, Here's the Kicker...

Of course, everything we learned in school, in both economics and history, suggests that if inflation rises, then rates must rise as well, right? Well, sadly, in this brave new Orwellian world of government fact-omission, centralization, and shameless debt expansion, much of what we learned in school has changed. In short: Almost everything is in flux, including this subtle trend toward government control of commercial banking.

As previously described, given the growing and grotesque debt levels (compliments of a politician and central banker near you, rather than the COVID excuse), *policy makers literally have no choice but to inflate their debt away.* But as alluded in the prior chapter, public policy makers, being the clever little foxes that they are, will, of course, make every effort to have their cake and eat it too by *deliberately allowing inflation* (to pay down debt) yet also *repressing the cost of that debt* by turning to yield curve controls to artificially repress rates. Again, such desperate rate repression is a must for broke sovereigns crawling into the 2020's. Given current global debt levels (>$300T), naturally high nominal interest rates would (and we repeat!) literally kill the markets and governments with the same, rising-rate bullet. If rates were allowed to rise naturally (i.e., in genuine capitalism), the interest expense on government debt would scream way past 50% of GDP in seconds and the global debt party and so-called "economic recovery" would end in dramatic fashion immediately.

Thus, central banks will kill free market price moves in the bond market. Again: *They have no choice.* In simple speak, and worth repeating as much as possible, the only way to get out of debt is to keep inflation rates above interest rates— and the greater the gap, the faster the road out of debt. Of course, and also worth repeating as much as possible, is the fact that this open sham wherein inflation runs higher than nominal yields is also a perfect, textbook setting for *negative real rates*, which as we described in the prior chapter, is the ideal setting for a structural bull market in precious metals.

But as for further rate repression and hence debt expansion subsidized by printed currencies from central banks, a key question has always been: How long can such a charade masquerading as monetary policy last? How long can central banks solve every debt problem with money created by a mouse click? Economists like Ludwig von Mises of the Austrian school of economics provide some timeless and clear answers. Such economists have always warned that the money creation needed to repress yields/rates via artificial bond buying leads inevitably and without fail to currency destruction and a bursting bomb within the financial markets and broader economy. As von Mises himself famously observed, and repeating from Part I, no economy or nation can survive on a debt binge without destroying the purchasing power of its underlying currency at pain levels equals to its prior debt pleasures.

Based on such warnings, won't there be a terrible, terrible price to pay for this new abnormal of rising inflation? The short answer is "yes," but the only issue remaining is what flavor of terrible are we talking about?

Austrian School Disaster vs. Command Economy Nightmare?

Given Ludwig von Mises' warning that all artificially rising bubbles end in catastrophe—including (and depending on the size of the bubbles) hyperinflation, crashing securities markets, and the advent of social, economic and political chaos which always follows the death of paper money--what can informed investors expect? How can they prepare?

Today, of course, we already know and accept that the growing loss of confidence in paper money is real—from the Austrian school's warnings to the understandable and rising popularity of alternative crypto currencies like Bitcoin.

There are some, however, who don't foresee such a von Mises-like explosion in the near-term. Many intelligent economists contend that modern "democracies," now deeper and deeper under the command economy of governments aligned with central bankers (think Janet Yellen as former Fed Chairwoman now at the Treasury or Mario Draghi as a former EU central banker turned Italian Prime Minister), will simply take over the economy rather than allow its natural death ala the von Mises forecasting. The recent moves by governments to directly guarantee commercial credits is indeed a clear and early sign for such extended delays of the otherwise inevitable "von Mises moment" of demise by debt. In short, the question boils down to this: Can governments continue to delay the pain of too much debt by extending debt levels even further, or will the entire house of cards come to an abrupt and sudden end?

This is a debate which has raged well before the global economy stumbled into the 2020's. It's also a valid debate, but either way—a von

Mises implosion or more can-kicking centralization--the end game is the same for gold's rise, as we still face the inevitable slings and arrows of misfortunate-inflation that follows extreme money supply and debt expansion. In short, currencies will continue to weaken by the second and the role and price of precious metals will continue their secular and systemic climb north.

Who Can Hide from Inflation?

Even in the event of a command-control new world in which desperate governments seek to continue a dangerous game of encouraging more borrowing, more debt and hence more toxic money expansion, which class of investors can protect themselves from the rising inflation and further currency debasement that mathematically follows? Who, in other words, will be the freest to seek protection in key assets like gold?

If command control continues unabated from the major governments of the world, the increasingly regulated big boys in their big banks and other institutions won't have a lot of gold choices as they will be legally subject to regulatory capital controls. This is because the entire survival of an increasingly centralized, command-control economy (20% of US income now comes from government handouts) rests upon having less rather than more free choice in the form of currency hedges like gold and silver. That is, increasingly centralized economies, whose bread and butter is by definition "financial repression," will not allow alternative escape hatches or open channels for monetary alternatives which might otherwise threaten their needed inflationary agenda or intentionally debased currency. Instead, governments will have no choice but to repress rather than encourage creative and alternative solutions to inflation and dying currencies.

Bad News for Bitcoin

This also means that Bitcoin, despite its millionaire-making narrative of late, is facing a challenging future. Why? For the simple reason that clever loopholes and "alternative currencies" like Bitcoin are a direct threat to an increasingly centralized world of financial repression and currency control to which we are not only heading, but are *already* experiencing. One of the key appeals of Bitcoin, for example, is its anonymity profile. This revolutionary blockchain move has our greatest intellectual respect as an open defiance to corrupted monetary regimes and openly dying currencies. Sadly, however, centralized governments will not tolerate such tax less "coins" or anonymous ownership. Bitcoin as a viable and alternative cross-border currency is simply too great a threat to increasingly repressive financial systems. In fact, if Bitcoin where to truly succeed as viable alternative currency, then national currencies, and hence national governments, would inevitably fail.

Which bet will you want to take?

This is why governments, including at the U.S. Congress, are already submitting legislation to strip BTC of its anonymous profile. Rather than admit to their own failing (i.e., *debased*) currency, governments will attack alternative currencies like Bitcoin as a "threat to national security"—their favorite meme for just about anything that justifies further control over citizens and markets. They are also attacking cryptos "electronic mining" as environmental threats, as BTC mining creates more environmental harm than burning fossil fuels. In short, and rightly or wrongly, Bitcoin will be attacked at many levels, yet primarily as a tool of terrorist money transfers and illicit financing and slowly castigated as a digital boogeyman rather than as a sane alternative to insane monetary policies. This does not mean, however, an outright ban of the sexy crypto (yet), but such a shift would certainly remove much of Bitcoin's lipstick, price action and investor appeal.

Turning Back to Gold...

As we like to say, all roads, and discussions, ultimately and inevitably turn back to gold, which is forever biding its time as the ugly girl at the dance as all these structural changes and asset bubble hysterias (including BTC) seduced the forever myopic attention of sell-siders, deflationary pundits and bubble-lovers worldwide. Unlike Bitcoin, however, *physical* gold held *outside* an over-regulated, financially repressed command-control economic system, does not rely upon anonymity or "digital mining" to maintain (and grow) its value.

In the coming years, and assuming the entire system does not simply implode under the weight of its own massive debt levels (which is equally if not more likely), we may see more and more capital controls imposed on institutions, where sadly, most of the great national wealth (and even paper "gold") is held. Either way, of course, informed investors with a respect for wealth preservation can remain both prepared and protected by staying outside this autocratic yet openly broken (corrupted) system. Unlike banks, pension funds and other "government controlled" players, individual and private institutional investors like you and us will have greater choices and options to seek escape hatches and currency hedges like gold.

Operating out of Switzerland and watching markets, policy makers and precious metal pricing for decades, we have *never* believed in holding gold in commercial banks, for the simple reason that: a) such gold is not truly "owned" by its account holders, b) those banks face criminal and staggering levels of derivative risk (Chapter 10) and c) they are increasingly coming under the control of governments not depositors. Nor did we ever believe that owning gold in the paper ETF markets was ever a long-term solution, for all the reasons to be outlined below in Chapter 16.

Instead, the smart and independent money has always determined to hold real, *physical* gold in their individual names within segregated accounts and stored in private vaults *outside* of the commercial banking system—typically in a Swiss jurisdiction where privacy rights and capital controls are NOT determined by the central banks in Tokyo, Brussels, London, Beijing or DC... In other words, gold is (and always has been) a clean investment choice in an increasingly dirty, desperate and hence repressive environment. That said, how one purchases, owns and secures their precious metals is an absolutely critical matter. Individuals and private institutions with more freedoms than regulated commercial banks and pension funds in this ever increasing "command control new normal" are opting to hold portions of their wealth *outside* of such openly and increasingly centralized financial systems. They understood this decades before less farsighted "stewards" like Yellen or Draghi took office at a centralized bank or government near you.

Immodestly, we saw the writing on the global wall when gold was less than $300 an ounce and created an ideal system for acquiring and safeguarding precious metals for the long game not the global putting green. In short, we created a superior system for acquiring, growing and preserving wealth than the bankers and politicians have created for the rest of the world, which, as argued above, is sliding ever more toward greater controls and heightened absurdity rather than wider freedoms and effective simplicity.

Why such foresight? It's simple: *We lost trust in the experts and their mismanaged as well as dishonest policy making long ago.* The evidence of, as well as cause for, such distrust was plain to see in the banking and currency risks we've quietly been tracking (discussed respectively in Chapters 10 and 11) as well as in the embarrassing dishonesty we saw in money supply reporting by the Fed as recently as 2021 (Chapter 13). In sum, such open dishonesty masquerading as data was nothing new even to our jaded eyes, as the following discussion of government inflation reporting makes all too clear.

Chapter 15

Gold Headwinds--Misreported Inflation

Despite the prior inflationary discussions driven by massive levels of M1 and M2 monetary expansion, a rising commodity cycle, increased governmental controls and unprecedented debt levels which all point toward currency debasement favorable to precious metals, many headwinds remain in play. One of the most obvious headwinds, equally and deliberately omitted from most public media and market discussions, is the open yet largely overlooked manipulation of inflation reporting by governmental agencies seeking to downplay the true nature (and danger) of actual rather than reported inflation levels.

Masters of Double-Speak

Despite a penchant for double-speak that would make even a politician blush, the Fed consistently proclaims that its primary focus is unemployment not inflation. Let us remind readers, however, that an openly nervous Mr. Powell came out in the summer of 2020 with a specific, as well as headline-making, agenda to "allow" higher inflation above the 2% rate. This "new inflation direction" ignored the larger irony that the Fed had been allegedly and unsuccessfully "targeting" 2% inflation for years before changing verbs from "targeting" to "allowing." Such magical word choices reveal a critical skunk in the Fed's semantic wood pile. If, for example, the Fed was honestly "targeting" inflation to no success for years, how could Powell suddenly have the public ability to then "allow" more of what he failed to achieve before, as if inflation was as simple to dial up and down as a thermostat in one's home?

Dishonest Inflation Reporting

The blunt answer is that the Fed, in sync with the fiction writers at the Bureau of Labor Statistics (BLS), reports consumer inflation about as honestly as Al Capone reported taxable income. In short: The Fed has been openly lying about (i.e., downplaying) genuine inflation for years. As we discover below, the Consumer Price Index (CPI) scale used by the BLS to measure U.S. consumer price inflation is an open charade, allowing the BLS, and hence the Fed, to basically "report" inflation however they see fit—at least for now.

If, for example, the weighting methodologies hitherto used by the Fed to measure CPI inflation in the 1980's (upper line) were used today, the US, CPI-measured inflation in 2021, for example, would be closer to 15% not the reported 6+% (lower line).

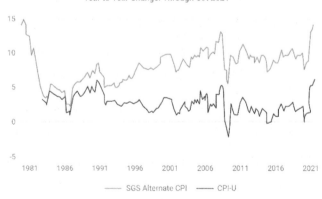

Consumer Inflation - Official vs ShadowStats (1980-Based) Alternate
Year to Year Change. Through Oct 2021

— SGS Alternate CPI   — CPI-U

Published Nov, 10,2021   Source: ShadowStats.com

Concerned about by rising consumer costs and hence rising *reported* inflation, the Fed simply tweaked its CPI scale for measuring the same, effectively downplaying rising costs in housing, health care or education to measure consumer price inflation like a fat-camp scale which downplays the caloric significance of beer, chocolate or pizza when measuring individual body weight. In short, the Fed didn't like the old CPI scale for measuring inflation, and so they simply replaced it with one in which 2+2 =2.

But why would they do so? Why all the mathematical gymnastics and creative writing at the current BLS and Fed? What explains the ongoing double-speak (i.e., lying) wherein the Fed wishes to *target* higher inflation yet simultaneously and deliberately *mis-reports* it at far lower levels?

Necessity: The Mother of Invention

Again, the Fed, in deep *need* of keeping its IOU-driven (i.e., debt-driven) façade of "recovery" in motion, has no choice but to *invent* a respectably controlled (i.e., lower) CPI inflation rate in order to make US Treasury bonds look even moderately attractive to other buyers of their IOU's when measured against inflation. Furthermore, given that Uncle Sam is responsible for paying back those IOU's, they like to do so at an affordable (i.e., manipulated-low) interest rate. Central bankers, however, know that rising inflation naturally and normally invites rising interest rates, which make debt harder to pay. The Fed fears this, greatly. Thus, rates are artificially controlled while inflation is deliberately downplayed/misreported—*a double whammy of open fraud.* Again, and given the sad fact that the US lives off debt rather than productivity (as measured by an openly anemic GDP), the Fed needs to make its IOU's (i.e., Treasury bonds) at least *appear* pretty to future bond buyers.

Unfortunately, rising inflation would make bonds look, well...unattractive when comparing bond yields against the pain of rising inflation. If, for example, a more honest and much higher 15% inflation rate were honestly reported by an honest CPI scale, this would mean that the *inflation-adjusted* yield on a 1.6% yielding US Treasury bond would be generating a *negative* 13.4% yield/return–which hardly makes it a pretty bond for the world to either admire or buy. After all, who would buy bonds that lose 13% from the moment they are purchased? Of course, that's a major problem for an Uncle Sam who literally survives off IOU's rather than productivity. And so, the Fed cleverly invents a CPI inflation number that is artificially less embarrassing than reality.

It's just that simple, and that dishonest. It would further explain why greater than 55% of US Treasuries issued since February of 2020 were purchased by the Fed rather than natural market buyers. That, folks, says a lot...

Needless to say, if real (inflation-adjusted) yields on the US 10-Year were honestly reported at -13%, gold would also be ripping to the moon right now (it skyrocketed in the 1970's when real yields were -4%). This surge, as explained in Chapter 13 above, is because gold rises fastest the faster and deeper inflation-adjusted yields go negative.

What many investors fail to recognize, however, is the simple fact that the Fed (and the bullion banks it serves) are terrified of rising gold prices because a rising gold price confirms the absolute failure of their monetary policies and the open, and ongoing, debasement of their sacred U.S. Dollar. In other words, a rising gold price is open proof of the Fed's mismanagement of, as well guilt for, a dying U.S. currency.

This further explains why the world's central and bullion banks, despite 2021's Basel III regulations, shamelessly manipulate the paper gold price in the COMEX markets on a daily basis, an open secret we discuss more fully in Chapter 16. In simplest terms, rising gold makes the dollar look embarrassingly bad, and so the Fed, along with the bullion banks, has to pull out all their tricks, lies, bad math and open market manipulations to make gold appear weaker than natural market forces would otherwise dictate. Such efforts are *shameless*, and yet it's an open secret to anyone who understands futures markets and bullion banks.

Furthermore, given that the only thing that seems to be "healthy" in the US as of this writing is the biggest stock and bond market bubble in its history, the Fed wants to keep that bubble growing rather than naturally popping. And toward this end, the Fed's officials may be dishonest and delusional, but they aren't completely stupid. They know, for example, that for the last 140 years, ALL (and we mean ALL) of the stock market's gains came during *disinflationary* periods, not *inflationary* periods. This need to appear disinflationary provided all the more reason for the Fed to lie about honest inflation in order to keep that otherwise monstrous market bubble rising rather than naturally imploding.

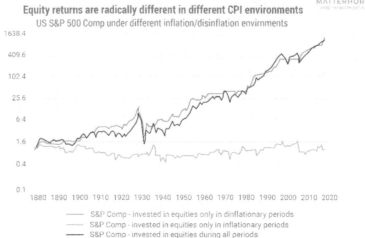

Equity returns are radically different in different CPI environments
US S&P 500 Comp under different inflation/disinflation envirnments

Legend:
— S&P Comp - invested in equities only in dinflationary periods
— S&P Comp - invested in equities only in inflationary periods
— S&P Comp - invested in equities during all periods

Gavekal Research/Bloomberg_Shiller data   Source: Gavekal

Understanding such tricks and distortions is what kept a minority of informed investors from ever falling for Powell's double-speak that he was more concerned about focusing on employment than inflation. His subsequent claim that rising inflation levels in 2021 were just "transitory" was no less shameless. These were just open lies. Period. The unspoken but well-known truth in the canyons of Wall Street or the lamp-lit streets of Zurich is that Powell (as well as Yellen, Bernanke, Greenspan et al.) have been absolutely obsessed with (i.e., worried about) inflation for years, as have been the other and major central banks of the world. Hence, and again, they simply mis-report (i.e., lie about) inflation as the *purchasing power* of the world's reserve currency continues its slow fall toward the floor of history.

Having Your Cake and Eating it Too

What the Fed has been doing ever since Greenspan (the veritable "Patient Zero" of the current global $300T debt disaster and currency crash) is thus very clever yet extremely toxic, as well as openly duplicitous. Specifically, in the early to mid-period of 2021, the Fed was printing over $120B per month (to buy $80B in unwanted Treasury bonds and another $40B in unwanted, toxic MBS paper) with no apparent inflationary effect (despite the repeated fact that inflation is defined by money supply) beyond its so-called 2% "allowance." Such extreme money creation openly dilutes the dollar and thus helps policy makers inflate away US debt with increasingly diluted money, a desperate policy followed, again, by all the world's major central banks.

By simultaneously and dishonestly mis-reporting low CPI inflation at the same time that inflation was and is in fact rising, policy makers get the best of both dishonest worlds. That is, they can dilute the dollar to inflate away US debt without having to fully confess (i.e., report) actual inflation risk (which they downplay as "transitory") nor endure a scenario where inflation grossly outpaces bond yields, which would otherwise make their Treasury bonds too embarrassingly ugly (i.e., grotesquely *negative*) for broader circulation and consumption. Such open fraud, of course, allows the Fed to have its cake (debased currencies to inflate away debt) and eat it too (by under-reporting the otherwise disastrous CPI inflationary consequences of such a desperate policy.) In short, by putting lipstick on the pig of what would otherwise be *highly negative* real yields on openly bogus Treasury bonds if the CPI inflation rate were *accurately* reported, the Fed could continue to live on more debt, more "attractive" IOU's and more dishonesty. Such veiled inflationary fraud allowed the U.S. to effectively extend and pretend an historically unprecedented debt binge at repressed rates as the US credit markets marched forward like a veritable Frankenstein—that is dead, yet still marching on the oxygen of so-called "inflation-less" yet permanent money creation.

But Even Frankenstein Eventually Dies

By Q1 of 2021, however, that groaning monster of a bond market, despite all of rich Uncle Fed's (and Uncle Sam's) support, began to sell-off rather than rise up. Bond prices were slipping, and hence yields were slowly rising alongside misreported yet nevertheless rising inflation, thereby evidencing the ever-weakening powers of the Fed's allegedly all-powerful money printers.

Needless to say, the Fed (sitting on top of $30T in public debt) couldn't bear these rising yields, as they force rising rates, and remember: Rising rates, which reflect the cost of money and debt, scares the hell out of debt-soaked markets (and debt-soaked sovereigns) like those pretending "recovery" in the land of the free (but not free markets) ... For another brief window, and as previously seen in the repo markets of late 2019, the Fed was once again losing control of the low-rate narrative and hence the bond market in 2021. This only meant we could expect more money printing (despite a bogus "taper" in late 2021) to buy those otherwise unloved and unwanted Frankenstein bonds in order to keep their yields down (or "controlled")—the veritable definition of Yield Curve Control, or "YCC."

But such yield (and hence interest rate) control, is nothing more than a dangerous game of Russian roulette for currencies. The Fed may play for a while, but eventually there's a natural market and currency-killing bullet aimed at its head. That is, the only way to postpone a fatal yield and rate spike is for central banks to print more fiat currencies to buy more unwanted bond debt. By extension then, the only way to keep bond and debt-soaked markets alive is to destroy the nation's underlying currency by "over-printing" the same. In short, grotesquely inflated markets may *live* under a rate-suppression blade, but the currencies, well...they *die* by the same sword.

That of course, is having your cake, but not eating it...

And the Pablum Continues

Meanwhile, the pundits, central bank propaganda ministers and BLS fiction writers continued to spew their theories and projections of a deflationary rather than inflationary future. Again, they want inflation to help them repay debts, but they don't want to honestly report inflation, as that makes their bonds unloved and hence un-bought by everyone but the Fed itself. These peddlers of the surreal thus prattled on about year-over-year CPI inflation comparisons, even noting that annualized CPI inflation would break the 2% marker for the first time in almost 10 years, despite the hidden fact that real inflation was already above 9% as they said this, and by even the CPI's own bogus measures, was already above 6% by end of 2021. Such dishonesty was almost comical, if it was not otherwise so tragic.

Why?

Because the entire inflation-deflation discussion, as well as data reports and projections, are ultimately meaningless if the very scale used to measure the CPI inflation figure is itself as bogus as a 42nd Street Rolex. And so, the madness (as well as dishonesty) continued well into 2021 as the creative writing, clever math and the equally distortive projections and pundits spun their tales about bogus inflation "data" as retail investors simply stared at the rising (i.e., *inflating*) costs of health care, education, housing, stock and bond valuations or even the tolls on New York City's George Washington Bridge. In other words, for those wanting to see honest inflation, all they had to do was walk out their front doors, as real inflation was everywhere, except, that is, within the open joke that was (and is) the official CPI inflation scale.

Meanwhile, the Fed's money printing and artificial rate suppression continued, as did that Frankenstein otherwise known as the US bond market, so essential to the ongoing survival of that massive bubble otherwise known as the US stock market. The Fed, alas, was forward guiding, as well as dishonestly managing, more of the same debt-and-print madness (and securities bubble) masquerading as policy.

The Fed: Gold's Best Friend

For owners of physical precious metals, of course, they could only bide their time and smile, because that same Fed, as a policy proxy for all the world's major central banks, was ultimately, and ironically, gold's best friend. More money creation, just means more debased dollars, and more debased dollars just means more inflationary and negative-real-rate tailwinds for gold, as per the one graph which demands repeating over and over...

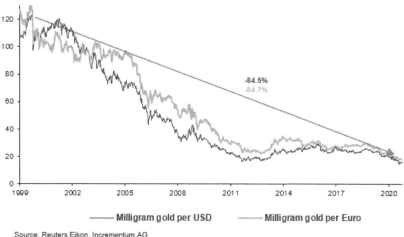

Milligramm Gold per USD & EUR, 01/1999-09/2020

-84.5%
-84.7%

——— Milligram gold per USD   ——— Milligram gold per Euro

Source: Reuters Eikon, Incrementum AG

Eventually, once the jig is up regarding the current inflation lie and hence the equal lie about the *real* (i.e., inflation-adjusted) yield on Treasuries as well as the real (and massive) *over-valuation* of U.S. stocks and bonds, the entire Fed experiment (of using debt to solve a debt problem) comes to a brutal and likely disorderly end. That is, markets nosedive and faith in *already* diluted currencies does the same. Already, by the end of 2021, Janet Yellen at the Treasury Department could no longer hide from the inflation reality she once pretended was "temporary." Of course, and as revealed in Part I, she blamed this inflation exclusively on COVID rather than her own reflection in the mirror. How rich.

This currency and market sinking death is an ending which no one can *time* (it's hard to fight a desperate Fed or a dishonest inflation scale) but for which anyone can *prepare* by simply understanding the current and historical role of precious metals in an open setting of dying currencies and unsustainable debt.

Thereafter, the equally desperate global "re-set" (compliments of the very players who brought markets to and over the debt cliff which they alone created) will likely come, as already telegraphed by the IMF in 2020 under the illusory name of a pending "Bretton Woods II." Under such a projected scheme, new debts will be created, and new digital currencies (redeemable only by central banks, known as Central Bank Digital Currencies, or CBDC) will likely become a new component of the "new abnormal." That, or the entire central banking system will be revealed for the open failure that it was, is and will be, as math-savvy historical figures from David Hume and Thomas Jefferson to Ludwig von Mises or even Andrew Jackson had warned us years ago.

"Reset" or no "reset," currencies will continue their slow death spiral, and gold, always patient, always real rather than virtual, will continue its gradual and inevitable rise above the semantic dust and financial rubble of a broken (yet fiercely supported) banking system and failed monetary experiment driven by logical delusion (*See* Chapter 18), myth and alas, blatant dishonesty, of which the CPI inflation scale is just one example among so many.

As we discover in the following chapter, another open distortion, hidden in plain sight, is the COMEX futures market, a setting in which deliberate price-fixing by just a handful of commercial/bullion banks worked day and night for decades to artificially repress the paper gold and silver price in order to prevent further embarrassment to otherwise embarrassing (i.e., dying) global currencies in general, and the U.S. Dollar in particular.

Chapter 16

Headwinds & Tailwinds: The COMEX Market & Paper Gold Risk

As we've endeavored to argue with objective data throughout Part I, there is bluntly no such thing as free market capitalism in a world wherein central banks, eight key commercial banks, and a few global institutions (such as the IMF, the Bank of International Settlements or the World Bank) have effectively taken over, as well as *distorted*, almost every aspect of the natural supply & demand forces before which we and Adam Smith once knelt. Today markets are artificially rigged, not naturally priced.

In case you worry that such statements are meant to reveal a bias rather than honest perspective, let's consider even more objective numbers rather than controversial words. It would take hundreds of additional pages to fully reveal the myriad ways in which fiscal and monetary policy from global law-makers and bankers have hijacked, distorted and then destroyed free market price discovery and hence genuine capitalism via the over-stimulation of global credit and equity markets with fiat currencies and massive debt policies. But rather than break such a page count here, let us briefly examine just one corner of this grossly distorted financial matrix and illustrate how genuinely rigged the current playing field otherwise known as free-market capitalism and free market "price discovery" truly is.

In short, let's draw back the curtains to that corrupted stage otherwise known as the COMEX futures market for precious metals and see for ourselves.

Buckle up.

The COMEX Futures Market –Making the Complex Simple

For many, the COMEX future's market is a very scary, mysterious and almost foreign universe. It's complex in all its various risks, jargon, players, strategies and layers—too complex, indeed, to fully unpack here.

At its most basic level, however, the COMEX futures market is a place where paper contracts representing actual hard assets (from soybeans and lumber to gold and silver) are traded. In a normal world, for example, a contract to buy a bundle of grain at a fixed price can be traded on the COMEX market to ensure fixed (i.e., contractual) future pricing against intervening market price swings detrimental to producers and buyers of key commodities. In the past, such "futures contracts" were designed to allow farmers and other modest commodity producers and users to intelligently and fairly protect themselves from unexpected price swings (due to weather etc.) by contractually "fixing" a future price higher or lower than its actual price as a form of safety as opposed to speculation. Once such a contract (be it for grains, metal, or pork-bellies) nears its expiration date, the holder of the contract can either take delivery of the contracted-for commodity, or rollover (i.e., extend) that contract for a longer period, thereby delaying actual delivery.

Pretty simple, right?

From Simple to... Manipulated to… Outrageous

Such simplicity, however, gets more complex when that same exchange (thanks to creative young bucks like Leo Melamed and Alan Greenspan as described in Chapter 3) allows those originally simple contracts to be traded with leverage, anywhere from 100:1 to even 200:1. In short: Far more contracts are traded than the actual assets within them. The simplicity gets even more complicated when participants are allowed to go simultaneously long AND short those contracts via the use of admittedly complex derivative instruments, treating corn or gold like a chip on a blackjack table in a casino. Finally, the simplicity gets fully distorted, and complex, when a small minority of extremely deep-pocked participants within that "futures market" control the vast majority of the buying and selling of those contracts, and hence their pricing—the veritable "house" which controls their own casino. In short, the COMEX futures market is not that simple place for the buying and selling of paper contracts once innocently used to protect farmers against such things as weather-induced price swings. Instead, is has devolved into a highly corrupted place for the leverage and manipulation of those paper contracts and hence the false-pricing of the assets they represent.

Worthless Paper

Paper, as we know, is ordinarily just a flimsy thing. Paper is also how we get to hold and touch fiat currencies, which like most paper products, are not terribly valuable. As Voltaire famously said: "All paper money eventually returns to its intrinsic value—zero." Yet this ever-weakening paper money, ever since Nixon robbed it of its gold-backing in 1971, is what makes the ever-mad financial world go ever-round in this new, ever-distorted era. Central banks, and broke nations, therefore need to make otherwise weak paper *appear* valuable, and will do all kinds of complex market gymnastics to keep the illusion that paper wealth (be it a levered derivatives contract for a bar of gold or a simple dollar bill) is actual wealth. Toward this end, it is very, very, very important for those powerful players to make true stores of wealth—i.e., gold and silver—look far less valuable than what the natural market forces would otherwise dictate. In this nefarious reality, a small handful of key market manipulators (described below) like to use paper products (i.e., levered futures contracts on the COMEX) to make physical gold and silver products *appear* less attractive, for again, if gold and silver where to be accurately priced according to genuine supply and demand forces, then the entire (and embarrassingly broken) paper scheme of global fiat currencies and markets would fall like a house of cheap (paper) cards.

Hard to believe?

Let us (and the numbers) show you.

Gold & Silver's Fictional "Paper" Price

Take our two favorite, misunderstood, yet historically-confirmed stores of genuine rather than paper (or even crypto) value: Physical gold & silver. Popular demand for these otherwise rare assets is in fact massive, which means their price power should be openly and equally so. After all, true, free-market capitalism was designed to reward those assets which enjoy high demand yet relatively low supply, right? That, after all, is Econ 101: As demand rises, prices rise.

Let's look, then, at the example of rising demand for silver in 2020 as measured by ETF flows:

And let's do the same for flows into gold ETF's, just to make its *natural* demand visually clear:

With such rising ETF demand for gold and silver (allegedly fully backed by actual physical gold and silver held by the custodians of these funds), shouldn't gold and silver prices therefore be skyrocketing in the paper (future's contract) markets that represent them?

Well, as alluded above, paper is a funny thing, and for the policy makers (i.e., central banks, major commercial -or "bullion"—banks and all dollar-dependent politicians) who are deeply threatened by rising gold and silver prices, paper can be easily manipulated, which means so can the price of paper gold and silver.

How the Hateful-8 Killed Free Market Price Discovery

And to make this obvious, objective and undeniable as opposed to just theoretical or dramatic, let's see how a tiny circle of big players, rather than natural supply and demand forces, artificially, legally and yet dishonestly fixed the gold and silver prices, and thus mocked any vestige of respect for that bygone ghost otherwise known as free market price action. Specifically, let's see how just eight major commercial banks and institutions are able to overpower the natural price power of thousands of other contract buyers on the COMEX futures market to artificially suppress the natural pricing of these two precious metals.

Believe it or not, nearly *every* contract (and we're talking thousands of them) for gold and silver in the COMEX futures market trade net long— meaning they are *buyers*. Such powerful demand should make gold and silver prices quite high. Yet all it takes to defeat the demand power (and rising price) of those numerous metal contracts is for just four to eight of the largest traders (mainly bullion banks) in the futures market to perpetually short (i.e., bet against) those other contracts with levered deep pockets to keep their prices suppressed.

Hard to believe? Then see for yourself:

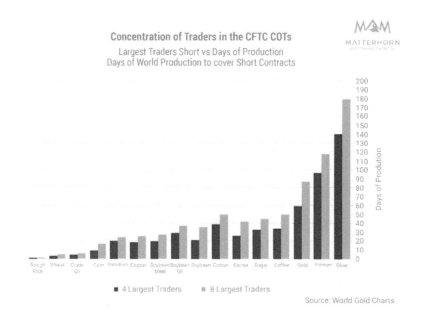

Concentration of Traders in the CFTC COTs
Largest Traders Short vs Days of Production
Days of World Production to cover Short Contracts

■ 4 Largest Traders   ■ 8 Largest Traders

Source: World Gold Charts

In sum, what we see in the **COMEX** futures markets are eight extremely deep-pocketed players essentially using massive amounts of paper leverage (i.e., borrowed money) to bet *against* the rest of the world in order to control the fair price of precious metals. Alas, this tiny handful of eight (the "Hateful-8"?) are and were short more than 50% of the entire futures market by 2021, and by going this deep and this short for so long, they literally (and artificially) control the *paper* price of precious metals, for without such levered intervention, the price of gold and silver would literally and naturally have been *skyrocketing*. Do you now see how terrified the policy makers and their subservient commercial banks are of rising gold and silver? As recently as early 2021, they were 112% short silver to the tune of over 412 million ounces. Of course, we *already* know what they are afraid of: *Rising gold and silver would be the ultimate and absolute confirmation of the otherwise open failure of unlimited money printing and fiat currencies in a post-Nixon world.*

How Long Can Natural Price Forces be Repressed?

But the next question is equally obvious: How long can this legalized scam/manipulation continue by a handful of powerful banks to artificially suppress the natural price of gold and silver? That is, if four to eight big boys are colluding to the tunes of billions and billions and billions of dollars in short contracts on the COMEX each day, how long can this rigged game continue without a wrench in their plans?

A key component to the survival of this open scam and price suppression (in play since 1973) is the ability to keep the short contracts on these precious metals perpetually rolling over rather than expiring, for if the contracts were to ever expire, an actual physical delivery of the underlying metals would be legally required. But that would immediately spell party over for the Hateful-8 as well as the COMEX itself. That's because these same big boys would default on actual delivery for the simple reason that they don't *actually own* enough gold and silver to honor their grossly levered contracts. *Not even close.* That is also why the cost spread on the COMEX for rolling over (rather than delivering) these contracts in gold and silver were so cheap—in fact, almost free. In simple terms, these market manipulators (or the COMEX itself) wouldn't survive without such manipulation and perpetual contract roll-overs.

Alternatively, if the Hateful-8 couldn't make actual delivery of the metals (and they can't), they would eventually be forced to cover their own COMEX shorts and go net long once gold and silver prices climbed (i.e., "squeezed" them) beyond their control. This short-covering would also cause the price of precious metals to skyrocket. But even the big boy's pockets aren't deep enough to ever afford going net long to cover their own sins and levered shorts, as this would require trillions, not billions. Not even a bailout from the Exchange Stabilization Fund could help these TBTF (Too Big to Fail) bullion banks at that point. In short, this small handful of big boys shorting the gold and silver contracts with levered money representing gold they don't actually own are playing with gasoline and matches.

All of the big boys, that is, but one...

Enter JP Morgan—No Honor Among Thieves

When JP Morgan inherited the post-08 balance sheet of that other headline failure, Bear Sterns, this included 30,000 to 40,000 *short* contract positions in gold and silver. For all the reasons (and risks) stated above, JP Morgan knew it was dangerous to be net short gold and silver (because as metal custodians for other funds, Morgan knew better than anyone that there simply wasn't enough physical gold and silver in their coffers to meet the delivery demands of the grossly levered contracts traded on that over-levered COMEX). Stated otherwise, Morgan needed to dump and cover (i.e., pay for) those short positions (by going long) at just the right moment, i.e., when metal prices were low. Thus, after spoofing the market in early 2020, Morgan artificially manipulated the metals prices *down* before buying the same and going net long to cover their inherited shorts in March of 2020.

By 2021, JP Morgan had closed its short positions and was market neutral rather than net short gold and silver. In fact, they are stacking their *physical* gold and silver bars in London warehouses as we type this, controlling over 1 billion ounces of Silver and over 25 million ounces of gold.

Why?

Very simple, they plan to front run the inevitable gold and silver bull market of which we've been tracking and investing for years. And as for the COMEX futures market in paper gold? Well, its days are numbered and the fallout from its failure will be more than "interesting," but nothing less than a disaster. As for this inevitable moment of "uh-oh" in the derivatives trade, we've touched upon this previously in Chapter 10, but as of this writing, the banks are already feeling the squeeze of the May, 2021 Basel III regulations which dramatically limited their ability to lever paper gold contracts (long or short) in the futures markets. These changes will have a mixed impact on gold pricing. On a bullish note, Basel III means less bank leverage, and hence fairer price discovery. On a bearish note, those same regulations make the trading costs, spreads and liquidity flows of gold and silver trades far more onerous and expensive, which can reduce institutional demand for precious metals due to "liquidity concerns."

Ultimately, however, the broader tailwinds for precious metals in a global backdrop of rising inflation, repressed yields and the ever-weakening purchasing power of global currencies means gold's ultimate direction is a rising one, as it always has been when economic systems get nearer to their breaking points. In the end, real assets in general, and physical gold in particular, have far greater power than paper assets when inflation becomes impossible to hide or stop. This fact is equally true of the gold ETF space, which is more of a paper risk than most investors realize.

Gold ETF's—Just Another Bad Paper Play

When speaking of derivative disasters, gold shortages and flimsy paper, no discussion of gold pricing and gold investing would be complete without addressing the ETF market in gold. We discussed ETF risk in general in Chapter 9, but when looking more specifically at the ETF gold trade, a unique range of risks and distortions requires more direct attention here.

Sadly, gold ETFs are the most convenient instrument for most uninformed individual and even institutional investors to allegedly "own" gold. But buying a gold ETF is, in most cases, just an investment in *paper* rather than actual gold. The holder of the paper confirming his/her ETF "gold" interests in fact has no security in the physical gold itself. Despite such realities, the total investment into gold ETFs and gold funds by 2020 was $316 billion, representing 4,878 tonnes of the metal, which, at the time, was a record amount. The increase in 2020 in the total ETF valuations was considerable and amounted to $160 billion, signifying a 50% increase since the end of 2019.

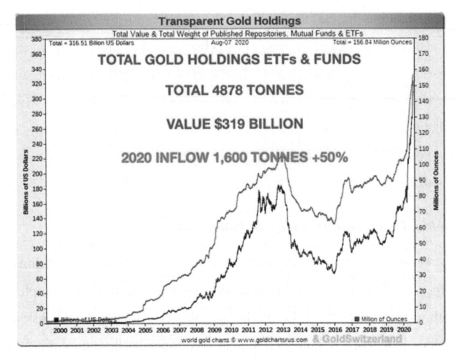

Tying such data together, Gold ETFs and funds reached $319 billion in 2020. But if we compare even that milestone to the S&P 500's total market cap of $27 trillion in 2020, we quickly discover that even this amount is just short of insignificant. The top 5 companies in the S&P index at the same period, for example, were worth $6 trillion. Just take Apple. With its $200 billion cash pile and some stock thrown in; if they so desired, Apple could easily acquire all the gold funds and ETFs in a single transaction. This tells us how small the gold market truly is. In the next few years, as stock markets crash and gold surges, the relative sizes of stocks versus gold will look very different, which is why now, rather than later, is an opportune time to buy gold.

The biggest gold ETF, for example, is GLD. By 2020, GLD held a total 1,258 tonnes with a value of $82 billion. This made GLD the 7th biggest holder of gold in the world.

GLD's value had gone from $42 billion at the beginning of 2020 to $82b by mid-year as both inflow and hence gold price increased. This ETF was the primary investment vehicle that most retail investors used when they wanted exposure to gold. What these investors didn't, and still don't, fully understand, however, is that "owning" gold within an ETF like GLD is no better than having a futures contract in gold, which means *not* owning actual gold.

This is because the ETF is a tracking vehicle that doesn't actually possess the gold it represents to buyers. The gold is not bought outright by ETF's like GLD but is instead *borrowed*. The holder of a GLD share thus has no genuine claim on the borrowed gold and therefore does not in fact own anything tangible. Instead, all the ETF investor holds is a piece of paper with no underlying security in the form of *immediate* gold delivery (and use) in case of insolvency. The gold in such ETFs is borrowed or leased from a central bank and not bought with clear title by the ETF itself. Again: This means a shareholder in an ETF like GLD is just a holder of a piece of paper that doesn't entitle him/her to immediate physical gold delivery. A paper claim on gold is very different from owning real physical gold. The gold price could surge but the ETF could still go bankrupt.

As we have often pointed out to audiences, clients and readers around the world, when an ETF like GLD buys gold, the gold doesn't come direct from the Swiss refiners. Instead, it comes from the bullion banks who borrow the gold from a central bank. The GLD ETF has a nice, official-looking audit with bar lists and numbers, giving ETF investors the false impression that they "own" real gold. But since central banks never publish a full physical audit of their actual gold holdings (because they don't actually have the full amount gold in their vaults needed to cover their obligation), there is no way of verifying or knowing if the same gold has been rehypothecated several times over by the central bank. In short, there is no way of knowing what the banks actually hold in gold, and hence no way of knowing what one owns in gold through the ETF vehicles operating alongside these banks.

But here's the short answer: You own nothing but paper, and the banks don't actually own the full amount of gold behind that paper. Of course, no one at a major bank (or ETF) will openly say or confess this.

GLD and Counterparty Risk

One of the major advantages of owning physical gold outside the banking (and hence ETF) systems is that it is the only asset which is not someone else's liability. Buying a gold ETF like GLD involves multiple counterparty risks with no actual ownership of the underlying metal. Investors in GLD, for example, buy shares in the fund's/ETF's trustee, in this particular case, the SPDR Gold Trust. The custodian bank, HSBC (eh hmmm), then sources and stores the gold for the trust/ETF. This obviously makes HSBC a major counterparty risk, which as our chapter on banking risk (Chapter 10) confirms, is anything but a safe system (or bank...) in which to entrust your precious metal (or any other form) of real wealth. Furthermore, HSBC also uses sub-custodians, namely other bullion banks and even the Bank of England, to source and store the gold. This means that investors have multiple exposures to multiple sources of banking and sub-custodian risk.

There are no contractual agreements between the Trustee and the sub-custodians or the custodian. This means that the ability of the trustees or the custodian to take legal action against the sub-custodians is limited. The trustee, moreover, is not insured. That is left to the custodians. Gold held in the ETF's/trust's unallocated gold account is not segregated from the custodian's assets. If a custodian becomes insolvent, its assets (i.e., your gold) may not be adequate to satisfy the claim of the trust, which means a real moment of "uh-oh" when you ask for your gold and/or the money you paid for that gold when you need it most.

The above relatively detailed explanation on how a gold ETF like GLD functions is intended to enlighten investors as to the real, and often ignored, risks in "owning" gold through an ETF vehicle.

For serious wealth preservation investors, such gold ETF vehicles do not satisfy any of the criteria of holding a reserve asset like gold totally risk free.

The main problems with buying gold through an ETF, as outlined above, are the following:

- It is a paper security held within a highly fractured financial system;
- It has multiple layers of counterparty risk;
- The gold holdings are not segregated from custodians' assets;
- It owns no gold directly;
- The gold is stored within a banking system riddled with risks;
- The gold held is probably rehypothecated;
- The gold is not fully insured; and
- Investors have no direct access to their gold.

Again, holding gold through an ETF is no better than holding gold futures, which as this chapter on the COMEX futures market makes objectively clear, is little more than a levered and highly explosive timebomb. For sophisticated and genuine wealth preservation purposes, gold must therefore be held outside such a highly levered and operationally fractured banking system in the safest private vaults in the world. The gold must be controlled directly by the investor with direct access to his/her gold in a private, secured and fully-insured vault. No other party must be allowed to touch the gold without the owner's express authorization and the gold must be held in the safest political and legal jurisdictions like Switzerland. Such an ownership approach is far superior to any gold ETF with none of the negatives.

Of course, we also know that not everyone can afford to buy large quantities of physical gold which can then be stored in private vaults in Switzerland or elsewhere. That said, anyone can commit to researching pathways to slowly acquiring and accumulating smaller amounts of gold coins or lower-ounce bars which can be privately held as per each individual's choice and budget.

Given such facts and factors, it continues to sadden us that so many major gold investors, even including larger private (and fiduciary-bound) institutional investors, would even consider an inferior method of gold ownership like a gold ETF.

In sum, the gross price manipulations of the COMEX paper market as well as the embedded counterparty risk within gold ETF vehicles combine to create real headwinds to accurate gold pricing as well as safe gold ownership. Ultimately, however, we anticipate an inevitable failure in the risk-heavy, derivative-saturated and now increasingly regulated COMEX and banking markets which will send gold prices higher rather than lower. For this reason, what was once a price headwind becomes a price tailwind for gold. As for ETF gold ownership risks, the only solution for serious precious metal investors is to replace ETF ownership of paper gold with actual and direct ownership of the physical metal as per the conditions described above. That too will turn a gold headwind into a tailwind.

In the next chapter, we consider another common gold headwind, namely deflation. Once examined more closely, however, we see that even this so-called headwind for gold is ultimately of far less importance (and debate) than many pundits would otherwise have you believe.

Chapter 17

Deflation: Is It Really a Gold Headwind?

Despite the numerous reasons discussed in the preceding chapters as to what we see as the *current* as well as *future* inevitability of rising inflation, there are many, including those who strongly favor gold, calling for a very different horizon, namely one colored by a deflationary rather inflationary future. If this were the case, would gold prices face more headwinds than tailwinds?

As argued below, our final answer is, "no."

Notwithstanding our strong inflationary views, the key arguments made by deflationary thinkers are not to be mocked or disregarded. Their primary argument in favor of deflation boils down to one simple idea, namely: When economies and markets stall (or even collapse) as we equally anticipate, this leads to dramatic slow-downs in consumer demand, and hence dramatic falls in consumer pricing, and hence deflation. Such an understanding of deflation is based upon demand and price factors, not money supply alone. By the 2020's in general, and during the global pandemic in particular, the world witnessed extreme levels of excess capacity (i.e., surplus supply rather than demand) in labor, manufacturing, retail and commercial real estate. Banks, in 2021, for example, were already telegraphing that post-COVID, they would require 40% less office space as more and more systems were put in place to manage operations outside of traditional office settings. All of these factors, the deflationist camp rightfully argues, point toward continued deflationary rather than inflationary forces going forward.

As to the staggering growth of the money supply unleashed by global central banks printing trillions of fiat currencies at record levels since 2008 in general, and in the COVID period in particular, the deflation camp argues that such extreme money creation has not lead to rising inflation, including hyper-inflation, for the simple reason that all those printed fiat currencies never enter/circulate within the real economy, but remain contained within a closed-circuit loop of Treasury departments, central banks, commercial banks and risk asset bubbles—not the real (i.e. Main Street) economy where money velocity can do its inflationary damage. In short, the deflationists further argue that so long as central banks act as lenders of last resort to government treasury departments and debt-driven security exchanges, all that printed money stays safely contained behind a Hoover-like dam of corporate, commercial and central bank balance sheets, not the real economy where such levels of money growth would and can be extremely inflationary.

These deflationary views, in fact, make logical sense, and it would be foolish to simply discount them. That said, there are some key mistakes, we feel, in the premises behind such otherwise sound logic.

First, the broader deflationary argument that trillions in central-bank-created money can and will stay contained within a closed-loop circuit outside of Main Street is not factually the case. By 2020, for example, the Fed pivoted from being a *lender* of last resort into a *spender* of last resort, making direct (albeit still small) purchases into various credit ETF's and even specific corporate bond issuances. This means central bank money was beginning to gradually leak *outside* of the foregoing "Hoover-dam" (cemented together by central banks, treasury departments and commercial banks) and directly into the real world. Such a small yet growing trend, by the way, is highly inflationary rather than deflationary.

Additionally, the deflationary camp ignores the massive (and rising) amounts of fiat currencies going directly into the real economy on the heels of unprecedented *fiscal* stimulus (i.e., deficit spending) as governments, most notably in the U.S., send trillions of dollars directly into the hands of consumers and businesses in the form of COVID relief checks, PPP loans and other "Care Package" policies which travel straight into Main Street. Of course, trillions of dollars flowing directly into Main Street eventually leads to an increase in the velocity (Main Street circulation) of those dollars, which again, is an inflationary rather than deflationary force.

Finally, it is worth repeating to all deflationary thinkers that the very scale used to measure inflation in the U.S., namely the Consumer Price Index published by the Bureau of Labor Statistics, is an open charade. As we've discussed in Chapter 15, the real measure of inflation by year-end 2021 was closer to 15% not the fictional yet rising 6-7% year-on-year rate promulgated out of a truth-challenged (i.e., desperate) Washington DC. Stated simply: Inflation is *already* here. Debate over.

In sum, the deflation and inflation arguments, as well as debate, will continue to rage, and although we see a distinctly inflationary future, we are not blind to deflationary forces or those who foresee more of the same.

Does the Inflation/Deflation Debate Really Matter?

As, and perhaps most importantly, we have to raise an additional, and perhaps even blasphemous question when it comes to future gold pricing, namely: Does gold even care about this larger inflation/deflation debate? That is, it's worth underscoring that gold price movements in general, and the role of gold as counterforce to increased currency debasement in particular, is and can be relatively agnostic to the issue of whether the world turns inflationary or deflationary in the near or long term.

Yes, of course, inflation still matters, in so far as gold prices rise best when the rate of inflation exceeds the nominal yields on 10-Year government bonds. Such negative real yields, as we demonstrated in Chapter 13, are ideal settings for gold pricing. But keep in mind, all that is required for such a setting is not that inflation shoots to the moon, but simply that inflation rates be higher than nominal yields/rates, which is a future we see as inevitable and consistent—and hence a major tailwind for gold over the long term.

Despite fears of rising rates (and hence inflation), which have an undeniable impact on gold pricing, we also have little to no doubts that in the near term, governments will continue to create liquidity (via QE, Repo, or FIMA swaps) to purchase bonds and hence keep nominal yields compressed. Let us repeat, this is because global government debt levels are at such record highs that their central banks will have no choice, *at least near term*, but to do whatever it takes to *artificially* keep the cost of that debt (i.e., rates and yields) repressed below inflation levels so that global governments, including in the U.S., do not become insolvent in an intervention-free world of *naturally* rising (and hence unpayable) interest rates.

And as for nominal rates, people may have been scurrying in 2021, screaming and worrying about so-called "spiking" yields, but folks, 1.6%, or even 2%, on the U.S. 10-Year is hardly nosebleed or "spiking" territory (and still *negative* when adjusted for inflation). Thus, compared to more normal eras, yields in this broken "new normal" are remarkably low (see below), and for all the *Realpolitik* reasons discussed above, won't be going much higher any time soon until the entire monetary system itself tanks under its own debt-weight.

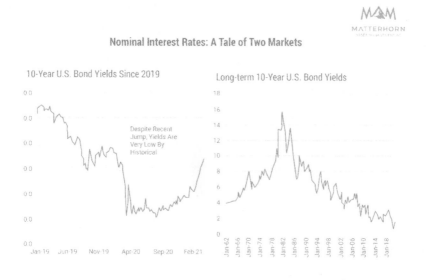

Nominal Interest Rates: A Tale of Two Markets

10-Year U.S. Bond Yields Since 2019

Long-term 10-Year U.S. Bond Yields

Despite Recent Jump, Yields Are Very Low By Historical

Given such low nominal interest rates, investors see very little upside in effectively yield-less bonds, and as a result, will continue to buy silver and gold regardless of whether inflation or deflation characterizes the current moment. In fact, *nominal* (i.e., non-inflation adjusted) yields would have to climb quite high for gold investors to exit the precious metal sectors in large numbers, and we don't expect nominal yields to reach such levels in the near future, again, because governments like the U.S. (or corporations on the S&P) could not afford such sustained rates without creating much higher inflation rates and thus more negative real rates. In short, don't fight a desperate Fed. But even if and when the Fed finally loses control of rates and debt markets, yields/rates would indeed spike as bonds tanked (bad for gold?), yet inflation would follow those rising yields. Either way, then: Gold wins.

Furthermore, and with specific reference to gold pricing, the real driver for its price has been, and always will be, direct consumer demand. Such demand is in fact driven by variables that go well beyond interest rates and inflation debates. In fact, such demand is driven far more by emotion than math, a factor which we introduced already in Chapter 12. More specifically, demand for gold rises when faith in political trust, economic policies and currency stability falls further and further toward the basement. And as we've shown throughout Part I, faith in each of these critical areas has fallen, and will continue to find, further lows—all of which helps explain why gold, despite all the enthusiasm for Bitcoin or fears of rising rates or even muted, "transitory" inflation, continues to attract consumer demand.

In short, and despite all the complex technical, mathematical and academic discourse regarding rates, yields, derivative markets, inflationary and deflationary forces, a key driver for gold will be the rapidly declining faith in the financial system. Needless to say, our faith in the global financial system is all but gone, and we are by no means alone in this blunt prognosis. Strangely, this faith indicator alone, and the fact that the global financial system is so broken and distorted (from Elon Musk to Jerome Powell, the COMEX market to the CPI lie) are the primary reasons we are supremely confident gold will reach far higher highs in the years ahead. Again, this is for the simple reason that trust in the global financial system is reaching all-time lows as measured by policy management and investor confidence.

But speaking of confidence, and by extension, conviction, is it truly *logical* to be so certain of gold's price direction and ultimate role in currency protection? Is there risk of too much bias from professionals (and even authors) like ourselves who advise in the precious metals space? In short, are "logical" voices like ours truly objective in pointing out the vast list of delusions and risks currently at play among global policy makers and in risk assets? Is it possible, in other words, that we too are simply ignoring the possibility of our own bias, and even delusions, in the precious metal arena?

These are fair questions, and no fair discussion regarding gold would be complete if such questions, as well as potential biases, were not squarely addressed. In the following chapter, we therefore turn to the topic of logic to make it clear that we speak not as "gold bugs" but as fiduciary realists.

Chapter 18

Logic in a Time of Madness and Bitcoin

In late 2017, as Bitcoin was making its first big moves in both price and public perception, John Hussman penned a lengthy as well as seminal report entitled, *Three Delusions: Paper Wealth, a Booming Economy, and Bitcoin.* The core themes set forth in his report (as in any well-reasoned, blunt analysis) are refreshingly evergreen in their ongoing applicability today. Rather than re-invent an already functioning wheel, we've opted to revisit some of Hussman's core arguments which have not only stood the test of time, but remain even more pertinent in today's perception-challenged markets.

The Follies of Our Predecessors

Hussman's report opens with a quote from Charles Mackay's work, *Extraordinary Popular Delusions and the Madness of Crowds*:

"Let us not, in the pride of our superior knowledge, turn with contempt from the follies of our predecessors. The study of the errors into which great minds have fallen in the pursuit of truth can never be uninstructive."

As for the "follies of our predecessors" and "the study of [their] errors," the list is long and cyclical, as we've chronicled throughout these pages, from the 1912 warnings of White's ghost in Chapter 2 all the way to the distortions in the modern COMEX market. That is, we've beseeched investors to question rather than blindly follow the so-called "experts" (Chapters 3 and 4) while keeping an ever-careful eye on the madness of crowds (Chapter 7) who blindly follow them. But as Hussman and others remind, delusion (i.e., "madness") is a complicated yet common thing. Even more alarming, *delusion can in fact stem from logic.*

Crowd Thinking—Crowd "Logic"?

Most logical minds, for example, tend to feel immune from delusion, but the irony lies in the argument that delusional ideas, including delusional markets, policies and pricing, are often marked not by *deficiencies* in logic, but rather by an *over-abundance* of it. Throughout the long and cyclical history of delusional market bubbles and their subsequent implosions, otherwise "logical" and/or intelligent market participants have always found themselves in the comforting presence of crowds. We have seen such comforting, yet deluded crowds from the France of the 1790's to the current era with eerie consistency. Recall, for example, that just before the Nikkei died in 1989, the popular expression in Tokyo was: "How can we get hurt if we're all crossing the street at the same time?"

Crowds, of course, love comforting consensus, feedback loops and risky speculation masquerading as logic, often at the expense of historical lessons, ignored data or even common sense. Instead, crowds focus on current trends, lofty credentials and the *loud* voice of rising price momentum at the expense of risk and reason's more unpleasant *whispers*. In other words, logical minds will often overlook dangerous market information (i.e., facts) and cling exclusively to the current price data which confirms their hopes and biases, creating a mass perception that is often misperception. As Hussman observed: "The reason that delusions are so hard to fight with logic is that delusions themselves are established through the exercise of logic."

The overwhelming and *objective* evidence, for example, of dangerous and grossly distorted risk asset pricing (Chapter 6) can be easily re-described (and thus re-perceived, re-framed and re-packaged) in the echo chambers of rational yet otherwise bubble-blind investors and debt-cornered policy makers as *logical* "stimulus," "support," or "accommodation." The popular "logic" that Modern Monetary Theory, for example, offers a sustainable "solution" to debt via the creation of unlimited dollars has actually taken hold. This is because MMT is wrapped within an academic, pseudo-logical aura of blissful projections of deficits without tears (and money creation *sans* inflation). As such, this otherwise fantastical and highly discredited "theory" has slowly left the *fringe* of economics and entered its *forefront* as a sound, indeed "logical" new path forward. Equally, "logical" are the euphemistic titles given to such popular policies as "Yield Curve Control" or "Quantitative Easing," which, as most of us *already* know, are just clever, even *logically titled* concepts masking the far more pernicious delusion of extreme debt expansion supported by extreme money creation which leads logically to extreme currency debasement.

Nevertheless, such irrational yet crowd-sanctioned ideas and logically-labeled policies have acquired popular/global acceptance not because they are *intrinsically logical* or rational, but simply because they have become *popularly embraced* and hence crowd-acceptable, common and, at least for now, profitable and even "effective." After all, when markets are rising, no one asks why or questions the risks or poor logic which lie beneath. Stocks have certainly risen faster than gold for years, so why not buy more stocks? Logical, right?

History's Patterns

For Hussman, as well as other students of market history, speculative bubbles or even human psychology, such delusions of popularity, group-logic, profit and even efficiency are not only dangerous, but historically quite common. Like the pages of this book, Hussman's lengthy report traces the anatomy of prior bubbles and crowd-ignored delusions with painful candor and historical confirmations rather than just self-selecting logic. His insights are not only highly relevant, but also highly recommended. The conclusions which Hussman and others (from J.K. Galbraith to Benjamin Graham) derived come down to this:

Deluded investors forever seek to justify extreme price valuations in ever-increasing and novel ways, which in the end, are nothing "but excuses for continued speculation" rather than honest confessions of desperate top creations and equally delusional top chasing.

The "Experts"—A Smaller Yet Equally Mad Crowd

Hussman takes particular care to point out that such delusions are not simply held by large crowds of retail investors riding a speculative wave which will eventually drown them. In fact, the so-called "rational" experts, like former Federal Reserve Chairwoman Janet Yellen, in Hussman's study, are equally, if not more, guilty of such self-delusion in the name of self-selected "logic." Of course, this is no surprise to many of us. Hundreds of pages could be written which detail the myriad occasions in which Janet Yellen, both before and after she took the Chair at the Federal Reserve, completely understated, exacerbated and then ignored real market risk, from the pre-08 era to today. Despite zero evidence that her policies of extreme money printing created any "trickle-down effect" on the real economy (though it sure did create a "trickle-up effect" [and wealth transfer to] the top 10% of national wealth), Yellen stubbornly clings to the delusion that Quantitative Easing is a public good, when in fact it has merely created and extended the largest risk asset bubbles and wealth disparity ever recorded. In short, her "logic," like her words, are openly flawed. For simplicity and brevity, let us just proffer (and return to) the following example:

"You will never see another financial crisis in your lifetime."
-Janet Yellen, spring 2018

"I do worry that we could have another financial crisis."
-Janet Yellen, fall 2018

Valuation Still Matters

What Hussman and countless other logical minds consistently warned against boils down to a simple truth proven throughout history, from the Romans of old to the Elons of today, namely: *Valuation still matters*. First published in December of 2017, Hussman's report warned that the expert-sanctioned as well as investor-fed speculative bubble in full gear then would inevitably devolve "into a roughly -65% loss in the S&P over the completion of the current market cycle."

Of course, other "logical" detractors would laugh at such predictive logic, reminding Hussman and others (including ourselves) that these warnings, made over *four* years prior, had been disproved by an S&P that has since reached all-time highs and never seemed to halt its climb north, despite a few hiccups along the way, each of which were easily "recovered" by more *logical* Fed "support"—namely trillions of more instant liquidity by a central bank money printer.

Such criticism of Hussman's warnings, however, misses the historical point that boom-to-bust cycles don't have clearly defined expiration dates, especially when those *natural* cycles are *un-naturally* extended via equally un-natural and illogical "stimulus" from global central banks. In short, just because a logically inevitable market implosion has been *postponed*, this by no means suggests it has been *outlawed* or disproved. In fact, such bubble "pretending and extending" by seemingly "logical" central bankers only makes the can-kicked market implosion far worse down the road.

Preparing Rather than Timing the Death of Paper "Wealth"

Thus, rather than mire one's self in the "logical" debate of *timing* a crisis (a fool's errand), more informed, and hence logical minds, should be otherwise engaged in *preparing* for one. Hussman's lengthy warning, much like our own pages herein, inevitably and bluntly addresses the ultimate and quantifiably objective delusion, namely the delusion of paper wealth. He addressed this theme with a quote by Galbraith as to the "extreme brevity of the financial memory." In other words, he was warning investors against convincing themselves that paper wealth was real wealth.

At the time of its 2017 publication and warning, Hussman's report also referenced the St. Louis Fed's December 16th declaration that negative interest rates "may *seem* ludicrous, but *not* if they succeed in pushing people to invest in something *more stimulating to the economy* than government bonds." (Emphasis added). Like Hussman, we found such Fed speak absolutely comical, if not otherwise disturbing, dishonest and *logically* flawed. In actual fact, such guidance from the Fed was riddled with both irony and danger, as negative rates were not in fact leading investors into "stimulating the economy," but merely forcing them to take more and more risk in an otherwise desperate search for yield in a world in which that very same Fed had all but destroyed yield. By 2017 and 2018, investor exposure to junk bonds (euphemistically described as "high yield credits") had passed the Rubicon of euphoric to just plain crazy—and, again, not the least bit "logical."

Hussman was thus prescient in not only proving that such "expert logic" can be openly delusional, but also in how predictively the mad crowds would embrace, and hence follow, this expert delusion toward even greater speculation, greater risk, and alas, greater pain when the "logical" advice of policy makers leads directly to personal disaster. In short, the St. Louis Fed's positive spin on negative rates "succeeding" in pushing crowds to invest in something "more stimulating" to our economy was simple and open madness.

And as for those ludicrous yet *real* negative rates which the Fed tried to downplay as normal, well, we sure as Hell got em post 2017, well over $19T worth...

But simply fast-forward just over four years since the Fed made this so-called "logical" suggestion that negative rates could somehow spur more "intelligent investing" and consider what those low rates and retail "people" have "intelligently" invested in since. The free access to debt which low rates encourage has led to massive levels of speculation and hence massive levels of price inflation in otherwise profitless or low profit stocks.

Take Tesla. It's a bubble asset for the ages, and whatever logical defense Tesla bulls might have for its growth potential, the screaming disconnect between Tesla's cash flow and share price once again proves Hussman's warning that valuation still matters and that stocks like Tesla are anything but an investment which "succeed in pushing people to invest in something more stimulating to the economy." Instead, negative real rates merely succeeded in creating the greatest risk asset bubble in history of which, again, Tesla's stock price is an obvious symptom among many.

Tesla Market Cap vs. Free Cash Flow
Is This A Joke?

MATTERHORN

2686.373
2500

2000

1500

1000

500
342.1083
0

2015   2016   2017   2018   2019   2020   2021

Normalized As Of 09/01/2015   —— Current Market Cap 2686.373
TSLA US Equity   —— Free Cash Flow   342.1083

Source: www.SignalsMatter.com

Once assets like Tesla climb too far from the plow of real valuation, the end is not only brutal, but inevitable and will hardly be "stimulating to the economy," as this otherwise logical but plainly delusional Fed mouthpiece had promised from St. Louis. Similar and "logical" speculation suggested by the St. Louis Fed has taken place since 2017. And as the graph below of *profitless* IPO's currently peddled by the equally "logical crowd" at Goldman Sachs confirms, none of that speculation was as economically logical or "successful" as our Fed experts had so arrogantly suggested in late 2017. How do we know this? It's simple: *Almost none of the IPO's issued by this "logical" bank showed a single dollar of actual profit.*

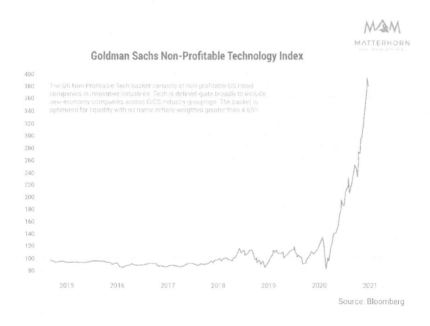

Goldman Sachs Non-Profitable Technology Index

Source: Bloomberg

Does that seem like "intelligent investing" which has resulted in "stimulating the economy" to you?

When stocks rise illogically on the backs of speculative (QE/debt-driven) policies which in fact have no logic despite the credentialed "logic" of their policy makers, the extreme paper wealth which follows and grows in their wake acquires the illusion of permanence, even stability. But as we and Hussman warned then, and which is even more true today, investors quickly and collectively fall under the collective delusion that the trillions of dollars in their portfolios today represent durable purchasing power tomorrow. In other words, "logical" investors always ignore the historically confirmed fact that most of that wealth will eventually evaporate once what goes up comes crashing down. Risk assets, in short, have never been riskier. As of this writing, for example, the global value of financial assets (stocks, bonds and real estate) is $520 trillion, which is 6.2X the $84 trillion in global GDP.

Re-read that last line. Do such numbers seem logical or delusional to you? Do they seem sustainable?

And Then There's Bitcoin...

Speaking of delusion, no conversation then (in 2017) or today, would be complete without addressing the current, yet logically-defended sacred cow of the digital currency universe otherwise known as Bitcoin, whose origins, founder, head-office or executive board is an open mystery—just saying... As believers in precious metals, we are not here to make a zero-sum argument, or even enter a debate, regarding gold vs. Bitcoin. In fact, we feel such a comparison is one of apples to oranges. Furthermore, we don't see the need or even logic in criticizing Bitcoin in order to defend gold, as they are entirely different types of assets befitting entirely different investor profiles.

In the simplest of terms, we see Bitcoin's ultimate profile as that of a speculative asset rather than a currency alternative or store of value; in short, no comparison to gold. Others, of course, will strongly (*very strongly*) disagree, but we are happy for anyone who has enjoyed the wealth which Bitcoin speculation has generated. In fact, many of our gold clients gained their wealth from Bitcoin. These pages were never intended to be an apology for gold nor an attack on digital currency. Other than what we've briefly observed in prior chapters, we are not interested in unpacking the myriad pros and cons, as well as logic and delusion, which mark the Bitcoin phenomenon. But as Mackay was quoted in 2017, and worth repeating here, such speculative cycles are not only common, but loaded with historical danger and *logical* warnings:

"We find that whole communities suddenly fix their minds upon one object, and go mad in its pursuit; that millions of people become simultaneously impressed with one delusion, and run after it, till their attention is caught in some new folly more captivating than the first."

Sound eerily familiar? From 17th century tulips and 18th century French markets to 19th century railroads or 20th century tech stocks, market historians know this fantasy pattern all too well. Of course, Bitcoin is more than a tulip, and as even Hussman himself confirmed, "the blockchain algorithm itself is brilliant." We too fully support Bitcoin's underlying thesis that fiat currencies and the central bank policies behind them are staggeringly weak and in need of an alternative approach, especially for younger or poorer populations who can't easily acquire physical gold. But the irony, as well as delusion, of the BTC era boils down to this: No asset bubble like Bitcoin, despite the logic of its thesis or the headline-generated confirmation of its supporters (as well as mysterious creators) can become a source of stability for something as critical as a national or global alternative currency. Bitcoin will not go away, but its valuations will go both north and south in astounding ways which, by itself, disqualifies this asset as a rational (or even "logical") solution to an admittedly and *already* irrational and openly bogus global currency market.

At the same time, and regardless of one's views (or biases) on gold, one (be they gold owners or stock pickers) should not simply ignore the growing and undeniable concerns rising around the BTC issue, even if those critiques come today from "biased" authors in the gold community.

In short, and despite the inevitable attacks we can and will receive from the BTC camp, we see *objective* risk in this otherwise bubbling and much loved "digital coin."

Bitcoin Bubble? Yep.

In a world of debt-driven bubbles, be they 1) stocks with CAPE ratios at 30; 2) sovereign bonds offering negative yields; 3) corporate bonds of predominantly covenant light and junk status; 4) SPAC froth; and 5) grossly over-valued tech names—it is no surprise nor effort for us to add the word "Bitcoin" to the list of current bubbles despite a global *economic* recession made all the worse by an equally nightmarish global pandemic.

BTC: This Time is Different?

As for the profile of a bubble, BTC's true believers feel this "coin" will only rise to the moon and take over the world as a new store of value and new global currency backed by admittedly remarkable technological innovation rather than a physical commodity.

Unfortunately, the facts as well as future possibilities portend a very different story, despite all the speculative wealth many have enjoyed riding the BTC wave. BTC, as current data and future regulatory, geopolitical and financial trends suggest, is not a currency, nor a unit of account, and despite all the vlogs, blogs and interviews to the contrary, is certainly not a stable store of value.

BTC as Currency? Store of Value?

Even the most faithful devotes of BTC cannot deny that a "currency" or "store of value" with price moves of 20% in a single trading day is hardly finding (or justifying) its way to such designations. As for currency status, not even BTC conferences will take it as payment, for its radical price moves can potentially wipe out (or grow) their profit margins overnight.

Others, of course, will say, Bitcoin's time will come after gradual adoption, and "what about Tesla, you can buy that with BTC." Well, actually you can't, and trusting tweet-happy front-runners like Musk, or over-valued balance sheets like Tesla, is an individual choice, and yours to enter (and hopefully exit correctly) at your own discretion and skill.

BTC: Old Tricks, New Widget

There is also no doubt that great fortunes have and can be made in such investments. But let us also recognize that Musk's "funding secured" tweets in 2018 amounted to fraud, and as of this writing, a Tesla in fact *can't* be bought with BTC despite Elon's expected attempts to "greenwash" this crypto's otherwise electricity-sucking mining operations as "environmentally healthy."

But lies, front-runs and price-fixing tricks from CEOs like Musk are forgiven because, at least as of this writing, Tesla's stock and BTC's valuation "prove their rightness" based on price, not truth, value or common sense. But no "asset" discussion of BTC is free of its short but sordid history of pump and dump, spoofing, wash trading and other front-running schemes and headlines (think BitMax) in which the big money pretends a "philosophical" interest in BTC merely to crush the little money when the time is right to buy and then sell—a near perfect nirvana for the Greater Fool Trade.

One other quick but relevant point is this: Where does BTC come from? Its genesis story, well, kinda matters, no? Did a mystery man named Nakamoto upload some code and then vanish into thin air with no one asking why? Who truly holds the largest controlling share of BTC? Where's the head office, staff and the ownership ledger for this otherwise totally de-centralized, $2T asset? What are and were the real motives behind this mysterious new-comer?

We have no idea either. Just saying...

BTC: The Asset Question

As for being an asset, BTC provides no income, cash flow, dividends, or coupon interest. Everyone, knows this, and everyone also knows that the same can be said of physical gold. Bitcoiners, of course, rightly don't care, as the money they've made is the key driver behind their "logic" and trade. Candidly, few can fault such motives—but at least be honest: The BTC trade is precisely that—a *trade*, not an asset, store of value or currency. Every blunt BTC investor we know has confessed the same. In short, deep down, they recognize that BTC is a risk asset not an alternative currency, store of value, or wealth preservation vehicle.

In case that sounds unfair, just watch what BTC does rather than what it, or we, say. In short, it acts just like a (highly volatile) risk asset—hence its real appeal as well as danger. Rather than "hedge," protect or buffer portfolios when markets tank (as, say, gold or other hard assets do), BTC just tanks faster with each and every market moment of "uh-oh" and "risk-off." In March of 2020, for example, when stocks fell by 35%, BTC fell by 50% and the larger crypto pool in general fell by more than 60%.

Whatever critics of gold can say, and they can say a lot, gold never falls that fast, that hard and that violently because gold is not a risk asset, but a risk protector. In short, gold and BTC are very different. Again, chose your motive rather than pick your side, as we are comparing apples to oranges.

But as for other key distinctions, gold, unlike BTC, does have some industrial use, centuries of jewelry utility and a 5000-year track record as a store of value from the planet earth (rather than blockchain code) that has saved far-sighted investors in one "uh-oh" moment after the other with eerie consistency. But again, all the Bitcoin vs. Gold debaters know this too. That's fine. Again: Just pick your motive–speculation or preservation—and stop screaming at each other 😅

BTC as a Payment System?

Many also know that as a payment system, BTC's heralded future (and proponents) overlook other regulatory and *Realpolitik* trends which don't often make the debate floor or the hyped-headlines. When it comes to future payment systems, it's more than fair, as well as realistically cynical, to assume that governments will, when backed to a corner, get the final say over which digital currency prevails, and it's most likely not going to be BTC...

Central Bank Digital Currencies (CBDC) will most likely (and vastly) outpace BTC and slowly, over time, find their way into ever-more commercial and private uses, including currencies like an eventual E-Euro, E-Dollar, or E-Yen which will crowd out pseudo private (yet currently trending) currencies like BTC many years down the road. The IMF has effectively confessed as much, and it late 2021 produced a working paper (and graph below) detailing how central banks will make direct CBDC payments to consumers as alternative, new "currencies."

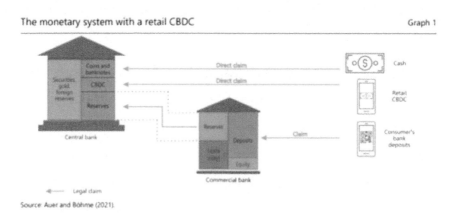

The monetary system with a retail CBDC   Graph 1

Source: Auer and Böhme (2021).

This, of course, is not a fact, but merely a realistic assumption based on power-dynamics rather than fair currency markets. In the meantime, BTC can continue its rise, and alas, its *bubble*.

As for the big, mean governmental big boys, rightly or wrongly, fairly or unfairly, their regulatory crack down on BTC has yet to really begin. First Mnuchin, and now Yellen and others, are already telegraphing their "ethical" concerns about BTC as a financial cover for human trafficking, drug sales, terrorist funding and other unsavory uses. Such concerns may or may not be sincere, as politicos are sadly driven by self-interested signaling not inherent moralism. These regulatory concerns, as well as increasing AML and KYC rules on cryptos to crackdown on their criminal uses, will eventually help "justify" the deflation of this BTC bubble, even if a Bitcoin ETF or even derivatives trade sends its price much higher in the interim.

Again, BTC can rise much higher, and BTC can make you rich (or broke). For those who understand such risk and such reward, and for those (even better) who can trade (enter/exit) BTC carefully and intelligently, we boring executives of an enterprise storing "boomer rocks" in Switzerland are not mocking you.

Again, we applaud the stories and wealth made on the BTC wave. Speculation, like preservation, each have their place in the diverse mind-sets and motives of the global investor class, so Bitcoin vs. Gold is a bit of a false dichotomy.

BTC and Gold: Different Uses, Different Views

But our offices do not represent nor champion wave assets or bubble markets. That's a mind-set and choice, not a bias, criticism or "gold bug" attack. In fact, may investors can share both choices, owning BTC to speculate for wealth and simultaneously holding gold to preserve that wealth (again, we've spoken to more than one BTC millionaire looking to buy gold *after* their BTC sale).

For these reasons, many of us (gold and/or BTC) are all growing tired of gold bugs mocking BTC and BTC fanatics mocking gold in the way a Yankees fan mocks a Red Sox fan (or a Manchester United fan mocks an Arsenal fan). These angry debates and participants are essentially ignoring the fact that these are two athletes playing on entirely different playing fields. In short, the Bitcoin vs. Gold debate in mode today makes as much sense as measuring David Beckham's fast ball against Mariano Rivera's free kicks.

As for BTC, we candidly (logically?) see it as a speculative bubble asset poised to rise and then either deflate or "pop." That's a bias, of course, but one backed by the data, history and long-term trends which we have been tracking for years—well before BTC even existed. Trade BTC as you will, but we personally (and, hopefully, without delusion) don't believe it will be a currency, "coin," store of value or "new gold."

Physical gold, of course, has its own data, history and trends—each far richer, deeper and more reliable than risk assets in general and bubble assets in particular. We ultimately see gold as a preservation asset and have written ad nauseum of its confirmed role as such over countless years, cycles and historical turning points. For the last decade or so, BTC has made many rich, and for the next decade or so, could make others even richer. That's a speculative bet. Fine. But for the last 5000 years, and for many more to come, gold will do what it *always* does: Preserve wealth when other assets and "currencies" can't.

That's *not* a bet.

Our antidote to the dying paper wealth of all global paper currencies is, of course, physical gold held outside the banking system. This is no secret, and to some, perhaps an illogical, and even outdated *bias*. Yes, physical gold price moves were far less sexy than the BTC or growth stock delusion gaining popularity, as well as speculative momentum (and then bust again) in 2021. Ironically, however, therein lies gold's open and logical advantage, for physical gold, unlike digital Bitcoin, has both an inherent as well as historical logic to both its role (and pricing) when measured against fiat paper as well as equally *fiat* digital "coins," which *logically* speaking, aren't even coins at all...Like paper or digital dollars, Bitcoins are backed by faith in a scarce digital *blip*, not a scarce physical *asset*. In short: *fiat*.

Detractors, of course will claim that the Hussman's, as well as our own, logic used to critique BTC's speculative illogic (i.e., delusion) can be equally used against the logic we employ to defend physical gold. In short, many can rightfully argue that we are just "gold bugs" holding on to a stubborn bias and outdated asset rather than the modern logic of evolving new technological breakthroughs. BTC, they say, is the future; gold, in turn, is the past. Such criticism is both fair and to be expected. In the end, however, to describe a physical asset derived from the periodic table (rather than a software program) and which has historically served to save dying currencies and delusional debt policies century after century, and currency crash after currency crash, as a "gold bug delusion" is a bit of a stretch, no? But Bitcoin defenders will naturally, in their own crowd-supported "logic," argue that physical gold is the outdated relic of an *old* world, whereas BTC is the modern and wise currency direction of the *new* world. That's a comforting defense indeed, as were the rapidly rising valuations of BTC. But like Hussman, we'll favor valuation, sanity, history and *valuation* logic over the mad crowds falling madly in love with the *speculative* "logic" of BTC.

In the end, history favors one form of logic over the other and we favor real stores of value that come from the earth over digital alternatives that come from a mysterious programmer. Frankly, even the central bankers who brought the world into the current and financial mess already know this, which is why they are quietly buying more gold, not Bitcoin...

Chapter 19

Gold as Wealth Preservation

"The scholar does not consider gold and jade to be precious treasures, but loyalty and good faith." - Confucius

We began this book with a Confucian insight and thus felt it symmetric and fitting to close with more of the same. As indicated in the foregoing quote, gold is a *precious* metal not merely because it's titled, commoditized, traded and priced as such, but far more importantly because its historical attributes and wealth preservation role speaks to values which go far beyond those of other risk assets or trading vehicles—namely: *Loyalty and good faith.*

For thousands of years, gold has loyally shown its good faith by serving the personal (and frankly priceless) values of its owners, including values of consistency, responsibility and protection. In this closing chapter, we underscore gold's timeless as well as growing importance as a protector of wealth, which articulates (and makes possible) the fruition of larger human goals and values—that is: Serving and protecting the people, goals and ideals most important us.

In short, and regardless of one's level of individual wealth, we can all agree that some level of tangible security is a key component to providing for those persons and endeavors in our lives whose value is immeasurable, invisible and yet essential. Although the coming price evolution of gold will be significant and exciting to all who own it, we are hopefully driven by the other gifts which gold-preserved wealth makes possible.

As Confucius' words remind, there are many values more precious than financial wealth alone. Loyalty and good faith to and among family, friends and personal ideals are clearly part of this. As we have stated (and will re-state) so many times here and elsewhere, the best things in life are ultimately beyond price: Connection with others, with nature, music, books and other, ever-evolving and inspiring new paths for conducting one's own life. But given the risks and problems now facing a rapidly changing world, it is our equal responsibility to realistically protect such immeasurable aspects of living in whatever way we can to avoid the obvious systemic risks ahead.

Systemic Risk & Currency Risk

As we have detailed in the many chapters above, there are two principal and highly interrelated risks that need our attention right now: Systemic risk and currency risk.

The systemic risks currently embedded within our global financial, political and even social fabric arose as a direct result of a 100+ year period (since the Fed was created in 1913) of immoral deficit spending and debt expansion encouraged by the mis-managed and over-creation of central-bank controlled money. As we've made clear throughout these pages, *debt matters because debt destroys currencies* which impact our society and individual lives in a myriad of ways.

Since Nixon closed the gold window in 1971, things have grown a lot worse, both inside and outside the land of the global reserve currency. Debts and deficits have gone exponential and the artificial (i.e., debt-driven) market expansion (inflation) that has resulted from such debt policies could only have been achieved by the fabrication of artificial money (and "solutions") from our misguided central and commercial banks and bankers.

As we now understand, all of this money was created out of nothing. No one needed to work a single minute for it and no one needed to produce a single good or service against it. Today, not even a printing press is needed to create such "money." All that is required is the simple pushing of a button on a computer and *abra cadabra*. Trillions of dollars, yen, euros etc. just appear out of nothing. Imagine logging into your own checking account and simply mouse-clicking more zeros to your balance whenever convenient and without risk of penalty? Who could resist such temptations?

Hocus – Pocus is Not a Sustainable "Plan"

But as more and more informed readers, investors and citizens are becoming aware, if something seems too good to be true, it's usually because it is. Such "magical" money creation from the top-down represents the biggest Hocus-Pocus scheme (con) ever produced in financial history. And yet this magical con has now evolved to become the very bedrock of the modern economic system—one completely lacking in the timeless virtues of loyalty and good faith.

If this both shocks and bothers you, it should.

To further deceive the people, the so-called experts behind this "magic" have come up with the soothing concept of MMT ("Modern Monetary Theory") to make something this corrupt appear otherwise logical, official or even intelligent. Such semantic tricks are nothing new to policy magicians. When they need to deceive the people, they cleverly pull calming letters from the alphabet and invent policy titles which sound academic, effective and sound-- like MMT or QE (Quantitative Easing).

But both of these now common policy titles mean nothing more than forging money out of thin air, an open absurdity that would clearly be embarrassing if honestly labeled as such. Can you imagine, for example, a central banker coming to a media platform or interview podium and calmly announcing that he/she has carefully arrived upon a new economic solution for the world's financial woes and are calling this new and exciting policy plan "creating money out of thin air"?

Can you imagine, moreover, if the policy makers replaced the term "Modern Monetary Theory" or "MMT" with the new title, "Counterfeit Money Solution" or "CMS"?

That, of course, would be a hard title for investors to swallow. Today's alleged financial leadership may be desperate, but they aren't stupid. It's much simpler for them to cleverly hide absurd ideas behind deceptive words or a well-labeled theory which few take the time to understand, including the very inventors of these desperate schemes.

In such a distorted backdrop of dishonest and/or delusional leadership, the responsibility for sound thinking therefore falls upon each of us as opposed to our alleged "experts." Toward that end, we can only pose a simple question: Is it possible that credit (i.e., debt) growth could be healthy for the economy?

At certain times and at certain levels, the simple answer is in fact "yes." That is, some moderate measure of debt can be useful in growing the economy and the markets, but not if debt monetized by fake money has reached such parabolic levels that you constantly need $3-$5 of *more* debt just to create $1 of GDP. And such debt policies are certainly not sustainable if they grow by 31X while tax revenues grow at only 6X, which has been the tragic case in the U.S. since Reagan became President in 1981.

Such debt policies (binges) make even less_sense if ballooning government deficits can only be financed (i.e., repaid) at zero or *negative* interest rates artificially created ("accommodated") by a mega central bank. Such rate suppression is not only an anathema (and insult) to natural market laws and capitalistic principles, it is mathematically unsustainable and impossible to reverse without creating unimaginable currency, economic and market destruction. In the long term, investments must always equal savings. Sadly, this fundamental law of nature and economics has been set aside by the politically-appointed MMT wizards and their equally magical predecessors, all of whom have forgotten to remind themselves and investors that the Piper will always demand to be paid. In sum: MMT (or creating money out of nothing) only lasts until the world wakes up to the fact that there was no substance or value to the magical money that has since inflated all the bubble assets of stocks, bonds and property to levels never seen before in history.

Money, Assets and Words Supported by Hot Air

If the money in circulation today was created out of hot air, then by logical deduction, we can also say that the ultimate value of the assets measured by that money must be equally air-filled. The only thing that needs to trigger the coming collapse in such currencies and risk assets is an evaporation of confidence in the same. In short: Once confidence in hot air goes, so goes the financial system it supports.

But how does one predict the death of confidence, especially when governmental talking-heads are forever selling illusion rather than truth as a matter of policy?

We know, of course, that governments and central banks will clearly not give up their magical hot air without a final stand. Like children caught with their hands in the cookie jar, policy makers will deny guilt even as the financial crumbs are falling from their chins. This could involve money printing going forward that defies all belief. Remember: When, not if, their counterparty obligations fail, the gross derivative market of $1.5 to $2 quadrillion will remain gross not net. Hyperinflation could follow as the currency beneath these failed counterparties collapses. If this future sounds crazy or far-fetched, is it any less far-fetched than a system that levered a single contract for a gold at 200:1? Such a system, in our minds, was doomed as well as rigged to fail.

The Greatest Risk Levels in History

As we've repeatedly observed, no one can say with certainty when or how deep the worst-case scenario is guaranteed to occur. Global banks have already telegraphed new schemes of **CBDC** to extend their fiat money illusions. But what we can say is that the risk of such an implosion (at one fatal degree or another) is greater than at any other time in history, and history is riddled with financial implosions.

Never before have so many countries been levered and indebted to such a parabolic extent and with absolutely *zero* ability to ever repay the debt or finance it at proper market rates. The current manufacturing of fake money and the open manipulation of interest rates breaks every single rule of nature and natural markets, creating a setting of massive disequilibrium that cannot be sustained. Again: Zero loyalty or good faith.

It is all tragically simple. Extreme moves (in currencies, markets or debt) always return/revert to their means in normal times. But we haven't had normal times in the last half century, thus, the extreme swing of the pendulum (i.e., mean-reversion) from one side (the "euphoria") to the other ("collapse") will result in a similar counter reaction from the sublime to the ridiculous. That is, the mean-reversion (or fall) from these hot-air market highs will be extreme.

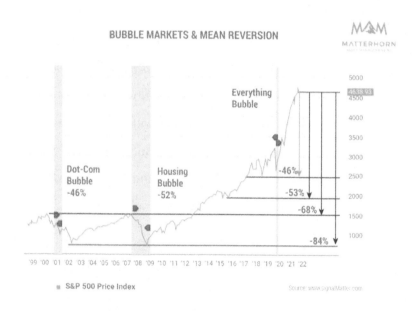

BUBBLE MARKETS & MEAN REVERSION

Thus, after this massive creation of more fake money with almost zero economic benefit unwinds, all assets, including paper money, will implode with devastating effects on the global financial and economic system. That is how the world goes from a depressionary hyperinflation phase to a deflationary implosion and depression phase. This, at least, is our blunt yet admittedly sanguine view of the most likely scenario in the next 3-10 years and probably sooner rather than later. Remember, however, that we are talking about probabilities and definitely not date or dollar certainties. We can clearly be wrong, but more likely as to the *timing* and degree rather than in the eventual and admittedly dramatic *outcome.*

Thus, in our view, the systemic risk we face today is greater than at any time in history. What will unfold precisely, and when, only historians can tell us with certainty, as hindsight is the most exact of all sciences...

Currency Failure Is Guaranteed

As to currency risk, however, we can speak to this theme with more certainty for the simple reason that it is *already* in motion. Currency destruction, now and in the future, is the obvious consequence of the systemic risk template (extreme debt paid with extreme levels of hot-air money) discussed above. Given how painful such truths are, many can and will reject these warnings, but few can deny the currency risks playing out in *real time* before their very own eyes and wallets.

We remind and close with the simple fact that since 1971, all currencies have lost 97- 99% of their value in real terms. And since 2000, they have lost around 80%.

Thus, it is absolutely guaranteed that all currencies will lose the remaining 1%-3% of their "real" value. The only question is how long it will take? Again, we would be surprised if it takes as much as 10 years. Between 3 and 5 years seems more likely. But no one knows. Not you. Not us.

So, there we have it. Not a rosy scenario but the candid and tragic consequence of creating a world driven by extreme debt sustained by fake money and the daily trickle of policy deceit and leadership "hot air" –all symptomatic of a total lack of values like the realism, preparedness, loyalty and the good faith with which Confucius' observations opened and closed this book.

Despite such a setting of distorted markets, values and responsible financial and political leadership, we must remember that countries and empires have gone through major forest fires before and life on earth has continued and, eventually, advanced. Notwithstanding the immense challenges ahead, including challenges that are likely to be greater than any the world has encountered before, from the coming financial, political and social rubble emerges the possibility for a foundation of future and healthy growth. We see such "creative destruction" as the ultimate necessity as well as characteristic of creating a better financial and human history. In order, however, to weather the storm that precedes the calmer waters, we must preserve our wealth before rather than after the storm.

After all, when did Noah build his arc?

Before the rain.

Wealth Preservation

Wealth preservation is precisely this: Protecting current and generational wealth from the tides and cycles of history to come. European families, who have survived financially through centuries of human and financial challenges, have always held major portions of their assets in land and physical gold.

Why?

Because they've learned that gold is a 100%-proof bet against the continued failure of ever-failing fiscal and monetary policies.

In other words, realistic investors have no illusions as to the patterns, distortions and failures of their financial "leaders." For such realists, holding physical gold is like buying flood insurance for a house sitting on a river bank whose water levels are rising. That is, you know you will eventually see the flood just as history proves with 100% certainty that governments seeking to buy credibility and time with fake money will continue to destroy their currency and economy whenever they get over their skis in debt.

Thus, even for those investors not in agreement with the systemic (and admittedly scary) collapse we have outlined above, no one can deny the currency collapse staring straight at us today, nor the long history of similar collapses of yesterday which history has taught us with cold realism.

Governments throughout the ages have been incapable of confessing their own failures or stopping the tides of their reckless deficits and subsequently desperate money printing. Like all political animals, their primary instinct is survival not candor, and staying in power means comforting words slowly devolving into autocratic rules. The U.S., for example, has increased its debt every year since 1930 with only a four-year exception. America today, like the France of the 1790's, is a bankrupt country. Unlike the 18th century French, however, its post-war powers allowed it to hang on to its reserve currency status until now. But this comes at an enormous cost. Since Nixon "temporarily" took away the gold backing of the dollar in 1971, the U.S. Dollar has lost 98% in real terms.

Given the current state of the U.S. economy, and given the fact that both red and blue leadership continues to commit trillions of new money to buy votes (and time) in one administration after the next, the dollar is guaranteed to continue its implosion. Again, the principal objective of an elected official is to be reelected, and the surest way to achieve such results is to bribe the masses and placate the bankers with ever-more money—at least until that bribe money ("liquidity") becomes as useless as their equally "liquid" promises. Thereafter, the militant and autocratic rather democratic setting takes hold, as it already is in cities and nations around the world. Thousands of years of history proves this cynical yet cyclical truth.

Gold Stands Above the Rubble of History as a Protector

In times of financial and geopolitical upheaval, gold has always served as a loyal protector and life saver. It has emerged time after time after time as the best protection against rigged and totally corrupt financial systems, including the most rigged of all: The current "hot-air" system.

As we discovered together in the opening chapters of this book, the tragic history and pattern of "debt-spend-fake-it and then implode" is undeniable as well as familiar. Again, just consider the Romans from 180 to 280 AD, when the Denarius lost 100% of its silver content. Or fast-forward to the example of Uganda during Amin's rule or the case of Yugoslavia during the hyperinflation of the early 1990s, or the sad cases of Venezuela, Greece, Argentina or South Africa today. The examples are many, and a full description of each would require an entire book. But for those who arrogantly feel that "stronger and wiser" nations or policy makers like those of the U.S., EU or Asia are somehow immune from (or otherwise above) the warnings and math of history, we can only say that such hubris is equally historical and equally dangerous.

Within the next 10 years, investors are likely to lose the vast majority of their "paper" wealth. This projection has nothing to do with sensationalism or Cassandra fortune telling. Instead, the likelihood of having nothing left in real terms is driven simply from the obvious and substantial reality of currency risk. As systems implode, you can expect greater capital, financial and social controls, very much like those to which we are growing pre-accustomed by over-zealous (and in our opinion absurd and deliberate) COVID lockdown measures. It's almost as if the powers-that-be are "test-driving" the masses today for much further controls tomorrow. As we've written above, mad crowds are often easily controlled crowds—at least until their mad delusion turns to just plain mad anger. When delusion turns to rage, it is best to keep the masses locked down and afraid, rather than assembling, thinking or acting for themselves.

Get Out of the System

Given such objective currency risk and the storm ahead for watered-down global currencies, now is the time to get out of the financial system and allocate a major portion of your assets away from "hot-air" assets into real commodities in general and precious metals like physical gold and silver in particular.

Sadly, the average investor considers such advice as the sales-talk of gold-bugs or Swiss-based commodity pushers. Such criticism assumes that we favor gold because we are leaders of an enterprise that deals in gold. But what detractors like these refuse to see is that we entered this service because we saw the need for, rather than profits from, such a service. If greed were our motive, we'd be running banks, momentum funds or growth tech companies rather than private vaults. We'd be selling junk bonds for Goldman Sachs, not refined gold for ourselves and trusted clients. Most consensus-thinking advisors and their trusting clients haven't got a clue of the *real* return on their paper investments. "Real" in this case means returns measured in stable rather than hot-air money. Of course, the only stable money in history, *without exception,* is that "barbaric relic," gold.

Today, measuring one's wealth in thin-air-defined currencies has nothing to do with its *real* performance. Given such undeniable conditions, wealth preservation through physical gold ownership is not a sales-pitch, it's an ignored yet historically confirmed necessity, one deliberately downplayed by a rigged financial system whose very (and increasingly discredited) survival-narrative involves convincing as many investors as possible to ignore gold while placing and measuring their assets in the *paper* (and eventually digital) wealth of an openly shaky financial system. Like Pickett's 1863 charge at the battle of Gettysburg, investors are literally being asked by their "expert" leadership to march straight into the mouth a currency-destroying cannon.

Needless to say, the so-called "leadership" and /or creators of this inherently rigged system are not ignorant of the very realities we've outlined throughout these pages. They know where the skunks lie within the global monetary woodpile for the simple reason that they *are* the skunks. Thus, like the rest of us informed realists, the rigged creators of the current and desperate monetary experiment are all too aware of the one asset which debunks their entire charade, that infamous anti-dollar otherwise known as physical gold.

In short, gold scares the heck out of desperate policy makers. In order to give credit to their false narrative of strong fiat currencies, they have consistently endeavored to discredit gold.

The former Governor of the Bank of England, Eddie George, when referring to the currency crisis of 1999, openly confessed as much. Rising gold prices in 1999 confirmed the decline of dying currencies and the entire system built around them. As he said of that era:

"We looked into the abyss if the gold price rose further. A further rise would have taken down one or several trading houses, which might have taken down all the rest in their wake. Therefore, and at any price, and at any cost, the central banks had to quell the gold price, manage it. It was very difficult to get the gold price under control but we have now succeeded. The US Fed was very active in getting the gold price down. So was the U.K."

Those are powerful words, and that's a stunning confession. Of course, some might see such realism as bad for gold's future. After all, gold clearly has powerful (very powerful) enemies. Given the fact, moreover, that the central banks control and own the BIS (Bank of International Settlement) which has immense power over (and interest in) this fully rigged system, it goes without saying that such bad actors are not going to allow the gold market to be honestly priced, *if they can stop it.*

And that, in a nutshell, is the critical question: Can the casino owners continue to rig the game? Does the "house always win?" Will monetary oligarchs continue to repress the gold market?

Our view is as blunt as it is simple: This rigged game is rigged to fail, and eventually all rotten systems, like all rotten casinos, no matter how powerful, fall under the weight of their own top-heavy (and increasingly recognizable) fraud.

It's our view that there will initially be some fudging of the rules (be it a second "Bretton Woods" or the new Basel III). The big boys on top will work long and hard to telegraph messages of efficiency, calm and order during any financial, banking or monetary transition period to prevent investor panic or ripping gold prices. Ultimately, however, we believe that the central banks will lose control of the gold market in the not-too-distant future and that the repression that worked in the past won't work again tomorrow. Faith in these fraudsters is waning just as awareness of their schemes is growing. Part of our aim here is to help spread this awareness.

Finally, it's worth reminding that despite such open repression, gold has fought back and held its own with remarkable consistency. One of our favorite annualized charts reveals how gold had consistently closed up in the 12 consecutive years between 2001 and 2012. Thereafter, gold corrected for only 3 years, yet since 2016, it has been consistently rising. Thus, since gold turned its most recent corner in 2001, it has closed positively in 17 of the last 21 years, and in our opinion, its real bull market has yet to even begin.

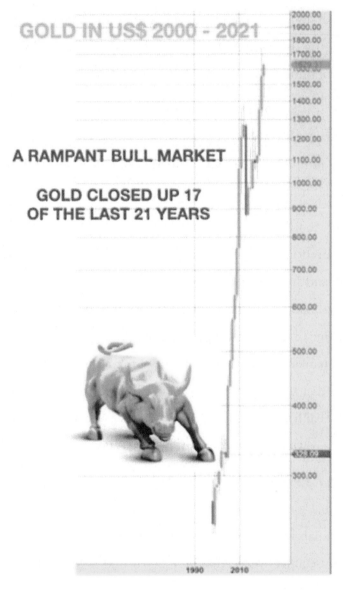

GOLD IN US$ 2000 - 2021

A RAMPANT BULL MARKET

GOLD CLOSED UP 17
OF THE LAST 21 YEARS

Much that will drive this bull market in gold will be the tragic bear market in dying currencies and historically bloated stocks and bonds, all previously driven by the most corrupted and distorted financial mismanagement in the history of capital markets. The consequences for such mismanagement are and will be dire.

The question we end with, therefore, is the same as the question with which we began: Are you prepared for such a future?

From where we sit in Switzerland, there is no better asset than gold to protect against—and prepare for--the systemic and currency risks which the world is facing today. Yes, we also see gold generating substantial wealth enhancement as its rising price continues to insult the falling credibility and purchasing power of hot-air currencies around the world. That's a clear bonus for far-sighted gold realists. But far more importantly, we see, and have always seen, gold as the single most loyal, faithful and valuable vehicle for our personal values of preserving wealth for the families, friends and goals most valuable to us.

Closing Thoughts

Congratulations. You have made it this far, and regardless of how much you agree or disagree with every idea presented, you are now a more informed investor than when you began this book.

We've made a brief yet important journey together in the preceding chapters, from the forgotten lessons of a forgotten academic at Cornell University to a few words on an all-too familiar digital coin. Between these two extremes of past and present, we've endeavored to speak plainly on patterns, risks, distortions and illusions which have characterized decades and even centuries of financial markets misled by desperate policy makers who have consistently attempted to solve unsustainable and self-inflicted debt catastrophes with, alas...more debt.

Again: If such approaches to debt sound too good to be true, it's because they are. For most readers, whether market novices or market veterans, such popular and short-sighted solutions from on high are clearly void of anything resembling common sense or long-term viability. From 18th century Paris to 21st Century Washington, we've tracked a consistent wind pattern which has blown through markets, economies and country codes with predictable speeds and predictable destruction—ending *every time* with ruined markets, economies, societies and currencies, for which physical gold has always emerged as the most genuine form of real (rather than paper or digital) wealth.

Despite such clear warnings and lessons from the past, the short-term seduction of cheap debt paid for with artificial and increasingly debased currencies has consistently gained investor (and voter) appeal, as risk assets can reach astronomical heights on such otherwise dangerous policy-tailwinds. The direct correlation of such central bank liquidity and low-rate stimulus to rising markets, increased wealth disparity and social discord is not theoretical but historically consistent. Caught in a familiar hysteria of greed and a collective fear of missing out, retail investors, seduced by smooth-talking and data-be-damned policy makers, commercial banks, Wall Street sell-siders and central bankers are whistling past a debt graveyard straight toward a market cliff.

This, again, is nothing new. Policy makers, from Rome to DC, have always sought newer and more creative ways to sustain a fictional hope rather than confess to plain-spoken risk. From Caligula to Nixon, FDR to Powell, those in power like to stay that way, and thus seek to keep the good times going with ever-more debt expansion paid for with ever-more debased currencies. Such historical and psychological patterns more resemble addictions than sober reflections or clear-eyed leadership. But again, this is no surprise for those who respect history, the psychology of power or the lessons of basic math. In modern markets, the mass leverage allowed by increasingly risk-averse banks exposed to staggering levels of derivative exposure have created unprecedented levels of banking and market risk. At the same time, central bank policy makers have pretended a "recovery" by extending and expanding their addiction to printed dollars with unprecedented levels of new money creation which, in turn, creates unprecedented (and unacceptable) levels of currency debasement.

As we've shown with objective facts rather than just dramatic statements, such destructive wind patterns through history and markets have been equally marked by patterns of deliberate dishonesty by policy makers and financial "experts" who have, time after time, attempted to hide their own culpability for such boom-to-bust cycles. The manifold ways in which the so-called financial leadership seeks to distract investors from their own mismanagement of the financial markets is no surprise to those who know where and how to look beneath the surface of allegedly "recovered" economies and markets. The deliberate misrepresentation of honest inflation reporting by central banks, along with equally mis-reported derivative exposures by commercial banks, are just two among many examples of open lies used to hide dangerous truths.

Meanwhile, of course, the currency in your wallet, bank account or portfolio statement loses purchasing power with each new fiat dollar, yen or euro created by the second at central banks like the Federal Reserve, Bank of Japan or European Central Bank. The facts, rather than adjectives, plainly show that these privately managed institutions (carrying immense and growing political powers) have massively expanded their roles as well as balance sheets (i.e., levels of printed currencies) to pay for unsustainable debt obligations at interest rates artificially stapled to the floor of time via equally unsustainable rate suppression policies. Just see for yourselves how high these money supplies (top lines) have risen and how low interest rates (bottom line) have fallen under such "leadership":

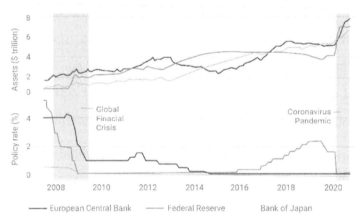

Loosening in monetary conditions
Major central banks expand their balance sheets and lower interest rates

Source: Thomson Reuters, Bank of International Settlements

Of course, such unlimited money creation (or "unlimited QE," as the fancy lads call it), is nothing more than a veiled manner of diluting the inherent value of the underlying currency. Just as one cannot add a swimming pool of water to a glass of wine and expect the wine to hold its flavor, central bankers and fiscal spenders who add trillions of new fiat dollars to the money supply cannot prevent the flavor (or purchasing power) of their currencies from being grossly diluted. Fortunately, *physical* gold can't be so diluted, manipulated or distorted by bankers, computers or fancy words. Stated simply: One can't "print" (or hack) physical gold. Again, that is why increasingly diluted currencies, when measured against a single milligram of gold, have lost greater than 95% of their purchasing power since the U.S. dollar was de-pegged from a gold standard in 1971. Sadly, and not surprisingly, however, almost no one has ever been told of such simple facts by a central banker (or even financial advisor) in the light of day. Although we foresee no return to a full global gold standard, we see no reason to doubt that gold will always be, as it has always been, the surest and safest way to individually protect informed investors from the now undeniable and ongoing debasement of their currencies.

Nor are we alone with this conviction. In fact, the very central banks and policy makers who authored such currency destruction/dilution are well aware that gold is a far more durable and trusted form of real money than the fiat paper that currently passes for the same. This fact, of course, is a direct threat to such guilty parties, as rising gold prices reveal the open failure of their experimental monetary policies as evidenced by gold's outperformance against increasingly debased global currencies. Gold's self-evident and time-tested superiority is the primary reason these same banks and policy makers have gone to such extreme lengths to artificially distort (repress) the *paper* price of gold by engaging in legitimized but otherwise patently fraudulent price fixing of gold pricing in the COMEX futures market. Such practices represent yet another open lie passing for fair-priced truth in what is nothing more than a corrupted, debt-soaked and soon-to-fail global market and currency system. Ultimately, the sheer weight of such market bubbles, debt piles, over-diluted currencies and veiled yet open lies collapses upon itself, as White's ghost reminds us from Chapter 2.

The difficult question we thus close with here is the very same question with which we opened in our Introduction, namely: Are you prepared for what's to come in global markets, economies and currencies?

We hope the many patterns, data points and examples provided in the intervening pages have made it easier for you to answer this critical question with conviction rather than suspicion, and realism rather than fantasy.

As for us, we've always preferred the former to the later and we hope you join us blunt-speakers in preparing for what lies ahead.

Matthew Piepenburg and Egon von Greyerz

About the Authors

Matthew Piepenburg

Prior to joining Egon von Greyerz' team at Matterhorn Asset Management, AG, Matthew brought over 20-years of experience as: the General Counsel and, later, CIO of a highly-capitalized single family office and then later the Managing Director of a multi-billion, multi-family office.

In addition to managing his own hedge fund during the dot.com hysteria and the post-08 bubble, Matthew has overseen the allocation of over $5 billion in investable assets over a full range of portfolios and alternative investment vehicles. He has led the quantitative and qualitative due diligence on hundreds of diverse asset classes, hedge fund managers and strategies, thereby developing a unique expertise as to the best practices and diverse strategies of the world's premier portfolio managers. His extensive background in risk asset markets drove him naturally toward gold as the most viable, long-term preservation investment in a central-bank distorted financial system derailed from natural valuation.

Fluent in English, French and German, he is the author of numerous international white papers on macro conditions, including the Amazon No 1 Release in Wealth Management, *Rigged to Fail*.

Egon von Greyerz

A dual-citizen of both Sweden and Switzerland, Egon von Greyerz is the 2000 founder of the Zurich-based wealth management firm, Matterhorn Asset Management, AG, where he has built a personal reputation as one of the world's leading authorities in precious metal markets. Toward this end, Egon created an industry-leading service model for UHNW individuals and institutions seeking optimal pathways to  precious metal investing and ownership. Outside of the highly-fractured and increasingly at-risk commercial banking system, Matterhorn Asset Management has evolved over the prior decades to become the largest, safest and most respected private gold ownership organization in the world for UHNW investors.

Prior to launching Matterhorn Asset Management, Egon worked in the Geneva banking sector before serving 17 years as the Finance Director and Executive Vice-Chairman to Dixons Group, Plc, a premier FTSE 100 company based out of London.

Made in the USA
Monee, IL
12 June 2022

97915760R00216